Forty Arguments for the Sake of Heaven

*Why the Most Vital Controversies
in Jewish Intellectual History
Still Matter*

Rabbi Dr. Shmuly Yanklowitz

Teaneck, New Jersey

FORTY ARGUMENTS FOR THE SAKE OF HEAVEN ©2024 Shmuly Yanklowitz. All rights reserved. No part of this book may be used or reproduced in any manner whatsoever without written permission except in the case of brief quotations embodied in critical articles and reviews.

Published by Ben Yehuda Press
122 Ayers Court #1B
Teaneck, NJ 07666
http://www.BenYehudaPress.com

To subscribe to our monthly book club and support independent Jewish publishing, visit https://www.patreon.com/BenYehudaPress

Ben Yehuda Press books may be purchased at a discount by synagogues, book clubs, and other institutions buying in bulk.

For information, please email markets@BenYehudaPress.com

Cover art adapted from a 16th century painting from the church of Saint-Louis des Français in Rome, now held by the Louvre Museum.

ISBN13 978-1-953829-47-4 paper

24 25 26 / 10 9 8 7 6 5 4 3 2 1   20231215

This book is dedicated to my great father, Stephen Yanklowitz, who has always had a rigorous passion for discussing values. I'm grateful to my amazing Dad for imparting to me his sensitive, intellectual commitment to moral inquiry.

Contents

Introduction ... 1

On Truth

1. Hillel vs. Shammai: Arguments for the Sake of Heaven ... 8
2. Absolute Truth vs. Compromise: Which is the True Good? ... 15
3. Trust vs. Questioning ... 20

On God, Torah, & the Cosmos

4. Rambam vs. Ra'avad: Is God Some Thing or No Thing? ... 28
5. Abraham vs. God: Is God Present and Active? ... 34
6. The Gra vs. the Besht: Mysticism of the Mind vs. Mysticism of the Heart ... 44
7. Divine Torah vs. Biblical Criticism ... 49
8. Heaven vs. Earth? ... 56
9. Rationalist-Monotheism vs. Mystic-Monotheism: On the Unity of God ... 63
10. The Mussar Movement vs. the Hasidic Movement ... 71

Moral Philosophy

11. Einstein, Freud, & Marx vs. The Sages:
    Are We Free to Shape the World? ... 78
12. Ayn Rand vs. Karl Marx: On Wealth & Virtue ... 91
13. The Angels vs. God: Should Humans Have Been Created? ... 100
14. Past vs. Future ... 106
15. A Purpose to Life vs. No Meaning to Life? ... 111
16. Prioritizing the Poor vs. Equity Toward All Parties ... 118
17. Judging Others Favorably vs. Judging for Justice ... 123

Israel

18. Yitz Greenberg vs. Meir Kahane:
    On Sovereignty and Contemporary Jewish Political Power ... 130
19. Israel vs. the Diaspora : What is the Center? ... 137
20. No State, One State, or Two States:
    Herzl vs. Wise, Art Green vs. Peter Beinart ... 146

Contemporary Moral Issues

21. Local vs. Global, Particular vs. Universal	152
22. Pro-Choice vs. Pro-Life	158
23. Gun Rights vs. Gun Control	162
24. Capital Punishment vs. Abolishing the Death Penalty	172
25. Care for the Vulnerable vs. Education: What does every community need?	180

Jewish Daily Life & Community

26. Obedience vs. Meaning : What is the Purpose of the *Mitzvot*?	186
27. Reform Judaism vs. Orthodox Judaism	191
28. A Life of Study vs. A Life of Action: Which is Greater?	201
29. Tamar Ross vs. Judith Plaskow: Paradigm-Shifting Feminism vs. Traditional Feminism	209
30. Auschwitz vs. Sinai: Which is the More Central Jewish Narrative Today?	220

On the Self

31. Love: Emotion vs. Deed, Emotion-based Love vs. Deed-based Love	228
32. Body vs. Soul	235
33. Zealousness vs. Tolerance	242
34. Calm vs. Tension: Is Life About Struggle or Peace?	248
35. Humor vs. Seriousness	253

The State & Authority

36. Hobbes vs. Anarchists: A King vs. No King	258
37. Halachah vs. State: What is the vehicle for progress?	265
38. The Individual vs. the Collective: Which Should We Value?	269
39. Hierarchy vs. Populism: Moshe vs. Korach	277
40. Spinoza vs. the Rabbis of Amsterdam: Allowing Heresy or Preserving Communal Boundaries	281
Conclusion	287

Appreciation

I want to express my sincere appreciation to Rabbi Avram Herzog, Judry Subar, and Cody Fitzpatrick for their feedback and edits. I also am grateful to Larry Yudelson, Laura Logan, and the Ben Yehuda Press team. I give special thanks to Professor Tamar Ross for her permission to quote extended passages of her work. Further, I want to express gratitude to the dozens of Jewish learners who joined my classes where I originally shared these ideas. I am grateful to Shoshana and my kids for gifting me the time to think and write and for inspiration. And mostly, I am, so beyond words, thankful to my Creator for life and for the opportunity to be a teacher of Torah.

A note on translations

Except where otherwise noted, biblical translations come from the 1985 JPS edition of the Tanakh; Talmudic citations are from the William Davidson Talmud, Koren-Steinsaltz edition.

Introduction

Forty Arguments for the Sake of Heaven explores Judaism from an uncommon direction. Many speak of the heart of Judaism being found within Jewish law. Others speak of it as being found within Jewish values. Here, I argue that a deeply authentic Jewish discourse goes further than both. Rather than embrace absolutes (laws or values), the rabbinic tradition can be most richly explored through dialectics. So, in this work, we look at forty of the greatest debates in Jewish intellectual history. Through this learning, we will retrain ourselves to view issues from different perspectives, as countless Jewish sages did before us. To be sure, it is not a work of moral relativism that equates all perspectives. Rather, we will learn how to passionately hold on to absolutes while at the same time being tolerant and pluralistic within the diversity of our community and society at large.

Today, we are in the midst of fierce debates (theological, political, moral), and those debates often bring more heat than light. We can relearn how to be passionate advocates for social justice while also adding more intellectual weight and Jewish sources to such debates. We can also learn how to debate without dehumanizing the other and how to allow debate to expand our intellectual and spiritual lives rather than narrow us and infuriate us. This is not an easy task. To be sure, this is not a practical debate guide. Rather, it is a book of ethics. It contains tensions, not answers.

The premise of this book is that both the traditional and liberal sects of Jews have largely distorted the Jewish intellectual tradition. The Orthodox camp frequently claims that *halachah* (Jewish law) is most central to understanding Judaism. The liberal Jewish camp frequently claims that Jewish values are most central to understanding Judaism. Both, of course, are hugely important. But here we will argue that it is neither law nor values that matter most, rather that Jewish thinkers historically thought not in absolutes but in dialectical tensions. Jews engaged less in monologues and more in dialogues and debates. Indeed, the entire Talmud is written in the style of debate, of give and take. And often, those debates remain unresolved. This book is about exploring how we can restore the Jewish intellectual tradition of healthy debate.

Some might think this sounds too relativistic. Shouldn't we be more resolute that Jews should follow the strict *halachah* of our day? Shouldn't we be clear that this Jewish value or that one is crucial for all? But we are not downplaying laws or values. Rather, we believe we can enhance *halachah* and Jewish values by putting values and laws in tension with one another as Jews have always done.

It is also important to note that while all Jewish ideas emerge within a unique historical context, they are often not limited to that context. For this reason, we will be curious about historical contexts within debates but will also appreciate that Jewish ideas debate one another across cultures and eras. Living Jews debate non-living Jews. People may die, but their voices live on.[1]

People can always "cherry pick" the texts that line up with their ideology and call it "Judaism." Our goal is different. We want to explore the fullness of Torah and Judaism, even if we do have strong ideological leanings. We need to bring our moral compass to the debates and texts, and we need to engage in interpretation and application to our day. This is quite a complex endeavor.

But aren't some arguments not worth preserving and not worth taking seriously? Over thirty years ago now, Rabbi Avi Weiss staged a curious affair. He invited Harvard Law School Professor Alan Dershowitz to debate Rabbi Meir Kahane at the Hebrew Institute of Riverdale for an all-encompassing disputation about the roles of Jews and Israel. It was, and remains, a fascinating display of contrasts: a liberal law professor and a reactionary politician. In his opening remarks, Dershowitz responded to those who criticized him for debating Kahane:

> I am debating Rabbi Meir Kahane because too few blacks debated and responded to Rev. Jesse Jackson and Louis Farrakhan. I am debating Rabbi Kahane because virtually no Arabs are willing to debate Yasser Arafat. I think it is imperative that the world understand not only that the vast majority of Jews repudiate Rabbi Kahane's views, but also why we repudiate those views.[2]

These words are still so relevant in today's cultural climate. In addition to explaining one's core position, debating extremists can, if done with precision, point out the ugliness of their positions. And if one has the courage of one's convictions,

---

[1] The Talmud tells us that Ya'akov Avinu (our forefather Jacob) didn't die. In other words, Ya'akov lives on through his lasting teachings, ethics, and ideas. But it is not necessarily a given. Rather, it is our charge to keep our tradition—going all the way back to our forefathers and foremothers—alive.

[2] Alan Dershowitz vs. Meir Kahane (1985 Debate), https://youtu.be/2ykrwmaKrLg?si=FenaaqQxj7TPUlcu.

they can truly undermine the inherent repugnance of the extreme view. Douglas Murray, founder of the Centre for Social Cohesion in the United Kingdom, writer for *The Spectator*, and currently Associate Director of the Henry Jackson Society, is a gay atheist and neoconservative defender of Western institutions. He accepted an invitation to debate, nevertheless, a radical Muslim group that supported terrorism, subjecting himself to verbal and physical intimidation. Afterward, he stated that free speech is not an easy process, and that many audiences would be hostile. Yet, Murray believes that some audience members may be affected in a positive way: "Even if it is just one member of the audience who is receptive to the anti-totalitarian possibility, it is vital to do this. It is the reason why I debate." In addition, he noted that debate brings out just how violent extremists actually are:

> Yesterday showed why bringing them out in the open and challenging their ideas is necessary. It reminds the government, the press, and British citizens of the true nature of these fundamentalist thugs who are not just going to disappear. Not since Oswald Mosley's British Union of Fascists (BUF) have we seen intimidation like this on the streets of London. Like the BUF, they will resort to violence the moment their fascist views are challenged.[3]

The failure to debate, or at least debunk, outrageous positions may be perilous. In 2004, Democratic Presidential candidate John Kerry was smeared by the "Swift Boat" campaign that attacked Kerry's experience as a Vietnam War veteran.[4] Although the campaign was funded by an extremist[5] and had absolutely no validity, Kerry's reluctance to face down the charges (and most likely his underestimating its effect) hurt his campaign, built a minor annoyance into a major problem, and probably contributed to his defeat.

Looking beyond political debate, scientists, too, have been frustrated by the persistence of skepticism toward the theory of evolution (which today measures 42 percent).[6] To some, such as astrophysicist Neil deGrasse Tyson, director of the Hayden Planetarium at the American Natural History Museum, scientists

---

[3] Douglas Murray, "Why we must debate the extremists," *The Guardian*, June 19, 2009, https://www.theguardian.com/commentisfree/belief/2009/jun/19/religion-islam-muhajiroun-choudary.
[4] Eric Boehlert, "It's Not 'Swift Boating' If It's True," *Huffpost*, September 16, 2012, https://www.huffpost.com/entry/its-not-swift-boating-if_b_1679611.
[5] Kate Zernike, "T. Boone Pickens Says No Deal on Swift Boat Bounty," *The New York Times*, June 25, 2008, https://archive.nytimes.com/thecaucus.blogs.nytimes.com/2008/06/25/t-boone-pickens-says-no-deal/.
[6] Elizabeth Quill and Helen Thompson, "Bill Nye on the Risks of Not Debating With Creationists," *Smithsonian Magazine*, November 6, 2014, https://www.smithsonianmag.com/science-nature/bill-nye-risks-not-debating-creationists-180953249/.

should not debate "belief systems" precisely because they are "not science."[7] He believes that bringing religion into science class is "undermining what science is and how it works."

Bill Nye, known to millions as "the Science Guy," takes a differing approach, and acknowledges a place for religion. In 2014, Nye debated evolution with Kevin Ham, the President and CEO of Answers in Genesis, the organization that operates the Creation Museum in Kentucky, which shows dinosaurs and humans cohabiting the Earth no longer than 6,000 years ago. To Nye, debate represents a continuing process:

> A person hears the arguments or is exposed to the arguments. He or she is not going to change his or her mind immediately. It takes several times through, so I hope this will plant a seed—that it will be a start of people discovering the fundamental idea in all of life science.[8]

To Nye, the denial of evolution is the denial of the scientific method. This repudiation will affect humanity's "ability to generate energy, to build cars, to fight diseases, to regulate traffic."

Engaging with someone of a completely different ideology does not need to be viewed as validating their views. In fact, Jewish law suggests the opposite: "shtika k'hodaah" (silence is like consent). It is not engaging but disengaging that is viewed as validating. If not for persuading others, we are to at least speak up in order not to appear as agreeing with false contentions and harmful propositions. There is a lot at stake in the marketplace of ideas. One must cultivate the complex sagacity to determine when to ignore faulty marginal ideas and when to openly confront them. It is not an obvious matter with universal principles.

Today, each of us can find ourselves in narrow places of conformity and agreement. Sometimes, however, we must step out of our comfort zone to learn about those who view things differently from us. Even further, there are specific times when we may, and perhaps even must, choose to debate fundamentalists and extremists. It is not an easy decision, and one must ensure one's safety, both physical and emotional, in the process. In the famous Biblical story of the Exodus, Moses could have merely waged war and led a slave uprising against the Egyptians. Rather, he approached Pharaoh and engaged him in the pursuit of justice. He looked evil in the face without flinching or backing down from his own holy convictions.

---

[7] Antonia Blumberg, "Neil DeGrasse Tyson Responds To Joel Osteen On Faith And Science," *Huffpost*, June 9, 2014, https://www.huffpost.com/entry/neil-degrasse-tyson-joel-osteen_n_5474231.
[8] Quill and Thompson.

Thus, we have to trust in the ability of truth and moral values to triumph over extremism if we are to suffuse holiness into our everyday lives.

But, of course, not all opponents are extremists, and not all positions are extreme. Many simply draw different conclusions than we do. All the more so, these are ideas that we should be engaged with. To be sure, we are not equating the magnitude of various debates in this book. Some are far more significant and rooted than others. The goal is simply to show the diversity, depth, and breadth of various debates that are still alive today, while rooted in our history and collective memory.

By engaging in these debates, we personalize the Torah for ourselves. We are not looking to persuade the reader one way or another. Instead, we ask you to take what you will from the debates to live deeper lives with more spiritual integrity. In this book, through the lens of debate, we will explore these opportunities for improving ourselves, our communities, and indeed our entire world entrusted to us by God.

May the debates continue.

On Truth

Debate 1.

Hillel vs. Shammai:
Arguments for the Sake of Heaven

So much of what it means to be Jewish—whether as a matter of self-definition or of identity as described by others—has to do with making distinctions. We distinguish between day and night, between sacred and profane, between permitted and prohibited. We're helped along in the process of making distinctions when we engage in dialogue and debate, using tools developed by Socrates and his students in an era also marked by the beginnings of the rabbinic Judaism from which today's Jewish thought and practice developed. And argumentative dialogue is particularly emblematic of the approach to decision-making and to thought development exemplified by the rabbis whose ideas were memorialized in the Talmud.

When we think about the process of Talmudic argumentation, we naturally start with Hillel and Shammai. They were towering figures of the Mishnah[9] who helped create the Judaism recognizable to us in the 21st century. They helped set the stage for the Jewish people to transition from an ethnic group that followed a Temple-based and priest-oriented system to a complexly defined religion that adheres to a sage-based Talmudic legal tradition. It was a bumpy path. Not only were these two Tanna'im often in strong disagreement with one another, their students, too, sharply differed on issues of law, ethics, theology, and ritual practice.

How bad did it get? The Talmud teaches us that, in the era of the Sanhedrin,[10] there were not many disputes because, when a question arose, it went through a system of lesser courts—until it reached the highest court, the Sanhedrin, located in the Temple, if needed. However, with the increase in the students of Hillel and Shammai who had not served their teachers adequately, unresolved disputes increased and the Torah became like two Torot.[11]

The Jewish people were divided on so many fronts and yet now here too, on the development of Jewish law, they were harshly divided as well. Even though both sides are typically recorded in the Talmud, we end up, almost always, following the approach of Beit Hillel[12] over Beit Shammai.[13] Why is that?

---

[9] A rabbi of the Mishnah is known as a Tanna (Aramaic for teacher). Hillel and Shammai were Tanna'im, and lived at the end of the last century BCE and the beginning of the first century CE.
[10] The Sanhedrin was the highest rabbinic court, the equivalent to the Supreme Court in the American Judicial system. It is fascinating to note that the Sanhedrin technically required 70 members, but the number was increased by one to avoid a tie when voting on Jewish legal matters.
[11] BT Sanhedrin 88b.
[12] The term Beit Hillel (and similarly Beit Shammai) means the "house of Hillel," referring to his school or yeshiva.
[13] The Mishnah (Shabbat 1:3) records 18 places where we follow the path of Shammai over that of Hillel. The rabbis taught that one could choose to be a consistent follower of Beit Shammai or of Beit Hillel, but was not

> Rabbi Abba said that Shmuel said: For three years Beit Shammai and Beit Hillel disagreed. These said: The halakha is in accordance with our opinion, and these said: The halakha is in accordance with our opinion. Ultimately, a Divine Voice emerged and proclaimed: Both these and those are the words of the living God. However, the halakha is in accordance with the opinion of Beit Hillel. The Gemara asks: Since both these and those are the words of the living God, why were Beit Hillel privileged to have the halakha established in accordance with their opinion?
>
> The reason is that they were agreeable and forbearing.... [W]hen they formulated their teachings and cited a dispute, they prioritized the statements of Beit Shammai [teaching Beit Shammai's positions before their own].[14]

How beautiful that our tradition embraces such halakhic pluralism around "the words of the living God," and how powerful that it was humility that gave Beit Hillel the upper hand over Beit Shammai. So too, in our debates today, we should record the opposing view and have the humility to study it and understand it fully even as we advocate fiercely for our own perspectives on ethics and truth.

There is a deeper worldview that emerges from the text found shortly after the articulation of that Talmudic conclusion just mentioned.

> The Sages taught the following *baraita*: For two and a half years, Beit Shammai and Beit Hillel disagreed. These say: It would have been preferable had [humanity] not been created than to have been created. And those said: It is preferable for [humanity] to have been created than had he not been created. Ultimately, they were counted and concluded: It would have been preferable had [humanity] not been created than to have been created. However, now that he has been created, [a person] should examine [their] actions.[15]

---

to pick and choose and thus follow the leniencies (or stringencies) of each. The verse reading "The fool walks in darkness" (Ecclesiastes 2:14) is applied to such people. (Rosh Hashanah 14b). Interestingly enough, Rabbi Isaac Luria (16th century, also known by his acronym Ar"i) suggested that in messianic times we will switch and follow Shammai over Hillel.
[14] BT Eruvin 13b.
[15] *Ibid.*

Here Beit Hillel and Beit Shammai are not debating law but theology. This is quite the anomaly! And yet, the placement of this debate on the same page as the statement celebrating the authority of Hillel over Shammai because of humility seems to paint a broader picture. Perhaps another dimension of the favored worldview is highlighted here. Is Shammai a pessimist, even cynical perhaps? Is Hillel an optimist, even hopeful, perhaps? Hillel seems to believe that the human condition has more blessings than curses. Does Shammai indeed believe the opposite? Perhaps Jewish law must be cultivated by those who seek progress, focus on blessings, and have some degree of hopeful optimism built into their philosophy.

Along a similar thread, Beit Shammai and Beit Hillel would light their Chanukah menorahs differently.[16] Beit Shammai would start with eight candles the first night and light one less each night, based on the idea that sometimes sacrifices are decreased over time rather than increased.[17] But Beit Hillel felt we should only increase light and ascend in holiness, thus starting with one candle the first night and adding one candle each night, which of course, is our practice today. This, too, could also reflect a philosophy of progress, of hope.

Another possible reason why Hillel was chosen over Shammai may be due to his more inclusive approach. If God realized that the world needed to be sustained more by mercy than judgment, then shouldn't humans, and judges in particular, follow the same approach? Here is one episode among many others in the Talmudic section discussing how Shammai and Hillel relate so differently to conversion candidates:

> There was another incident involving one gentile who was passing behind the study hall and heard the voice of a teacher who was teaching Torah to his students and saying the verse: "And these are the garments which they shall make: A breastplate, and an *efod*, and a robe, and a tunic of checkered work, a mitre, and a girdle" (Exodus 28:4). The gentile said: These garments, for whom are they designated? The students said to him: For the High Priest. The gentile said to himself: I will go and convert so that they will install me as High Priest. He came before Shammai and said to him: Convert me on condition that you install me as High Priest. Shammai pushed him with the builder's cubit in his hand. He came before Hillel; he converted him.

---

[16] BT Shabbat 21b.
[17] The Talmud is technically referring to the bulls of the additional sacrifice of the holiday of Succot, which decrease in number.

Hillel said to him . . . Is it not the way of the world that only one who knows the protocols [*takhsisei*] of royalty is appointed king? Go and learn the royal protocols by engaging in Torah study. He went and read the Bible. When he reached the verse which says: "And the common man that draws near shall be put to death" (Numbers 1:51), the convert said to Hillel: With regard to whom is the verse speaking? Hillel said to him: Even with regard to David, king of Israel. The convert reasoned . . . If the Jewish people are called God's children, and due to the love that God loved them he called them: "Israel is My son, My firstborn" (Exodus 4:22), and nevertheless it is written about them: And the common man that draws near shall be put to death; a mere convert who came without merit, with nothing more than his staff and traveling bag, all the more so that this applies to him, as well.

The convert came before Shammai and told him that he retracts his demand to appoint him High Priest, saying: Am I at all worthy to be High Priest? Is it not written in the Torah: And the common man that draws near shall be put to death? He came before Hillel and said to him: Hillel the patient, may blessings rest upon your head as you brought me under the wings of the Divine Presence.[18]

Hillel wasn't only more lenient in regard to conversions but in many other matters as well. For example, Shammai believed that only the most worthy students should be admitted into the *beit midrash* (study hall), whereas Hillel took a less elitist approach.[19] Shammai was strict on allowing divorces but Hillel said divorce was allowed even for seemingly trivial concerns in the marriage.[20] Shammai took to a literalist extreme, demanding that even at a wedding people describe a bride as being only as beautiful as an objective viewer would consider her to be, whereas Hillel allowed every bride to be described as beautiful and gracious, thereby enhancing her joy and dignity.[21] Beit Shammai argued that if one forgot to bentch[22] and left the place they had eaten, they needed to return to where they ate to recite it there. Beit Hillel, however, said that one can bentch in their new location.[23] It

---

[18] BT Shabbat 31a.
[19] Avot d'Rebbe Natan 2:9.
[20] BT Gittin 90a.
[21] BT Ketubot 16b-17a.
[22] *Bentch* is the Yiddish term for "bless," and refers specifically to reciting the Birkat Hamazon, the Grace After Meals.
[23] Mishnah Berakhot 8:7.

has been argued that they shared very different political worldviews as well and that Beit Shammai was more aligned with the hawkish zealots whereas Beit Hillel consisted of more pacifists, and that because of these political differences, Beit Hillel was alienated from prayer spaces led by Beit Shammai.[24] Thus, their view of how to engage with the oppressors (the Romans) colored their rulings regarding gentiles in general. It got so nasty that the Talmud says that Beit Shammai would even kill members of Beit Hillel.[25] As these matters cooled down, the positions of Beit Shammai were dismissed and became irrelevant.[26]

Nonetheless, these debates matter deeply in our tradition not only because of the importance of the content matter but also because of the process of the debate itself. The rabbis share:

> Every dispute that is for the sake of Heaven, will in the end endure; But one that is not for the sake of Heaven, will not endure. Which is the controversy that is for the sake of Heaven? Such was the controversy of Hillel and Shammai. And which is the controversy that is not for the sake of Heaven? Such was the controversy of Korah and all his congregation.[27]

Rabbi Jonathon Sacks states it in a more straightforward manner: "The difference between them, according to Bartenura, is that the argument for the sake of heaven is an argument for the sake of truth; argument not for the sake of heaven is argument for the sake of victory and power, and they are two very different things."[28]

There was a de facto respect built into the debates of Shammai and Hillel because both were working to serve God. Motives in a religious debate are crucial. It is all too easy for ego or power to take over. But if one is serving God and maintains respect and decency in the course of a debate, that dispute especially should be recorded and studied. Perhaps out of a recognition that the Hillel-Shammai divide was problematic in the short term, but ultimately provided the Jewish people, and indeed the world, with an example of a debate that was hard-fought but based on good-faith differences in outlook that contained an element of purity,

---

[24] Tosefta Rosh Hashanah.
[25] JT Shabbat 1:4.
[26] BT Berakhot 36b; BT Beitzah 11b; BT Yevamot 9a.
[27] Pirkei Avot 5:17. Translated in *Mishnah Yomit* by Dr. Joshua Kulp. Korach, Moses' cousin, challenged his authority claiming that "the whole nation is holy. . . and why are you [Moses and Aaron] lifting yourselves up above the congregation?"
[28] Rabbi Jonathan Sacks, "How Not to Argue," rabbisacks.org, 2020, https://www.rabbisacks.org/covenant-conversation/korach/how-not-to-argue/.

a fast day was instituted based on the conflicts between these two camps[29] (this fast day is no longer observed).[30] And as if to underscore the tension between the image of an unbridgeable disagreement and the importance of respect—even love—for those with whom we disagree, even with all of their disagreements, members of Beit Hillel and of Beit Shammai continued to marry one another.[31]

There were even rare cases of the two camps switching their respective views, teaching us the need to be flexible in our perspectives. One such case involves the application of *"tikkun olam"*[32] to a question about freeing slaves.

> In the case of one who is a half-slave half-freeman because only one of his two owners emancipated him, he serves his master one day and serves himself one day; this is the statement of Beit Hillel. Beit Shammai say: Through such an arrangement you have remedied his master, as his master loses nothing through this. However, you have not remedied the slave himself, as the slave himself remains in an unsustainable situation. It is not possible for him to marry a maidservant because he is already a half-freeman, as it is prohibited for a freeman to marry a maidservant. It is also not possible for him to marry a free woman, as he is still a half-slave. If you say he should be idle and not marry, but isn't it true that the world was created only for procreation, as it is stated: "He did not create it to be a waste; He formed it to be inhabited" (Isaiah 45:18)? Rather, for the betterment of the world his master is forced to make him a freeman, and the slave writes a promissory note accepting his responsibility to pay half his value to his master. And Beit Hillel ultimately retracted their opinion, to rule in accordance with the statement of Beit Shammai.[33]

How often today do we debate closed-mindedly? What if we could truly be open to changing our view?

---

[29] Halachot Gedolot, laws of Tisha B'Av; Shulchan Aruch, Orach Chaim 580.
[30] Beit Yosef, Orach Chaim 580.
[31] Mishnah Yevamot 1:4; BT Yevamot 14b.
[32] *Tikkun olam* means repairing or improving the world.
[33] Mishnah Gittin 4:5.

Now, it's logical to conclude that Hillel and Shammai disagreed on everything. But Maimonides[34] explains that that was not the case at all.

> [W]hen two people are of equal intellect and investigation and knowledge of the fundamentals from which reasonings extrapolate, no disagreement will occur in their reasonings in any way. And if it does occur, it will be minimal; as it is only found that Shammai and Hillel disagreed about isolated laws.
>
> And that is because the thoughts of the two of them were very close—one to the other—in everything that they extrapolated by way of reasoning. And, likewise, the fundamentals that were given to this one, were like the fundamentals given to that one.[35]

Here we learn another important lesson from the history of Jewish debates. We should not only focus on all that we disagree with but should strive to see all our commonalities as well. It may seem in America that Democrats and Republicans disagree on everything. But is that true? Is it true that Reform Jews and Orthodox Jews have nothing in common in their worldview? Do Iranians and Israelis have completely different visions of what constitutes a good life? The differences are real. But shared values can be built on and developed to mitigate the fallout from debates where there are disagreements.

By embracing intellectual openness, personal humility, and optimism for human progress as we decipher and fight for what is good, perhaps we can move closer to the truth Beit Hillel and Beit Shammai argued in pursuit of.

---

[34] Maimonides was also known by his acronym Rambam.
[35] Rambam, *Introduction to the Mishnah*, 11, translation by Rabbi Francis Nataf, 2017.

Debate 2.

Absolute Truth vs. Compromise: Which is the True Good?

One might think that absolutism is a sign of strength. If one has "moral clarity," then they shouldn't budge an inch on their position. This is a very popular approach today in both religious and political discourse. If you are not absolute, you are often accused of being "wishy-washy" or "a moral relativist" or "weak in conviction" or guilty of a "cowardly betrayal of principle." One is told it is a cop-out to claim "it's complicated" or that "we need more nuance." To be sure, a very strong Jewish case could be made for absolute truth, especially from Jewish sources prior to modernity. After all, the Torah instructs that we should not only not lie but "run from lies."[36] In the ancient world, the question was less *What is good?* than *Will you do that which we know to be good?* In modernity, as skepticism emerged, the question of what was good was itself asked more frequently and more searchingly. The question was no longer as much about the will to do that which everyone knew to be good, as more ethicists focused greater attention on the intellectual deliberation process to discover the particular good.

As mentioned above, a strong Jewish case could be made both from sources prior to, and since, the advent of modern thought, in opposition to absolutist thinking and favoring compromise:

> Rabbi Yehoshua ben Korcha says: It is a mitzvah to mediate a dispute, as it is stated: "Execute the judgment of truth and peace in your gates" (Zechariah 8:16). Is it not that in the place where there is strict judgment there is no true peace, and in a place where there is true peace, there is no strict judgment? Rather, which is the judgment that has peace within it? You must say: This is mediation, as both sides are satisfied with the result.[37]

The Talmudic rabbis applied value not only to compromise in the courts but also when it comes to religious ideas. In the Talmud,[38] Rabbi Yochanan is quoted as saying that Jerusalem was destroyed in the time of the Romans only because the people judged according to the Torah. The astonished reply is, "What kind of judgment should they have applied—that of the sorcerers?" The explanation: "What Rabbi Yochanan meant was that litigants insisted on strict enforcement of

---

[36] Exodus 23:7.
[37] BT Sanhedrin 6b.
[38] BT Bava Metzia 30b.

the law and were unwilling to compromise." Rambam (Maimonides) affirms this value for religious compromise in his Yad Hachazakah.[39]

This inclination in favor of compromise is also found in Talmudic discussions of financial matters:

> Rabbi Nechunya ben HaKana was once asked by his disciples: In the merit of which virtue were you blessed with longevity? He said to them: In all my days, I never attained veneration at the expense of my fellow's degradation. Nor did my fellow's curse ever go up with me upon my bed... And I was always openhanded with my money.[40]

We might think that the benefits of compromise would be apparent not only in the financial realm, but also when it comes to political action. We see, though, that that's hardly always the case. To understand how a failure to compromise has played out in just one arena, American history is replete with the tragic consequences of such a failure. The Civil War, for example, was the result of eleven Southern states refusing to deal with an elected president who was opposed to slavery, and their attempt to secede and drive Union forces out by military force. Even though the Confederacy was defeated, the "Solid South" has to this day retained an antipathy toward President Lincoln for a century and a half. Of course, this example also demonstrates the need to know when to compromise and when to stand firm; the implications of a hypothetical decision by the North to compromise on the issue of slavery are too painful to contemplate.

But compromise, while at times painful, has produced enduring results. During the New Deal, President Franklin D. Roosevelt concentrated on economic issues rather than civil rights, and most often created policies based on a consensus of experts. In June 1934, Roosevelt created the Committee on Economic Security (CES)[41] for the task of developing "... at once security against several of the great disturbing factors in life—especially those which relate to unemployment and old age." While the CES members quickly (by *January 1935*)[42] approved a way to create the Social Security system as well as programs for unemployment insurance,

---

[39] Hilchot Sanhedrin 22:4. *Yad Hachazakah*, also known as Mishneh Torah, is Rambam's work on Jewish Law. It is considered to be the most comprehensive work of its kind, as unlike the Shulchan Aruch of Rav Yosef Karo (the Code of Jewish Law), which is based to a great degree on the Rambam's opus, it deals not only with laws which were relevant in his time, but also those which were no longer current, such as laws of the *Beit Hamikdash* (the Holy Temple).

[40] BT Megillah 28a.

[41] Social Security Administration, "The Committee on Economic Security (CES)," ssa.gov, last accessed 2023, https://www.ssa.gov/history/reports/ces/cesbasic.html.

[42] Ibid. "II. The Formal Report to the President and Associated Documents," https://www.ssa.gov/history/reports/ces/ces.html.

they did not find a means to include health insurance, and even the funding of the social safety net programs that were created depended on a regressive tax on individuals (once you pass the maximum threshold, you do not pay a penny more of tax). On the other hand, it cannot be denied that millions of elderly, disabled, and unemployed Americans faced starvation without this legislation, so overall the law has benefited our society despite its imperfections.

It is no secret that compromise seems to be a dirty word in Washington these days. For the last decade, we have witnessed partisan gridlock that has not been seen in generations. It's almost as if we've gone from a situation in which compromise was the preferred goal to one in which we have only two opposing camps, with each one devoted to its own absolute truth and demanding action in keeping with that truth.

How can we learn to recognize that truth as a value has different valences in different contexts, to balance a religious commitment to truth with a social commitment to cultural and moral relativism? Rav Shagar[43] grappled with this concept:

> Similarly, what is our position regarding *sati*, widow burning, which is still practiced by some in India? From our perspective, this custom is extremely immoral, yet some women believe that burning themselves alongside their husbands' bodies is the best thing for the souls of all concerned. The perplexed postmodernist will have "double vision": While railing against the practice he will also be able to see the issue from the point of view of those who practice sati... To prevent postmodernism from sliding into absurdity, we must set boundaries. Where is the line at which the postmodernist will refuse to accept the other's values? What criteria and methods should be used for setting such boundaries? And can one propose other ways of coping with the paradox of pluralism, which is amplified in the postmodern era?[44]

Richard Rorty argued that we should set aside the quest to find truth, and rather embrace the notion that truth is to be created.[45] This is fundamental to post-modern thought and something that Rav Shagar also arrived at through studying Rorty

---

[43] Rav Shagar was a 20th-21st-century Jerusalem biblical scholar and religious postmodern thinker. Shagar is an acronym for his full name, Shimon Gershon Rosenberg.
[44] Shimon Gershon Rosenberg (Rabbi Shagar), *Faith Shattered and Restored: Judaism in the Postmodern Age* (Jerusalem: Maggid Books, 2017), 107-108.
[45] Richard Rorty, *Contingency, Irony, and Solidarity* (Cambridge: Cambridge University Press, 1989), 7.

and through kabbalah (the broken vessels, to use the kabbalistic metaphor, leave us only with sparks of clarity but no full clarity).

New-age thinker Eckhart Tolle writes:

> The Catholic and other churches are actually correct when they identify relativism, the belief that there is no absolute truth to guide human behavior, as one of the evils of our time; but you won't find absolute truth if you look for it where it cannot be found: in doctrines, ideologies, sets of rules, or stories. What do they all have in common? They are made up of thought. Thought can at best point to the truth, but it never is the truth. That's why Buddhists say, "The finger pointing to the moon is not the moon." All religions are equally false and equally true, depending on how you use them.[46]

Given what Rorty, Tolle and Rav Shagar all say, we can recognize that truth as a matter of religious devotion is different than truth as a matter of how we choose to live in society. We do hold a commitment to truth, but we also have to understand that thought is only one dimension of how we reach truth. There is also a deeper realm of consciousness beyond thought. Here, we can embrace both a bold spiritual quest for truth while also holding a humble relativity and pluralism.

The noted economist Joseph Schumpeter wrote: "To realize the relative validity of one's convictions and yet stand for them unflinchingly, is what distinguishes civilized man from a barbarian."[47] We have to be intellectually honest and yet still morally robust. Our skepticism must empower us rather than paralyze us.

The rabbis taught, in a fascinating *midrash*, that truth would ultimately become a human construct:

> R. Simon said: When the Holy One, blessed be God, came to create Adam, the ministering angels formed themselves into groups and parties, some of them saying, 'Let him be created,' while others urged, 'let him not be created.' As it is written, "Lovingkindness and truth met, justice and peace kissed." (Psalms 85:11): Lovingkindness said, 'Let him be created, because he will dispense acts of lovingkindness'; Truth said, 'Let him not be created, because he full of lies'; Justice said, 'Let him be created, because he will perform acts of justice'; Peace said,

---

[46] Eckhart Tolle, *A New Earth: Awakening to Your Life's Purpose* (New York: Penguin Publishing Group, 2006), 70-71.
[47] Joseph Schumpeter, *Capitalism, Socialism and Democracy* (New York: Harper Perennial Modern Classics, 2008), 243.

> 'Let him not be created, because he is full of strife.'" What did God do? God held Truth and cast it to the ground, as it is written, "and truth will be sent to the earth." The ministering angels said before the Holy One, "Sovereign of the Universe! Why do you despise Thy seal? Let Truth arise from the earth!" Hence it is written, "Let truth spring up from the earth." (Psalms 85:12).[48]

With our finite capacity, we humans cannot access the highest realms of truth, and so God needed to let go of such an absolute commitment, as it were, to allow us to have freedom and autonomy. The rabbis understood that the power and responsibility of defining the parameters of truth was now in their hands.

Rabbi Jonathan Sacks tried to push us from the binary of the absolute vs. the relative. He wrote:

It remains difficult fully to comprehend the vision at the heart of the Hebrew Bible, namely that religious truth is not universal, nor relative, but covenantal. God reaches out to each people, faith and culture, asking it to be true to itself while recognizing that it is not the exclusive possessor of truth. Great harm has always been done to the world by religions when they seek to impose their truth on others by force, or when they treat those who do not share that truth as less than equal citizens.[49]

The key question today is whether there is a lowest point that can be reached in a failure to compromise. Will we heed the warning of Rabbi Yochanan, or will we sink further into the political morass?

One's character is not solely measured by their ideals, but also by how they're willing to compromise. There are, of course, values that should not be compromised. But for the sake of peace, often we must compromise our upper hand even when we are certain of the truth.

Rashi teaches that doing "what is right and good" (Deuteronomy 6:18) "refers to a compromise, acting beyond the strict demands of the law."[50] We need to learn to work in the real world with real people and not let the perfect be the enemy of the good. This is true at home, in community, in society, and internationally. Compromise can indeed be a vice when it's about one's own self-gain at the expense of supporting others, but it can, and must, also be a virtue when it is about lifting others.

---

[48] Genesis Rabbah 8:5, translated by AJWS.
[49] Rabbi Jonathan Sacks, *A Letter in the Scroll* (New York: Free Press, 2004), 96.
[50] Rashi on Deuteronomy 6:18:1, trans. M. Rosenbaum and A.M. Silbermann, London, 1929-1934.

Debate 3.

Trust vs. Questioning

Trust is not a simple matter. We have all been betrayed by friends, colleagues, and strangers. We've all learned to be cautious. Bill Gates in his end of the year blog post shared his optimism and his concerns for 2022. On the top of his list for concerns was the growing inability of Americans to trust the government. He wrote:

> If your people don't trust you, they're not going to support major new initiatives. And when a major crisis emerges, they're less likely to follow guidance necessary to weather the storm.[51]

Indeed, a 2019 poll of American adults showed that according to 75% of respondents, basic trust in the federal government was shrinking.[52] Of course, we should not trust anyone or anything blindly. On the other hand, we should be concerned when the most basic levels of trust in a society break down, when huge segments of citizens don't trust medical experts, for example, because medicine has been politicized.

In Jewish thought, we have a tension between trust and investigation. On the one hand, we learn of the value of *bitachon* (trust), and on the other hand we learn of the value of *machloket* (argumentation).

A central problem involved in not living with trust is that anxiety will take over. With no one and nothing to trust, we can become full of worry. That overflow of anxiety will not serve us, or those around us, well. Lithuanian scholar and philosopher Rabbi Eliyahu Dessler writes:

> The true source of constant worry is that we have no *bitachon* (trust) of attaining the external things that we desire. This desire for "possession," and "taking," its realization always depends on others and external circumstances. Bitachon flourishes when we desire internal things—the desire "to be," because in that we are not dependent on others. Therefore, one who desires material possessions feels deep within one's heart that the desire is futile, and is not up to him or her. This is the root of worry.[53]

---

[51] Megan Sauer, "What Bill Gates is 'most worried about heading into 2022,'" *CNBC*, December 25, 2021, https://www.cnbc.com/2021/12/25/what-bill-gates-is-most-worried-about-heading-into-2022.html.
[52] Lee Rainie and Andrew Perrin, "Key findings about Americans' declining trust in government and each other," Pew Research Center, July 22, 2019, https://www.pewresearch.org/fact-tank/2019/07/22/key-findings-about-americans-declining-trust-in-government-and-each-other/.
[53] Michtav Me'Eliyahu volume 5, 90.

We learn from Psalms again and again that we should trust in God: "Trust in [God] at all times, O people; pour out your hearts before [God]; God is our refuge. Selah."⁵⁴ For the Psalmist, trust is the recipe for living without anxiety. This trust should not be mistaken for being passive. Psalms teach: "Trust in the Lord and do good."⁵⁵ Yes, we have trust but then we must go and act. *Hishtadlut* (striving) must follow *bitachon* (trusting).⁵⁶

So, what do we have trust in? Some of us may trust God, may trust science, may trust a friend, or may trust our gut. We should investigate to see where we are ultimately placing our trust. Steve Jobs, after being diagnosed with pancreatic cancer, shared his ideology that guided his life, which he called connecting the dots:

> You can't connect the dots looking forward; you can only connect them looking backward. So you have to trust that the dots will somehow connect in your future. You have to trust in something—your gut, destiny, life, karma, whatever. This approach has never let me down.⁵⁷

Trust is not only helpful on a personal level but necessary on a collective level. Rabbi Jonathan Sacks explains:

> Without morals, markets cannot function. The very words we use imply as much. The word "credit" comes from the Latin *cred*, the same root we see in "credo," meaning "I believe." "Confidence," the presence or lack of which shapes markets, comes from the Latin root fides, meaning to have faith in someone or something. "Fiduciary" has the same origin. Trust, the lack of which produced the banking crisis of 2008, is predicated on trustworthiness. These are, or were, fundamentally moral terms. When there is a breakdown of trust, something significant is going wrong.⁵⁸

---

⁵⁴ Psalms 62:9.
⁵⁵ Psalms 37:3.
⁵⁶ Rabbi Moses Feinstein, preeminent 20th-century halachist, wrote in his responsa Igrot Moshe (in response to one asking if it is permissible to purchase life insurance or if one should rely on trust in God) that obtaining life insurance is an imperative. Rabbi Feinstein was a strong advocate for trusting in God while at the same time doing our share.
⁵⁷ Steve Jobs, Commencement address at Stanford University, June 12, 2005, "'You've got to find what you love,' Jobs says," Stanford University, June 12, 2005, https://news.stanford.edu/2005/06/12/youve-got-find-love-jobs-says/.
⁵⁸ Rabbi Jonathan Sacks, *Morality: Restoring The Common Good In Divided Times* (New York: Basic Books, 2020), 98.

Yuval Noah Harari writes:

> For thousands of years, philosophers, thinkers and prophets have besmirched money and called it the root of all evil. Be that as it may.... [m]oney is the only trust system created by humans that can bridge almost any cultural gap.... Thanks to money, even people who don't know each other and don't trust each other can nevertheless cooperate effectively.[59]

However, Harari balances his defense of money's egalitarian nature by saying:

> But in its extreme form, belief in the free market is as naive as belief in Santa Claus. There simply is no such thing as a market free of all political bias. The most important economic resource is trust in the future, and this resource is constantly threatened by thieves and charlatans. Markets by themselves offer no protection against fraud, theft and violence.[60]

Saying that we "trust" does not point us to an easy answer or an obvious path to follow. With trust comes a challenge. Sometimes our trust-challenge is to give up control and cultivate the trust to calmly keep walking on the same righteous path as we spiritually wait for change. Other times, our trust-challenge is to actively change the course and remain confident as we strive to take control of the situation and create change.

The headlines each day across the globe remind us that so many in power are corrupt, dishonest, and abusive. It's a sad story for humanity. But let's not be deceived. Countless (billions!) across the globe are living honest, compassionate, and loving lives of integrity each day. This is where the spiritual revolution for good will emerge. With a moral consciousness of deep interconnectivity, let's keep marching in solidarity together (locally and globally) in our fervent quest to unite for good (while honoring our noble differences). We can trust, by and large, even with news-making exceptions, that humanity is generally good.

So how do we work to rebuild trust in our lives and in our relationships? Dr. John Gottman writes of what he calls "'sliding door' moments:"

> In any interaction, there is a possibility of connecting with your partner or turning away from your partner. Let me give you an

---
[59] Yuval Noah Harari, *Sapiens* (New York: Harper Collins, 2015), 207.
[60] Harari, 367-368.

example of that from my own relationship. One night, I really wanted to finish a mystery novel.... At one point... I put the novel on my bedside and walked into the bathroom.

As I passed the mirror, I saw my wife's face in the reflection, and she looked sad, brushing her hair. There was a sliding door moment. I had a choice. I could sneak out of the bathroom and think, "I don't want to deal with her sadness tonight, I want to read my novel." But instead, because I'm a sensitive researcher of relationships, I decided to go into the bathroom. I took the brush from her hair and asked, "What's the matter, baby?" And she told me why she was sad.

Now, at that moment, I was building trust; I was there for her. I was connecting with her rather than choosing to think only about what I wanted.[61]

On the other hand, we learn over and over of the Jewish value of asking questions. The Talmud famously teaches the value of asking questions at the Passover *seder* (and beyond):

> If his son is wise—the son asks him.
> If not, his wife asks him.
> If not, he asks himself.
> Even if there are [only] two scholars who know the laws of
>   Passover, they ask each other.[62]

Nelson Mandela, in *Long Walk to Freedom*, recounted that, in his house growing up, he was discouraged from asking too many questions.[63] He then explained the value of answering the questions of even his prison guards:

> Some of the [White Afrikaans prison] warders [on Robben Island] began to engage us in conversation. I never initiated conversations with warders, but if they addressed a question to me, I tried to answer. It is easier to educate a man when he wants to learn. Usually, these questions were posed with a kind of

---

[61] John Gottman, "John Gottman on Trust and Betrayal," *Greater Good Magazine*, October 29, 2011, https://greatergood.berkeley.edu/article/item/john_gottman_on_trust_and_betrayal.
[62] BT Pesachim 117a. This statement refers to the recitation of the *Mah Nishtanah*, traditionally asked at the *seder* by a young child. It is fascinating and instructive to note that the entire *seder* text and experience is an exercise in best educational practices. The question/answer format of *Mah Nishtanah* is actually used throughout the *haggadah*.
[63] Nelson Mandela, *Long Walk to Freedom* (New York: Little, Brown, 2008), 11.

exasperation: "All right, Mandela, what is it you really want?" Or, "Look, you have a roof over your head and enough food, why are you causing so much trouble?" I would then calmly explain our policies to the warders. I wanted to demystify the African National Congress for them, to peel away their prejudices."[64]

Rabbi Jonathan Sacks writes:

> Abraham, about to become father to the first child of the covenant, is being taught by God what it means to raise a child. To be a father—implies the Bible—is to teach a child to question, to challenge, confront, dispute. God invites Abraham to do these things because he wants him to be the parent of a nation that will do these things. He does not want the people of the covenant to be one that accepts the evils and injustices of the world as the will of God. God wants the people of the covenant to be human, neither more nor less. God wants them to hear the cry of the oppressed, the pain of the afflicted and the plaint of the lonely. He wants them not to accept the world as is, because it is not the world that ought to be. He is giving Abraham a tutorial in what it is to teach a child to grow by challenging the existing scheme of things. Only through such challenges does a child learn to accept responsibility; only by accepting responsibility does a child grow to become an adult; and only an adult can understand the parenthood of God.[65]

Questions can present us with a paradox. Gay, Orthodox Rabbi Steve Greenberg writes:

> The key to Jewish exegesis is to assume that nothing is obvious. Questions are the great cultural paradox. They both destabilize and secure social norms. Questions tend to democratize. Ease with questions conveys a fundamental trust in the goodwill and the good sense of others. Autocrats hate questions. We train children at the Passover *seder* to ask why because tyrants are undone and liberty is won with a good question.

---

[64] Ibid., 457.
[65] Rabbi Jonathan Sacks, *To Heal a Fractured World* (New York: Schocken Books, 2005), 25.

Khrushchev once explained why he hated Jews. He said, "They always ask why." It is for this reason that God loves it when we ask why. Consequently, we celebrate challenging the Torah to make sense, and above all to be a defensible expression of Divine goodness. When we ask good questions, the Torah is given anew on Sinai at that very moment.[66]

German-language poet Rainer Maria Rilke wrote:

> Be patient towards all that is unsolved in your heart and try to love the questions themselves like locked rooms. . . .. Do not now seek the answers; that cannot be given you because you would not be able to live them. And the point is, to live everything. Live the questions now.
> Perhaps you will then gradually, without noticing it, live along some distant day into the answer.[67]

Rabbi Haim Volozhin, a student of the Vilna Gaon and the founder of the Volozhin yeshiva, taught, in his commentary on Pirkei Avot:

> It is forbidden for students to accept the words of the teacher if the students have *kushyot* (challenging objections/questions). Sometimes the student will have the truth, just as a little branch can light a large log.[68]

Biblical commentator Dr. Avivah Zornberg writes about *kushyot* (hard questions):

> The "hard-edged" sense of language that comes with the negative form generates questions. The Talmudic word for the question is *kushya*. At its heart is the idea of the hard, *kasheh*, the difficult, the resistant. For Rav Hutner, the ability to question must now govern the relationship between God and man, as between parents and growing children. The aim of the relationship is to create, in Rav Hutner's imagery, the "face of one who can receive," who actively generates meaning by asking questions. Now, the dialogue is the model for evoking narratives.

---

[66] Rabbi Steve Greenberg, *Wrestling with God and Men* (Madison: University of Wisconsin Press, 2004), 79.
[67] Rainer Maria Rilke, letter to Franz Xaver Kappus, July 16, 1903; the letter is included as the fourth letter in *Letters to a Young Poet*, a collection of letters from Rilke to Kappus. *Letters to a Young Poet* (Penguin Classics, 2014).
[68] *Ruach HaHayim* on Avot 1:4.

> Without the capacity to ask, to open up the closed issues, to break through the obvious, the self-understood, there can be no meaningful narrative.... For questions do destabilize; they find difficulty and distance, where one might have dreamt of ease and continuity.[69]

We must learn to live with trust. But we also must learn to trust in our asking questions, living in uncertainty, and dwelling in paradox. The more we trust our epistemic foundation, the deeper we can travel in our inquiry.

We cannot blindly trust authorities. We will need to get "a second opinion" and investigate matters deeply. When trusting authorities, we can ask if the person has the adequate knowledge base, if the intent is positive, and if there is integrity. At some point, we will need to live with trust given our inability to ever have total clarity (i.e., the perspective of God). We cannot fall into the liberal trap of living in fear of being "duped." Some won't give to people homeless in the street lest they be duped and the person is not actually homeless. Some won't believe in God even though they want to lest they be duped. Some won't engage business partners lest they be cheated. We can learn to be careful but also courageous, to be questioning but also trusting. That can offer us a path toward wholeness.

---

[69] Dr. Avivah Zornberg, *The Particulars of Rapture* (New York: Knopf Doubleday Publishing Group, 2011), 180 ff.

On God, Torah, & the Cosmos

Debate 4.

Rambam vs. Ra'avad:
Is God Some Thing or No Thing?

What does it mean to seek God? Where can we find God? What does that feel like and look like? Every spiritual seeker craves some contact and connection. So much joy can be found in connection. On the sensual level, we can find joy through our connection to food and bodily touch. On the emotional and cognitive level, we can find joy through relationships, conversation, learning truth, and peace of mind. And on the spiritual level, we can find joy in our connection to Oneness. But is a personal relationship with the Divine possible? If so, can we connect through our flesh and our words, or must we transcend the body and travel into a different spiritual realm?

Of course, no one knows for sure. Many strains of Jewish thought teach that we know little about what God is. There have been great debates about the nature of God and what we can actually know and even attempt to speak about. The Rambam (Maimonides) believed that we cannot talk about what God physically is at all,[70] but only about what God is not (an approach known as negative theology), and even argued that it is heretical to believe that God has a body:

> Therefore bear in mind that by the belief in the corporeality or in anything connected with corporeality, you would provoke God to jealousy and wrath, kindle His fire and anger, become His foe, His enemy, and His adversary in a higher degree than by the worship of idols.[71]

When the Torah speaks consistently of God's body parts such as "an outstretched arm" and of emotions such as anger, only a fool (in the Rambam's view) doesn't know that it's a pedagogical metaphor.[72] Rambam explains:

> The removal of materiality from God. . . signifies that this unity is neither a body nor the power of a body, nor can the accidents of bodies overtake divinity, as e.g., motion and rest, whether in the essential or accidental sense. It was for this reason that the

---

[70] Rambam does assign behavioral attributes to God, such as being merciful, kind, at times even angry, but posits that we cannot truly comprehend the meaning of these attributes vis à vis God as they are different from these same feelings and traits vis à vis humans.
[71] Guide for the Perplexed, English Translation, Friedlander (1903), 1:36.
[72] Guide for the Perplexed 2:25.

Sages denied to God both cohesion and separation of parts, when they remarked:[73] "no sitting and no standing, no division and no cohesion." And the prophet said, "And unto whom will you liken Me that I may be like, says the Holy One."[74] If God were a body [then] God would be like a body. Wherever in the Scriptures God is spoken of with the attributes of material bodies, like motion, standing, sitting, speaking, and [the] like, all these are figures of speech, as the Sages said,[75] "The Torah speaks in the language of men."[76] People have said a great deal on this point. This third fundamental article of faith is indicated by the scriptural expression, "for you have seen no likeness,"[77] i.e., you have not comprehended God as one who possesses a likeness, for, as we have remarked, God is not a body nor a bodily power.[78]

Part of what might have been at stake was the inconsistency between basic Jewish ideas and a fundamental tenet of early Christianity. Jews for centuries already had wanted to push back against the Christian idea of divine incarnation. The theory of divine incarnation, developed in different forms beginning early in the history of Christianity, holds that God could exist in the flesh in the form of Jesus, who has been portrayed within classical Christianity as a divine human of sorts. The notion that God can exist in a physical form, and that anthropomorphism is more than just a didactic tool, could perhaps have been viewed by some Jewish medieval philosophers as getting too close for comfort to the Christians who often proselytized not only through persuasion, but also by the use of the sword.

Rabbi Moshe Taku, a Tosafist,[79] asserts the opposite view, that we should take the Torah literally and should understand God as sometimes taking on human form. For Rabbi Taku, it would be heretical not to read the Torah literally.[80] More famous even than Rabbi Taku was the Ra'avad,[81] who strongly disapproved of

---

[73] BT Chagigah 15a.
[74] Isaiah 40:25.
[75] BT Berakhot 31b, et al.
[76] The expression "The Torah speaks in the language of people" is used approximately 20 times throughout the Talmud.
[77] Deuteronomy 4:15.
[78] Rambam on Mishnah, Sanhedrin Ch. 10, Third Principle.
[79] The Tosafists, the earliest among them being Rashi's grandchildren, are known primarily for the supra-commentary found in the glosses of the Talmud.
[80] Ketav Tamim, in Otzar Nechmad (Vienna, 1860).
[81] Ra'avad wrote a running commentary on Rambam's Mishneh Torah, in which he disagrees with much of Rambam's views, both theological and legal.

Rambam's characterization of corporealists as heretics.[82] Whatever the Ra'avad's own view of divine corporeality might have been, he rejected the idea that the views of those such as the kabbalists with whom he associated were necessarily heretical just because they described the divine identity as having corporeal aspects. He argued that "greater and better people than Rambam" were corporealists who embraced a model of Divinity that engages in anthropomorphic manifestations.[83] Consider Rashi's commentary on the Torah:

> "את ידי this must be translated literally, "hand", (not "power") I will lay My hand upon Egypt to smite them."[84]

There is far more to say about the countless rabbinic commentators who strongly reject corporeality and the many, although fewer, who defend literal corporeality. As just one example, we can see the tension between their respective perspectives that played out in the debate about how humans are created in God's image. What aspect of God's image are we talking about here—physical, spiritual, or maybe something else? Indeed, although it is rarely quoted, a minority traditional view suggests that what makes humans godly is precisely the physical form.[85] In any event, it can suffice to say that there is a rich Jewish debate about corporeality, and as is not uncommon for many medieval philosophers, the intellectual battle became so pitched that their rhetoric approached a level at which, as we demonstrated above, fighting words are involved.

The focused issue about divine corporeality raises a broader philosophical question for us: Is God something or not a thing? There is an inherent contradiction in the idea that God is "nothing." On the one hand, that can mean that God is now actually something, since nothing is conceptually something.[86] On the other hand, one can say that nothing is no thing, the absence of a thing.

Consider the gaps, or pauses, between spoken words. Are those gaps nothing or no thing, or are they something? Or consider the "taste" of the hole in a donut or a bagel. Is the hole of a bagel or donut something? On the one hand, there is nothing there. On the other hand, the bagel or donut loses its identity without that hole. The hole is paramount to the identity of those objects. A shadow, similarly, requires another object to be cast. Is a shadow, then, merely the absence of light,

---

[82] Rambam's Treatise Concerning the Resurrection of the Dead.
[83] The Ra'avad's commentary on Hilchot Teshuvah 3:7.
[84] Rashi's commentary on Exodus 7:4. (M. Rosenbaum and A.M. Silbermann, London, 1929-1934). Also see Rashi's commentary on Exodus 14:31.
[85] See, for example, Shiur Qomah.
[86] And if God is indeed something, then what is He?

or something? And the color white, on one hand, is technically not a color at all; rather it is the absence of color. So, is white actually no thing?

And so, the idea of God as something and as nothing is indeed a paradox. In philosophy, we talk about dialetheism, the idea that both sides in a contradiction are indeed true, or at least that they can be true. Of course, even from a dialetheist perspective, some contradictions should be rightly accepted merely as contradictions where one side must be wrong, yet others are simply unavoidable contradictions where both opposites are true. This is the case with statements about the nature of God, a being whose name reflects the actuality of being even while we cannot begin to grasp what it means to be an entity who existed before any element of the universe had come to be, a deity that we, in some way, experience and even feel in the physical world but that we also recognize as not being physical in any way.

Basic to Jewish tradition is the recognition of a danger inherent in conceiving of God as a physical entity. Such a mistaken mode of thinking is inherent in an idolatry in which the infinite is represented within the finite confines of a physical object, perhaps best exemplified by the sin of the Golden Calf.[87] But even as we recoil when we encounter someone who seems to worship an embodied deity, we should still be troubled by the ease with which some are willing to label others as heretics. Rabbi Nathaniel Helfgot writes:

> The words "heretics" and "heretical" have often been invoked on a whole range of issues in the ideological battles within Orthodoxy in the last two centuries. It is important to note that most of the leading lights of the last two generations have rejected the application of the term "*apikores*" to various people who were led to their conclusions based on sincere reading of the sources. The roots of this perspective are in the famous comment of the Ra'avad that while the Rambam considered anyone who believed in a corporeal God (a rejection of one of the essential pillars of the faith acc. to Rambam) as a heretic, there were many great people who came to that erroneous conclusion from their reading of Tanakh and Hazal. And thus,

---

[87] On the other hand, consider panentheism in Jewish theology which certainly allows for God as the infinite (ein sof) to be found within the finite and concrete (and everything). The key here though is that while God is within everything, God is also beyond everything hence distancing itself from pantheism which equates God and world (matter and Divinity).

while they were wrong and the idea should be rejected, the person was not to be read out of the community.[88]

Indeed, we can appreciate the intensity of belief that leads some people to speak in inflammatory tones about others who disagree with them, but as we come to our own philosophical convictions we can resolve to talk respectfully as we engage in theological debates. In Rabbi Dr. Donniel Hartman's recent book,[89] he argues that we should "put God second." Here he contends that God wants us to make human dignity primary and to view our obligation to honor God as secondary. To apply such an idea here, God would want us to argue theology with a level of respect that makes the first priority of our discourse be about *menschlichkeit*. This idea is seen in the shift in the writing, and even the thinking, of Rabbenu Yonah Girondi,[90] who, early in his career, had a very negative view of much of the Rambam's thinking and who arrogated to himself a license to level ad hominem critiques against him. After seeing that his style of speech seemed to have led to the public burning of the Rambam's works, which in turn might have helped to bring about the public burning of many copies of the Talmud, Rabbeinu Yonah humbly repented and resolved to seek penance for speaking harshly about the Rambam.

And in the twentieth century, the Hazon Ish would argue that since the presence of God in the world was not evident to his contemporaries in the way that God was apparent at Mt. Sinai, observant Jews should no longer view non-observant Jews as heretics. That way of thinking would apply, he argued, to those who knew God yet still rejected belief. In his time (which was basically our time), he argues, many grow up having no understanding of, or relationship to, God at all. If such an approach is appropriate in the realm of observance, all the more so with regard to theology.[91]

We should channel our fervency in our fighting over the nature of God (in inter-religious and intra-religious conflicts) toward searching more deeply for God. Deepak Chopra writes:

---

[88] Rabbi Nathaniel Helfgot, "Reflections on the Historicity of the Torah," Academia.edu, https://www.academia.edu/8225661/REFLECTIONS_ON_THE_HISTORICITY_OF_THE.
[89] Rabbi Dr. Donniel Hartman, *Putting God Second: How to Save Religion from Itself* (Beacon Press, 2016).
[90] Also known as Rabbeinu Yonah, Rabbi Gerondi was a 13th-century Spanish rabbinic scholar.
[91] Similarly, Rabbi Moses Feinstein, arguably the greatest *poseik* (halachic decisor) of the 20th century, ruled that one raised in our time in a nonobservant home falls under the rubric of a *tinok shenishbah* (literally meaning a child who was taken captive), and as such is not to be viewed negatively as an *apikores*.

> Everything we experience as material reality is born in an invisible realm beyond space and time, a realm revealed by science to consist of energy and information. The invisible source of all that exists is not an empty void but the womb of creation itself. Something creates and organizes this energy. It turns the chaos of quantum soup into stars, galaxies, rain forests, human beings, and our own thoughts, emotions, memories, and desires...[I]t is not only possible to know this source of existence on an abstract level but to become intimate and at one with it. When this happens, our horizons open to realities. We will have the experience of God.[92]

Even while we search for Divine connection, we should recall what the Kotzker Rebbe said, that we're all lying, we're all imposters. He argued that none of us knows the truth, none of us knows God, and that we're all fakes with our convenient certainties. This is yet another reminder of why we should not debate too fiercely about the nature of God. Rabbi Yisrael Salanter taught: "Compassion is the foundation of belief. For a person who isn't compassionate, even the belief in God is a kind of idolatry." Rather than debate God, we should become godly.

So, can we still appreciate the medieval debates as such? The nature of theology in the medieval era might have been different than it is today, but we can still draw inspiration from the fervent battles for truth in which giants of thought such as the Rambam and the Ra'avad engaged.[93] We can, and perhaps must, read the words that they used to describe their respective conceptions of God and, empowered by the energy of their faith, go on to defend the existence of God through our actions.

---

[92] Deepak Chopra, *How to Know God* (Harmony/Rodale, 2007), 1-2.
[93] There is an old joke based on the idea that the Ra'avad challenges so much within the thought and rulings of the Rambam. What is the absolute proof that God exists? It's the very first halachah in Rambam's Mishneh Torah and the Ra'avad doesn't argue with him!

DEBATE 5.

Abraham vs. God: Is God Present and Active?

> You are not to stand by the blood of your neighbor.
> —Leviticus 19:16

The specter of theodicy, or explaining the seeming lack of Divine presence during times of adversity, has long stymied theologians, philosophers, and lay people alike. In the Torah, there are many instances of what appears to be senseless cruelty and abandonment: Cain murdering Abel, Hagar and Ishmael left to die in the desert, Pharaoh enslaving entire generations of innocent Hebrews, the tribulations of Job; the list goes on. Indeed, looking to our generation, we can shout to the heavens: Where was God during the Holocaust? Where was God to liberate the ghettos and stop the pogroms? Where was and is God when I most need the Divine presence in my life?

Then there's the related question: With the pervasiveness of injustice and oppression in the world, what should our response be to God's silence and inaction?

And perhaps most importantly, how can there be a benevolent omnipotent God, while so much suffering in the world still festers like an unattended wound upon all of humanity?

These questions speak to the deeper notion of how the immortal, eternal Divine interacts with the gossamer reality of human existence. Surely, shouldn't that which proclaims Itself a protector of all keep all from harm?

Biblical scholar Yochanan Muffs writes on this subject:

> Biblical religion does not seem to require the man of faith to repress his doubts in silent resignation. Abraham, Jeremiah, and Job, all men who question God's ways, are hardly numbered among the wicked. There is even some evidence that God demands such criticism, at least from His prophets (cf. Ezek. 22:3).[94]

Moses, too, questioned God on more than one occasion, to the point of challenging not only His actions and judgment but even their long-term implications and seemingly inherent hypocrisy. One mainstream religious approach holds that

---

[94] Yochanan Muffs, *Personhood of God: Biblical Theology, Human Faith and the Divine Image* (Woodstock, Vermont: Jewish Lights Publishing, 2009), 184.

God is perfect, humans are imperfect, and a bold protest against God's actions is ignorant, immoral, and childish. But, as we see above, it is not hard to find the alternative view as well: that protesting God is not futile, but rather is a deeply religious and moral act. Indeed, there are strands of rabbinic thought that not only allow for, but even celebrate, human confrontation with God. It is not only some of the Talmudic sages who embrace this theology, but perhaps even God, God's self, as well.

In Rabbi Dr. Dov Weiss's *Pious Irreverence: Confronting God in Rabbinic Judaism*, the author lists a series of challenges, protests and confrontations with God, and then he notes that "[a]fter none of these challenges does God castigate or punish the challenger." Rabbi Weiss demonstrates how a theology of protest extends even toward the heavens. In showing the rabbinic exploration of the parameters of God's benevolence and moral perfection, he teaches us deep lessons about both humanity and divinity.

In confronting the awesomeness of God's deeds, Weiss argues that humanity is also able to construct a "fallible God" and a God that "recognizes His [own] limitations and fallibility."[95] In fact, how are we to relate to an imperfect world or an imperfect relationship to the Divine? We can recognize that none of us is born perfect. Every breath is but another opportunity, another chance, to improve our tangible being in this world. Similarly, one can argue that God, too, is constantly working to improve God's self.[96]

In one of the most startling passages in the Torah, Abraham challenges God. Abraham doesn't just challenge something that God wants to do (to destroy Sodom) but questions whether God is just at all. "Shame on You, You unjust Judge," Abraham seems to say.

Abraham does not debate God in the course of so many encounters where confrontation would seem to be most appropriate. He seems to have no problem circumcising the males of his home. He is ready to leave his home and homeland upon God's demand. So, it is not startling, or out of character, that he is even prepared to kill his son after being commanded to do so. Nonetheless, in this moment, Abraham is fierce in his interrogation, and God doesn't seem to mind—and even

---

[95] Dov Weiss, *Pious Irreverence: Confronting God in Rabbinic Judaism* (Philadelphia: University of Pennsylvania Press, Incorporated, 2017), 182.
[96] While one could theoretically claim that the notion of God being fallible and working to improve Himself is heretical, the Torah itself implies that this is how we are to perceive God. For example, in the aftermath of the sin of the Golden Calf, God tells Moses that he will destroy His people. Moses pleads with God to forgive the nation, and further adds that if God does not forgive them, then "erase me from your book which you have written." Moses adds that destroying the Israelites will make Him look bad in the eyes of the Egyptians, and in the end God relents. The implication is clear: God realized that God's initial reaction was not the desirable one. In this way, God is revealing to Moses that He, too, just like humans, is not completely infallible.

though God's decision prevails in the end, divine patience does not seem to be lost in the slightest when Abraham takes up God's time (as if God has time) to challenge the idea of collective punishment. We are told:

> Abraham came forward and said, "Will You sweep away the innocent along with the guilty? What if there should be fifty innocent within the city; will You then wipe out the place and not forgive it for the sake of the innocent fifty who are in it? Far be it from You to do such a thing, to bring death upon the innocent as well as the guilty, so that innocent and guilty fare alike. Far be it from You! Shall not the Judge of all the earth deal justly?"[97]

In a similar vein, consider the startling words of Jeremiah:

> You will win, O Lord, if I make claim against You,
> Yet I shall present charges against You:
> Why does the way of the wicked prosper?
> Why are the workers of treachery at ease?
> You have planted them, and they have taken root,
> They spread, they even bear fruit.
> You are present in their mouths,
> But far from their thoughts.[98]
> Even King David, held up as the hero of faith, questions God directly:
> Rouse Yourself; why do You sleep, O Lord?
> Awaken, do not reject us forever!
> Why do You hide Your face,
> ignoring our affliction and distress?
> We lie prostrate in the dust;
> our body clings to the ground.
> Arise and help us,
> redeem us, as befits Your faithfulness.[99]

Expressed most succinctly, Malachi asks: "Where is the God of justice?"[100] And similarly, Habakkuk is also waiting for God's justice:

---

[97] Genesis 18:23-25.
[98] Jeremiah 12:1-2.
[99] Psalms 44:24.
[100] Malachi 2:17.

> How long, O Lord, shall I cry out
> And You not listen,
> Shall I shout to You, "Violence!"
> And You not save?
> Why do You make me see iniquity
> [Why] do You look upon wrong?—
> Raiding and violence are before me,
> Strife continues and contention goes on.[101]

And he waits longer:

> You whose eyes are too pure to look upon evil,
> Who cannot countenance wrongdoing,
> Why do You countenance treachery,
> And stand by idle
> While the one in the wrong devours
> The one in the right?[102]

The book of the Tanach (Bible) in which issues of theodicy are most pronounced is the Book of Job. Job has everything and then he loses everything. In his misery, he doesn't question whether God exists, whether God is powerful, but whether God is just:

> By God who has deprived me of justice!
> By Shaddai who has embittered my life!
> As long as there is life in me,
> And God's breath is in my nostrils,
> My lips will speak no wrong,
> Nor my tongue utter deceit.
> Far be it from me to say you are right;
> Until I die I will maintain my integrity.
> I persist in my righteousness and will not yield;
> I shall be free of reproach as long as I live.[103]

Fast forward to perhaps the greatest atrocity in human history (the Holocaust), and Elie Wiesel recalls: "We really did put God on trial." He details further:

---

[101] Habakkuk 1:2-3.
[102] Habakkuk 1:13.
[103] Job 27:2-6.

> I was there when God was put on trial. . . . . At the end of the trial, they used the word *chayav*, rather than [*asheim*,] "guilty." It means "He owes us something." Then we went to pray.[104]

Wiesel famously wrote a play on the matter entitled *The Trial of God*. What's startling about the story is that after the characters found God guilty, they went, as stated above, to pray. This is the spiritual life of a Jew. We can argue with God, and even find God guilty, but then we return to engagement. Both our intellectual integrity and our spiritual commitments must be held intact even when seemingly contradictory.

The Kedushat Levi, Rabbi Levi Yitzhak of Berditchev, argued radically, on multiple occasions, that righteous people can overturn God's decrees implying that God's decree was too harsh but human mercy could reverse it. For example:

> The Talmud reveals that God's people comprise people of the stature of Royalty, people who are able by their very stature to overturn evil decrees made by God in heaven and turn their effect into blessings.[105]

The Kedushat Levi was ready to argue in court against God to end the exile and longtime suffering of the Jewish people:

> I come to You with a lawsuit from Your people Israel.
> What do you want of your people Israel?
> From my stand I will not waver,
> And from my place I shall not move
> Until there be an end to this Exile.
> Yisgadal v'yiskadash shmei raboh—
> Magnified and sanctified is only Thy name.[106]

In another tale from the Kedushat Levi, he tells of a simple tailor arguing with God on Yom Kippur. The tailor shares:

> You wish me to repent of my sins but I have committed only minor offenses. I may have kept leftover cloth, or I may have eaten

---

[104] "Wiesel: Yes, we really did put God on trial," *The Jewish Chronicle*, September 19, 2008, https://www.thejc.com/news/uk-news/wiesel-yes-we-really-did-put-god-on-trial-1.5056.
[105] Kedushat Levi, commentary on Exodus 19:6, trans. Rb. Eliyahu Munk.
[106] Kedushat Levi, Arguing for the Sake of Heaven, page 8.

> in a non-Jewish home, where I worked, without washing my hands. But you O Lord have committed grievous sins. You have taken away babies from their mothers and mothers from their babies. Let us be even. You forgive me, and I will forgive You.
>
> Rabbi Levi Yitzhak replied: "Why did you let God off so easily? You might have forced God to save all of Israel!"[107]

Viktor Frankl, in his *Man in Search of Meaning* argues that those who could have a better chance as survivors from the Holocaust were not physically stronger or the most devout of faith, but those who could make meaning of their trauma. Here the challenge is diverted from anger at God toward personal meaning-making and growth.

In pushing us not to abandon God but rather to reimagine God, Rabbi Harold Kushner writes:

> In his book *A Grief Observed*, C.S. Lewis wrote, shortly after his wife's death of cancer, that the danger of affirming all misfortune as God's will is not so much that people will stop believing in God. The danger is that they will continue to believe in God but will believe terrible things about Him. Worse than concluding "there is no God," people will conclude that there is a God and He is a monster. He is a cruel, heartless God who snatches children from their families and takes parents from children who need them, a God who uses His awesome power to destroy in an hour what it took a family years to build. Who can love a God like that? Who can turn to such a God for help in times of grief? Such a God would be a God who inspires fear, not a God who repeatedly urges His people, "Don't be afraid."[108]

To address the problem of theodicy, we must loosen our grip on one of the three traditional theological commitments: 1. God's benevolence; 2. That evil is indeed evil; and 3. God's omnipotence. Given the conceptions of the Divine shared across the Jewish world, we must abandon the idea that God is not good, because the whole basis of a God worth believing in and engaging with is the idea that God is just and loving. We also should abandon the temptation to reject human reason and conscience and the suggestion that humans simply have no clue about

---

[107] Ibid.
[108] Harold S. Kushner, *Conquering Fear* (New York: Knopf Doubleday Publishing Group, 2010), 47-48.

the difference between good and evil. We can't entertain the notion that genocide is actually, through some moral perversion, the ideal, or even an acceptable, state of affairs. John Hick wrote succinctly: "A theology cannot go unchallenged when it is repugnant to the moral sense that has been formed by the religious realities upon which their theology professes to be based."[109] As Rabbi Yitz Greenberg has taught: no theology is acceptable if it couldn't be uttered to people entering gas chambers in the Holocaust.

Of course, we must acknowledge that not all pain can be equated with evil. Maybe God should have created a world without pain, but that world could not have had human beings in it where pain is so fundamental to the human experience and the human striving to alleviate pain. And so not all pain, inevitable in the human condition, is a theological problem.[110]

So, the only option in engaging with evil is to name that which is truly evil, to realize that God also sees it as evil, and the problem is that God lacks some element of the power necessary to defeat evil.[111] That means the work is left here for us humans. So, is God weak, we may ask? Not necessarily. One significant concept found within Jewish tradition teaches that God chooses *tsimtsum*, limiting God's own power to empower human freedom. Gershon Scholem[112] explains the concept in brief:

> *Tsimtsum* originally means "concentration" or "contraction," but if used in the Kabbalistic parlance it is best translated by "withdrawal" or "retreat," ... The Midrash—in sayings originating from third century teachers—occasionally refers to God as having concentrated His *Shekhinah*, His divine presence, in the holiest of holies, at the place of the Cherubim, as though His whole power were concentrated and contracted in a single point. Here we have the origin of the term Tsimtsum, while the thing itself is the precise opposite of this idea: to the Kabbalist

---

[109] John Hick, *Evil and the God of Love* (Palgrave Macmillan, 2016), 98.
[110] Similarly, Rabbi Moshe Chaim Luzzatto, in his *Derech Hashem* (Ways of God), posits that God created darkness because without it, we would not have the ability to appreciate light.
[111] Alternatively, God may at times choose the path of *hesteir panim* (literally meaning "hiding His face") during an act of evil. Indeed, God Himself warns of such consequences (Deuteronomy 35:17), yet it must be stressed that this warning is mentioned only in reference to God's reaction to idolatry. Extrapolating from this context to another is potentially off the mark and dangerous.
[112] *Tsimtsum*, at least in Lurianic terms as described here, began, as Scholem explains it, in opposition to earlier kabbalah and derived from an idea first written about in the thirteenth century (even though the term was used in earlier, Talmud-era works), and even in this partial quote he's saying that Luria's view is different from the point made about *tsimtsum* in the Midrash. And certainly, outside the world of kabbalah entirely, Lurianic *tsimtsum* isn't an element adopted by Jewish tradition writ large.

of Luria's school Tsimtsum does not mean the concentration of God at a point, but his retreat away from a point.[113]

The human enterprise is meaningful because we are free and empowered to be God's partners in creation. The rabbis of the Talmud were thinking about this, albeit with many different theological frameworks:

> It has been taught: Rabbi Meir used to say, "The critic [of Judaism] may bring the following argument: 'If your God loves the poor, why does God not support them?' If that happens, answer as follows: 'So that through them we may be saved from the punishment of Gehinnom.'" This question was actually put by Turnus Rufus to Rabbi Akiva: "If your God loves the poor, why does God not support them?" He [Akiva] replied: "So that we may be saved through them from the punishment of Gehinnom."[114]

The Talmudic rabbis explain why Abraham, and we, can't have everything we want; we can't have both human freedom and a just world.

> If you want a world, you will not have justice; if it is justice you want, there will be no world. You are taking hold of the rope by both ends—you desire both a world and justice—but if you do not concede a little, the world cannot stand.[115]

Elisha ben Avuya, the quintessential heretical figure for the Talmudic rabbis and arguably the first atheist in the Jewish tradition, witnessed tragedy and chose a different path: He concluded that "there is no justice and there is no judge."[116]

Nonetheless, the problem is still here for us and it is ours to address: God has empowered humans to respond to evil when it's in our control. But what about

---

[113] Gershom Scholem, *Major Trends in Jewish Mysticism* (New York: Schocken Books, 1995), 260.
[114] Bava Batra 10a. The implication is that God wants us humans to proactively support the poor, and in doing so we will be justly rewarded for our efforts, even to the point of the annulment of an otherwise deserved "punishment of Gehinnom."
[115] Midrash Rabbah, Genesis 49, no. 20.
[116] Elisha ben Avuya's error was in his conviction that the world is consistently just. While the Torah itself may promise long days for one who honors his parents (Elisha, according to one Talmudic story, observed a boy doing so and yet died), that does not necessarily mean that this will always be the case. There can always be other variables, unbeknownst to the observer, affecting the outcome. Perhaps that is why the sages went so far as to explain that this promised reward is referring to long days in the World to Come and not in this world. We cannot fully grasp the workings of a world which leaves room for unjust behavior, seemingly unjust punishment, and unfulfilled promises.

when it's not in our control? A tsunami wiping out a village? A two-year-old suffering and dying from a painful degenerative disease? Over a billion people born in the global south into deep poverty? Do we accept this as God's will? Do we accept this as good and just? The Jewish tradition teaches that we are to do all we can, and when we can't do enough, we ask God for help, sometimes faithfully and sometimes through questioning, perhaps even protesting against God.

Bracketing the Maimonidean tradition which seems to propose a non-personal God,[117] the major thrust of Jewish thought pushes us toward dialogue. Martin Buber wrote: "If to believe in God means to talk about Him in the third person, then I do not believe in God. If to believe in God means to be able to talk to God, then I do believe in God." Our primary Jewish engagement, then, must be not merely philosophical but also behavioral. Rather than talking *about* God, we talk *to* God. So too, rather than philosophizing about injustice and theodicy, our primary role is to respond to moral problems and to do what we can to combat the evil that we perceive.

Post-Holocaust theologian Rabbi Eliezer Berkovits wrote:

> Yehuda Halevi, who was not a rationalist, found it necessary to exclaim: "God forbid that there should be anything in the Torah that is contrary to reason!" The Torah is not absurd[,] and the authentic Jew does not engage in religious acrobatics. To believe in the absurd is absurd.[118]

The Polish writer and journalist Tadeusz Borowski wrote, as cited by post-Holocaust theologian Emil Fackenheim:

> One can fulfill the imperative of belief in God without believing that God will necessarily always thwart undeserved evil ([s]ee *Berakhot* 7a). The concept, prevalent in some quarters, as a matter of inviolate dogma of a steady-state, real-time omniscient, continuously intervening Deity has, unfortunately, caused much suffering to the Jewish people. Many sincere believers slackened up ever so slightly on their vigilance and self-reliance, confusing fate in retrospect with fate in prospect. For a sincere

---

[117] Maimonides writes that the concept of *hashgachah peratit* (Divine supervision) applies on a national, and not individual, level. Whereas others claim that God is aware of and controls even the bug resting on a blade of grass, Maimonides disagrees.

[118] Eliezer Berkovits, *With God in Hell* (Sanhedrin Press, 1979), 123.

believer who is overly reliant on this inviolate dogma, may not quickly enough rise to thwart his looming enemy.[119]

Of course, we can move away from a dualistic model of God and toward a mystical monism where there is no separation between God and us. In this model, God is suffering and crying with us because we are intertwined with the Divine. In any case, what matters most is that we keep the questions alive and keep the search alive. Have we lost the questions and the search? Perhaps God is crying that we are no longer searching for the Godly presence? The Rebbe of Mezhibozh told a story:

> This can be explained by what happened to me and my grandchild. He asked me to play hide-and-seek with him and I agreed. I close[d] my eyes and counte[d], and he went to hide. I was suddenly distracted by a friend an[d] forgot all about the child. Soon I heard him crying from his hiding place, "No one has come to look for me." So does God cry, "I am hidden, and my children do not search for me.[120]

Here we can relocate a contemporary approach to ancient Jewish theology which has too often been dormant. This approach is necessary for all who struggle with religious faith, the existence of theodicy and lingering questions about the exceptional and elusive composition of the soul. There are no easy answers to difficult questions. It should remain that way, even as we struggle to build a world that reflects the comfortable answers that we would like to see actualized, but that we know only exist in any kind of fulsome way in our collective imagination, itself a force that we try to harness for good. As the political columnist and former member of Parliament John Stuart Mill famously remarked: "Better Socrates dissatisfied than the fool satisfied; better the fool dissatisfied than the pig satisfied." We can choose easy, comfortable answers, but we lose a part of our humanity in doing so.

So, the debate is, and must remain, between us and God. We have a lot to say. And God's response, it seems, is most commonly silence. All we can do is seize the opportunity to use our God-given power to alleviate evil in the world when we can.

---

[119] See Tadeusz Borowski, cited in Fackenheim, *God's Presence in History* (Harper & Row, 1972), 104.
[120] Rabbi David Wolpe, *Making Loss Matter* (Riverhead Books, 1999), 176.

Debate 6.

The Gra vs. the Besht: Mysticism of the Mind vs. Mysticism of the Heart

One of the greatest debates in Jewish history is about the nature of Jewish theology. Is the belief system of Judaism fundamentally rationalism-based, thereby lining up with human reason? Or is it fundamentally mysticism-based, thereby transcending human reason? Is the Jew's relationship to the concept of divinity to be lived in the study house or in the field? Is Judaism a set of ideas to be understood exclusively by the elite, or is it a religion for the masses? This debate can be observed most poignantly in the clash between the Baal Shem Tov (the Besht) and the Vilna Gaon (the Gra).

Rabbi Israel ben Eliezer, known as the Baal Shem Tov or the Besht,[121] lived in 18th-century Poland and was a highly regarded and beloved teacher and healer. He didn't write his teachings but rather had students, such as Rabbi Yaakov Yoseph of Polnoye and Dov Ber (known as the Maggid)[122] of Mezerich, who expressed his ideas as they understood them, both orally and in various writings (e.g., Shivhei haBesht and Toldot Yaakov Yosef). What mattered most to the Besht was not studying Talmud or intellectual debate, but *deveikut* (clinging to God). He prioritized praying in the field and meditating over studying in the *beit midrash*. Rather than celebrating the elite and intellectual sage, the Besht's thinking and approach gave power to the humble worker seeking God. This radical innovation served as the catalyst for, and germination of, Hasidut. Indeed, he is considered the founder of Hasidut by all Hasidic sects![123]

As a young boy, Israel was orphaned and adopted by the Jewish community of Tluste. Even as a child, after his formal studies he would wander into the fields. As he grew, he developed a deep soul and became attracted to prayer, healing, and storytelling. He wrote amulets and offered spiritual cures. He spoke about visions he had and Kabbalah he learned. He cared for the poor and tended to his students. He worked for a short time as a *shochet* (kosher butcher). But ultimately, the allure of ideas and concepts attributed to him that were lofty and deep, spiritual and accessible, led to the image of the Besht as a charismatic leader. As the movement of Hasidut developed, the Besht's spiritual and intellectual descendants became regarded as *tzaddikim*—righteous seekers of God—whose role in Hasidic communities displaced that of the sage to a significant degree. God, for so many of the Besht's followers, was not merely some abstraction beyond the universe but

---

[121] Baal Shem Tov means "One of a good name." Besht is the Hebrew acronym for Baal Shem Tov.
[122] A *maggid* is a storyteller or preacher.
[123] This attitude toward the Besht is quite a tribute, particularly given the differences, even strife, between various Hasidic sects.

was also a personal deity who is loving, close, and present in all we do. In this panentheistic approach, the quintessential humble shoemaker and peddler can be the closest one to God if they direct their *kavanah* (spiritual intentionality) appropriately. As a generalized matter, then, the thinking of Hasidut places much emphasis on the spirit of the law and relatively less on the letter of the law.

This novel approach to Jewish observance and devotion was controversial, and as expected, there was fierce opposition.

Rabbi Elijah ben Solomon Zalman, known as the Vilna Gaon or the Gra,[124] was born in what is today Belarus, lived during the 18th century and was a renowned Talmudist, halachist (decisor of law), and kabbalist. Himself a kabbalist, he shared with the followers of Hasidism a desire to understand the mysteries of divine reality, yet at the same time he opposed so much of early Hasidut and is therefore considered to have been the (or at least a significant) leader of the Mitnagdim, or "Opponents." The Gra believed in mysticism in his own way, but rejected emerging Hasidic Judaism that took applied mysticism in new directions. He was deeply engaged in the study of math and science in addition to pure Torah texts. He offered new critical methods to Talmudic learning and studied Hebrew grammar closely. He was known to be extremely modest in his lifestyle and had many ascetic practices. But the Gra took active steps to curb the influence of Hasidic Judaism, even supporting the idea of excommunicating Hasidic leaders.[125]

So, if the Gra believed in mysticism, why was he so vehemently opposed to Hasidic Judaism? Given the Gra's deep humility and rejection of power status, this seems not to have been about power and ego, but rather about a belief in the centrality of the mind and the centrality of study. Part of his intensity likely emerged from a fear of the return of the failed messianic movements that followed Shabbtai Tzvi and Jacob Frank during the 17th and early 18th centuries respectively. Along with concern about the return of the Sabbatean and Frankist movements came unease about what would happen if other charismatic, messianic-style healers exercised power over the Jewish masses. Some wondered if the new Hasidim might actually be Sabbateans or Frankists themselves, even when those Hasidic leaders spoke out against the earlier troubling movements. The Gra also believed that claims made, or ascribed to, Hasidic masters about performance of miracles and experience of visions were dangerous lies and anathema to Judaism. Perhaps, though, much of the opposition to Hasidut on the part of the Gra and his followers had to do with social antipathy and political opposition.

---

[124] The term *gaon* means scholar. Gra is an acronym for Gaon Rabbeinu (our rabbi) Eliyahu.
[125] The Gra's concern was that in time Hasidut's emphasis on spirit of the law would lead to its replacement of letter of the law; that less emphasis on formal study of *halachah* would lead to ignorance and thereby less strict and accurate observance.

The Mitnagdim were mostly based in Lithuania,[126] in relatively close proximity to the Hasidim, and the most intense clashes between the two groups occurred in the late 18th century after the Baal Shem Tov had already passed. But contemporaneous with the rapid spread of Hasidism which the Mitnagdim were unsuccessful in stopping, they started to innovate in their own ways, such as with Rabbi Chaim of Volozhin's novel analytic approach to Talmud study and Rabbi Yisrael Salanter's new *Mussar* movement.[127]

These innovations were somewhat subtle relative to the practical and external Hasidic practices and the popularization of the Lurianic kabbalistic approach (developed in the 16th century by Rabbi Isaac Luria and his student Rabbi Chaim Vital) which were large and sweeping. And with the growth of both Hasidism and its Mitnagdic opposition came a further articulation of the differences between the two approaches. Many Mitnagdim felt that Hasidut's panentheism (God is in everything in this world but also beyond) and the utter reverence given to many of its leaders by their followers could lead to pantheism (God is this world and nothing beyond) and radical messianism. Further, they had a deep distrust for the considerable emphasis within Hasidut on erotic imagery as applied to the relationship between humans and God,[128] as well as a disdain for the Hasidic tendency to overtly demonstrate piety during prayer.

From the perspective of non-Hasidim, it was a subversive reordering that the Hasidim proposed:

> What [H]assidism did was re-order and re-prioritize Jewish values—the Tzaddik over the scholar, prayer over Torah study, immanence over transcendence.[129]

Another major departure has to do with how one relates to the past. From a Mitnagdic perspective, people of the past were essentially holier, wiser, and closer

---

[126] Because of this geographic detail, later Mitnagdim, particularly those affiliated with non-Hasidic yeshivot of the Eastern European style, became known as "Litvaks" (meaning "of Lita," an alternate name for Lithuania), with their approach referred to as "Litvish" or "Yeshivish."

[127] Rabbi Lipkin (his real name, although he was known as "Salanter" because he spent significant time during his youth in the town of Salant) wasn't responding directly to the rise of Hasidut but to changing social issues in general. Czarist Russia, with all its corruption, created a culture where Jews often sought materialism, a lifestyle which he fiercely opposed. He strove to overcome this influence and offered an alternative in his teaching at a *Mussar* yeshivah in Kovno. In the Enlightenment period (known as the period of *Haskalah*), following their political emancipation, many Jews turned away from traditional Judaism, which he therefore felt needed new modes to engage Jews who found themselves pulled away.

[128] This discomfort with the erotic in the Hasidic movement coexisted with the considerable eroticism found in kabbalistic texts studied of course by, for example, the Gra himself.

[129] Rabbi Dr. Eliezer Shore, *Torah from the Heart: Chassidic Insights into Spiritual Education*, page 201; based on A. Green, "Typologies of Leadership" in *Jewish Spirituality I*, ed. Arthur Green (New York: Crossroads, 1987), 127-156.

to God and truth than even contemporary pietists could be. For the Hasid, by contrast, each person could reach the level of an earlier sage. Rav Kalonymus Kalman Epstein, an 18th-century Hasidic thinker, even wrote that with spiritual work, anyone can reach the understanding of Moses.[130]

This new movement was about radical reflection. Rabbi Steinsaltz writes:

> One of the great Hasidic rabbis (who was the rabbi of a small town in his youth and would often volunteer to serve as a merrymaker at weddings) would say that the essence of Hasidism is that one must constantly be asking, "Why?" about everything that one encounters in life. That is the way his life went, he said. One day, when he went to perform the ritual washing of the hands, this question of "Why?" occurred to him. He began to reflect on the ritual and stood there, towel on his shoulder, for two hours. He said that afterward, whenever he recited the blessing on the ritual, his level of devotion was higher than ever.[131]

Another fascinating difference can be found in how to relate to one who errs. However much early Mitnagdim might have had some tolerant and pluralistic inclinations, they did judge their Hasidic coreligionists harshly, to the point where they even viewed them as deserving of excommunication. Many early Hasidim, on the other hand, professed a new sense of tolerance based on love. Consider this teaching from the 18th-century Hasidic Rebbe Shneur Zalman of Liadi:[132]

> Even with regard to those who are close to him, and whom he has rebuked, yet they had not repented of their sins, when he is enjoined to hate them, there still remains the duty to love them also, and both are right: hatred because of the wickedness in them, and love on account of the aspect of the hidden good in them, which is the Divine spark in them, which animates their divine soul.[133]

And consider how this idea that love is to be extended to all creation is beautifully expressed in one Hasidic tale:

---

[130] Maor VaShemesh, 255, "Terumah."
[131] Rabbi Adin Steinsaltz, *Talks on the Parsha* (Maggid, 2015), 55.
[132] Rebbe Shneur Zalman of Liadi is the founder of the Lubavitch Chabad Hasidic sect. Chabad is the Hebrew acronym for *"chochmah, binah, da'at"* (wisdom, understanding, and knowledge).
[133] Shneur Zalman of Liadi, *Tanya*, Part I; Likkutei Amarim 32. (Kehot Publication Society).

> One [H]asidic master, Rabbi Zusya of Hanipol (d. 1800), was so pained by the sight of caged birds that he would purchase them from their owners and then set them free. He regarded this as a form of *pidyon shevuyim*, ransoming of captives, which is the highest form of charity when performed on behalf of human beings. Rabbi Zusya apparently felt that it was a moral imperative to spare animals, particularly birds, whose very nature demands freedom, the suffering of captivity.[134]

What's remarkable about the grand debate between the proponents and opponents of early Hasidism is that, in the end, neither side won. Or perhaps better stated: both sides won. Hasidim came to study Talmud, and elements of Hasidic thought evolved into the neo-Hasidism of Martin Buber in the early century and of Rabbi Dr. Arthur Green more recently. The Yeshivish world is frequently allied with the Hasidic, and, despite itself, Litvish yeshivot can be seen as having left an intellectual inheritance for what became Modern Orthodoxy. Both Hasidism and Mitnagdim, in many ways, came to learn from, and to be influenced by, one another. Neither group fully resembles the movement as it existed in its earliest state.

So where does that leave us today? Will we give power to the unknowable or only to that which we know? Will we cling to the most wise and complex thinkers or to the most pure, innocent, and simple of people? Will we find our truth in the text or in the heart? Each of us will need to find our path. And maybe, for some of us the best path will be a synthesis of these various approaches. We can be grateful for the intellectual and emotional chasm between Hasidim and Mitnagdim, because their streams of thought—both independently and by virtue of their interaction—have given us different models to explore and to cherish.

---

[134] Rabbi Joseph Telushkin, *A Code of Jewish Ethics: Volume 2* (Harmony, 2009), 319. Martin Buber also records this story about Rabbi Zusya, although in Buber's rendition, the rabbi's behavior was even more radical: "Once Rabbi Zusya traveled cross-country collecting money to ransom prisoners. He came to an inn at a time when the innkeeper was not at home. He went through the rooms... and in one saw a large cage with all kinds of birds. And Zusya saw that the caged creatures wanted to fly through the spaces of the world and be free birds again. He burned with pity for them and said to himself: 'Here you are, Zusya, walking your feet off to ransom prisoners. But what greater ransoming of prisoners can there than to free these birds from their prison?' Then he opened the cage, and the birds flew out into freedom. When the innkeeper learned what Zusya had done, he shouted at him, 'You fool! How could you have the impudence to rob me of my birds and make worthless the good money I paid for them?' Zusya replied [he knew the innkeeper to be an observant Jew], 'You have often read and repeated these words in the psalms, "His tender mercies are over all his works" (145:9).' Then the innkeeper beat him until his hand grew tired and finally threw him out of the house. And Zusya went his way serenely." (Martin Buber, *Tales of the Hasidim*, Volume 1 (Schocken, 1975), 245).

Debate 7.

Divine Torah vs. Biblical Criticism

There are a lot of morally troubling ideas found in the Torah. How can this book be Divine?

Personally, I live with the commitment that the Torah is from God and that I'm obligated by God to live by the mitzvot. For me, this is as much a loving relationship with a covenant as an acceptance of obligation to abide by a distant law. While this is my framework, I have a respect for the academics who have demonstrated that the Torah was written by many authors throughout different eras. While I am not a Bible scholar, my general orientation is toward believing academic experts where there is a general consensus, as there is here. I find rabbinic maneuvers to prove that every word of the Torah is the word of God to be meaningful at times and silly at others. For me, though, the tension between a covenantal relationship with Torah and an academic perspective on it is not an irreconcilable conflict. I understand the Torah to represent an evolving relationship with the Divine (both within this world and beyond this world). Of course, I do not know, indeed none of us know, in an empirical sense, what was said at Sinai, but I relate to the Sinai experience as having been the beginning of a key aspect of the relationship between the Jewish people and God, with everything good that emerged after that experience being somehow connected to that place and that time. In that sense, it doesn't totally matter to me when the description of the experience was written down, or by whom.

For me, also, given my commitment to *halachah*, I view the ethical and the legal to be one. There cannot be a difference. Furthermore, it seems clear that we have the mandate to actualize the unity of these two concepts. And so, the written Torah and the spoken Torah, the Chumash and the Talmud, the *halachah* and the ethical, all merge together. Of course, there is some fidelity to a chain of connectivity which means there sometimes needs to be patience in the merger, but everything must stem from that starting point and move forward in that trajectory.

The rabbis of the Talmud explained that the Torah was not revealed in a perfect Divine language but in an imperfect human language so that it could be properly understood. Or putting it another way, the Torah was written in a way that could be understood by humanity: *Dibrah Torah bilshon b'nei adam*—The Torah was written in the language of human beings.[135] This inevitably renders perfect inter-

---

[135] BT Berakhot 31b; BT Ketubot 67b. The term *Dibrah Torah bilshon b'nei adam* is used approximately 20 times in the Talmud. It seems that at first it was used by the Talmudic sages to explain the linguistic writing style, such as word repetition, of the Torah text. Its usage was later expanded to include other aspects of Torah, most notably by Rambam (Maimonides) who extends this notion to anthropomorphic references to God, e.g.,

pretation or consistency impossible. This is not a hermeneutical problem unique to the Torah. Rather we understand in modernity that our mystical insights and psychological depth can never adequately be captured in language. Human experience is more profound than human language.

Even if the Pentateuch was written down over time (a position that the tradition itself embraces, at least to a degree),[136] this does not detract from its Divine origin. Traditional commentators have offered many explanations for how the Torah was written. Rabbi Yochanan argued that the Torah was given scroll by scroll, while Resh Lakish argued that the Torah was originally given in its entirety.[137] According to Rashi's interpretation, even for Resh Lakish the entire Torah was not given all at once on Mount Sinai. Rather, Moses wrote down each passage as it was told to him, and then the passages were compiled together (*megillah megillah nitnah*).

In the 13th century, the Ramban (Nachmanides) explained:

> When Moses came down from the mountain, he wrote from the beginning of the Torah until the end of the story of the Tabernacle, and the conclusion of the Torah he wrote at the end of the fortieth year... this is according to the one who says the Torah was given scroll by scroll. But according to the one who says it was given complete, the entire thing was written in the fortieth year.[138]

While traditionally it is understood that God is the author, some traditional scholars believe that there still may have been more than one scribe. Ibn Ezra, at the end of his commentary on the Torah, argued that not every word was written by Moses himself, since Joshua wrote the last twelve verses of the Torah:[139]

God redeemed the Israelites with a "strong hand and outstretched arm," and to similar supernatural references to other creatures, e.g., the talking donkey of Bilam. According to Rambam, the episode with Bilam and his donkey was seen by Bilam in a vision and did not happen in three-dimensional reality.

[136] One particular passage stands out as to its authorship and is subject to a three-way debate in the Talmud: the verses recording the death and subsequent burial of Moses. On the one hand, how could Moses have written that he died if he were indeed still alive? On the other hand, how could he have written that he died if he had already passed on? The three opinions: God dictated the words to Moses and he subsequently recorded them in the manner he recorded the rest of the Torah; Moses indeed wrote this passage, but *bidema* ("with tears"); and Joshua, not Moses, wrote these last eight verses of the Torah. (There are different interpretations as to the meaning of the words "with tears" in this context, among them that the medium of writing these verses was tears rather than ink, or that he wrote these verses while crying).

[137] BT Gittin 60a-b.

[138] Ramban, introduction to his Torah commentary.

[139] The dispute in the Talmud is regarding only the last eight verses of the Torah, beginning with the death of Moshe. Ibn Ezra extends this to an additional four verses, the point when Moshe ascends Mount Nebo in order

> In my opinion, Joshua wrote from this verse on, for after Moses ascended [Mount Nebo], he no longer wrote. Joshua wrote it by way of prophecy, as we see from "the Lord showed him...," "The Lord said to him...," and "He buried him."

Rabbi Yosef Albo, the 15th-century Spanish rabbi, explained:

> This is why the Rabbis say, God made a covenant with Israel only for the sake of the oral law. This is because the written law can not be understood except with the oral law, and also because the law of God can not be perfect so as to be adequate for all times, because the ever new details of human relations, their customs and their acts, are too numerous to be embraced in a book. Therefore Moses was given orally certain general principles, only briefly alluded to in the Torah, by means of which the wise men in every generation may work out the details as they appear.[140]

Earlier, Rambam understood Rav Albo's point that "the law of God cannot be perfect so as to be adequate for all times." Clearly, there are Biblical stories and laws which are morally troubling. Why is slave ownership permitted? Why do multiple chapters of the Torah deal, in such specific detail, with the building of a tabernacle that hasn't been in use in millennia, and that God obviously knew would only be temporary, aside from preservation for a messianic era? And are we really to stone rebellious children? But Judaism is not only, and not even primarily, a Biblical religion maintaining that every particular law was crafted for a particular context but an oral tradition that evolves while maintaining the Torah's core values and legal principles. The Talmudic rabbis actually compare the Torah to the lips of a seductive woman.[141] Our loyalty is to the rabbinic interpretive tradition, and we shouldn't be tempted to believe that the esoteric Bible is the sole Jewish authority. The Bible is the revealed wisdom that began our tradition (and others), but it also gave license and authority for—indeed, it obligates us to engage in—continued interpretation.

Rav Kook suggests that Jewish law not only evolves but also expands. He explains:

---

to prepare for his death.
[140] Yosef Albo, *Sefer HaIkkarim*, Maamar 3:23, trans. Jewish Publication Society of America, 1929.
[141] Midrash Tanchuma, Teruma 8.

> We should not immediately feel obliged to refute any idea that comes to contradict something in the Torah, but rather we should build the palace of Torah above it. In so doing we reach a more exalted level, and... the ideas are clarified. And thereafter, when we are not pressured by anything, we can confidently also fight on the Torah's behalf.[142]

Rabbi Kook further defended the idea of progress, suggesting, "An evolution marked by constant progress provides solid grounds for optimism."[143]

The Kotzker Rebbe explains that we are to live both in this world and outside of it. Embracing both revelation and reason enables us to actualize our Torah values to the fullest. While the Torah comes from heaven, "it is not in the heavens";[144] its continued interpretation, application, and relevance are under human control. The Torah's applications continue to evolve, while the core truths and values are preserved.

The Revelation did not bind us to a destiny of stagnancy but gave us freedom. Immanuel Kant challenged this point, arguing that if Divine revelation was a reality, it would be calamitous for man's created freedom since one loses free will and the capacity for reason when encountering Divine truth. Emmanuel Levinas explains why revelation (thus limiting human freedom but maximizing human responsibility) needed to be so: "The teaching, which the Torah is, cannot come to the human being as a result of a choice. That which must be received in order to make freedom of choice possible cannot have been chosen, unless after the fact."[145] Our freedom needed to be suspended during the Sinaitic revelation in order that we could be free.

Another barrier to embracing Jewish tradition has been the idea that one should live by reason rather than faith. However, according to the dominant Jewish perspective, one need not take a leap into the irrational when embracing the truth of the Torah. Countless Jewish authorities and commentators, such as Rambam, Ralbag, Saadya Gaon, Ibn Tibbon, and Abravanel, have suggested that reason and revelation are indeed compatible.

Perhaps the question of who wrote the Torah is not really the most crucial Jewish question after all. Rabbi Abraham Joshua Heschel once suggested that if we were to find historical proof that the Ten Commandments were indeed revealed

---

[142] *Iggerot HaReayah* I, 163-164.
[143] Ibid., I, 369.
[144] Deuteronomy 30:12, BT Bava Metzia 59b.
[145] Emmanuel Levinas, *Nine Talmudic Readings*, trans. Annette Aronowicz (Bloomington: Indiana University Press, 2019), 37.

from God, few to none would live any differently, for we do not make our daily life decisions based upon historical evidence. Further, we are aware that historical positions of this nature can never be proven. The existence of God and the origin of the Bible are at best untestable hypotheses.

While intriguing, this question is not so problematic; history is ephemeral, while meaning is eternal. What matters most in the Jewish tradition, much more than historical truth, is the power of values. In assessing the value of historical context in the interpretation of text and law, some Jews are overly dismissive, but others embrace it to the exclusion of all meaning of Jewish core values. Reading ancient texts solely with a historical or scientific lens blocks one from embracing deep moral and spiritual truths. Evaluating the literal veracity of the creation story is much less relevant than the ethical dimensions of this phenomenal narrative.

Midrash Sifra, as understood by the contemporary Jewish theologian Rabbi David Hartman, explains beautifully that it is a principle of faith in the Jewish tradition that God liberated the Jews in an exodus from Egypt (*Yetziat Mitzrayim*). However, the sages go on to explain that the obligation is not primarily a requirement of belief but of action. The one who truly believes in the miraculous exodus is honest in weights and measures. The one who acts ethically in business has embraced the deepest meaning of this theological value. The truth is not a historical fact merely to be noted, but is rather a value that must transform our character.

I personally believe that God did indeed reveal the Torah to our people. My soul is bound up with Torah in a way that perhaps makes revelation retroactively true. This is an existential, not epistemological, claim. The Torah is the most powerful and persuasive work I have ever read and I feel spiritually elevated from an encounter with Torah unlike that which I experience with anything else. I feel the values of this tradition to be the most ethically poignant and compelling. I'm not alone. All of western religion, whose adherents make up about half of the world's population, has been built upon the belief in this powerful revelatory experience.

Yet the ultimate question for me is not whether one believes in the Torah, but whether one lives it. Further, the fact that we cannot find historical proof that the Torah is from God is not a reason to opt out of living by Jewish law and values. Historical ambiguity is no excuse for disengagement. A philosophical agnostic who questions whether human reason can understand anything beyond worldly experience and thus claims that the revelation is merely a myth that cannot be taken seriously, risks becoming spiritually numb if tradition is therefore dismissed. It is not a leap of faith that is needed, an embracing of that which one understands may or may not be true; rather one must suspend, or look beyond, disbelief in order to find self-actualization. Embracing Revelation may actually represent what is constitutive of our humanity (what makes us uniquely human), since the ability to grasp something phenomenal beyond our own limited experience is what demonstrates that humans have intelligence.[146]

One might ask pragmatic questions: Does living in a community that embraces Jewish Revelation enhance my moral responsibility? Does living by Jewish law and values make me a better person? Do I feel closer to the Divine when I learn Torah, pray, and fulfill traditional Jewish requirements? Theology that works, in a sense, is true whether or not it is historically accurate—and such accuracy is elusive, in any event. If one finds that through years of learning and performing *mitzvot*, their moral, spiritual, and intellectual commitments and capabilities grow, this cannot be dismissed as tangential to the goal of religion. True religion must be more concerned with the doable "good" than with the unknowable "true." Judaism is a performative theology. We understand it by doing it. This is why the Israelites say, "*Naaseh V'Nishma,*" "We will do and [then] we will understand"[147] when receiving the Torah. Ritual is spiritual exercise that can facilitate the expansion of one's moral imagination. Torah is like love. You can't understand it unless you've fully felt it and lived it.

The Pentateuch, written sometime during the second millennium BCE. (whether or not it existed in some phenomenologically inaccessible state earlier than that), is a remarkable set of moral and legal teachings, poetry and song, love and tragedy, and dreams of a better world. Today its message is unfortunately blurred in this age of skepticism, where no commitment seems to be held too tightly, and everything is contingent on what the latest historical evidence seems to indicate. However, if we imagine that God loves us, that a heaven awaits us, that a time of universal peace and justice will come, we can embrace the wisdom of our heritage much more deeply. If we can allow our encounter with God and tradition to be existential rather than purely historical, we can connect in deep and meaningful ways even without having all of our concerns resolved.

When some of the tales about the Chafetz Chaim were challenged, one leader responded, "I don't know if the story is true or not. But they don't *tell* stories like that about you or me." In like terms, we may not be able to prove the historical accounts told in the Bible, but there is nothing that compares to it in the modern world (or even in antiquity). As Mark Twain said, "If the Ten Commandments

---

[146] Possessing intelligence is a basic understanding of human beings being created *b'tzelem Elohim* (in the image of God).

[147] Exodus 24:7. Rashi's understanding of these words is that the Israelites' response was sequential: "First we will do and then we will hear." In other words, the Israelites committed themselves to observing the mitzvot before they even heard what the actual mitzvot were. Putting it another way, they accepted upon themselves to observe the Torah in its entirety without knowing what that specifically entailed.

were not written by Moses, then they were written by another fellow of the same name."

The wisdom and language of the Bible is unparalleled in its power to inspire idealism and social change. No one claims that the Reverend Martin Luther King, Jr., was naïve or unintelligent to root his social activism in the language of the Bible. This revealed tradition has the power to inspire us again and again to transform the world, to make a sanctuary where God can dwell. Perhaps questions such as "Is the Torah divine?" and "Are the critics right?" are the wrong questions to ask. Perhaps we can, and should, live with paradox and the humility of uncertainty. Rather than over-philosophizing as to "Who wrote the Torah," we can spend our time building our character through the deep wisdom it offers, enabling us to heal the world.

Debate 8.

Heaven vs. Earth?

Should our primary concern as we go about living our lives be the world to come? After all, we will, supposedly, spend our eternity in such a soulful realm. Or should our primary concern be about this world? After all, that is all we can truly control. Besides, that is where we are at present, and we can't easily focus on much beyond the here and now. Perhaps an appropriate resolution of this conundrum is what is at stake in a famous Talmudic debate, in which Beit Shammai and Beit Hillel disagree over whether Heaven or Earth was created first.[148]

> Beit Shammai says, "The heavens were created first, and then the earth, as it says, "In the beginning, God created the heavens and the earth."[149] Beit Hillel says, "The earth was created first, and then the heavens, as it says, "On the day that the Lord, God, created earth and heavens."[150]

Perhaps Beit Shammai is suggesting the primacy of the heavens and Beit Hillel is expressing the primacy of the earth. We generally tend to follow the view of Beit Hillel on halachic issues, and so it may be safe to assume that is the case here too. As such, although we remain mindful of the powerful instruction of Beit Shammai, we prioritize the teaching of Beit Hillel. We are to be concerned with our souls and the next world as Beit Shammai teaches, but the primary vehicle to get there is through a focus on this world and doing all we can to contribute to it, consistent with the view of Beit Hillel. Rather than try to bring the earth up to the heavens, making the transcendental realm the primary focal point of our attention and concern, we focus on bringing the heavens down to earth, by improving and refining our behavior and by removing violence and adding to peace and justice.

The Talmudic sage Rabbi Yochanan notes: "The Holy One, Blessed be He, said: I shall not enter Jerusalem above, in heaven, until I enter Jerusalem on earth down below."[151] Thus, the Heavenly Jerusalem (the ideal) cannot be built until the Earthly Jerusalem (the pragmatic city) is built. The concealed Jerusalem is the reward for achieving the building of the revealed city.

Another way to consider the debate is by wondering whether the questions we will be asked when we stand to be judged after death will be about Heaven, where

---

[148] BT Chagigah 12a.
[149] Genesis 1:1.
[150] Genesis 2:4.
[151] BT Ta'anit 5a.

we are going to, or about Earth, where we are coming from. When one stands above Earth but outside of Heaven, which realm will be primary?

To be sure, the conception of a world beyond our own has been a nearly impossible thought experiment since time immemorial. Throughout the eons, people—of all stripes and denominations—have wondered where the soul wanders after it leaves its flesh container. It's such an enormous question with manifold consequences. In truth, the idea of the Gates of Heaven emerges early in the Torah:

> "How awesome is this place!" [Jacob] exclaimed. "This is none other than the abode of God, and that is the gateway to heaven."[152]

Is Heaven itself, and not only a terrestrial spot that happens to catalyze feelings of spirituality, actually an awe-inspiring place? Is it a place we should fear? Is it a physical place at all? How could we ever imagine something so wonderful when there is no temporal equivalent? Let's bracket these particular theological questions and, instead, reach for some meta-questions: Do I believe in a God who judges? Do I think there can be a gates-of-heaven experience? How might engaging in such thoughts improve the way I live my life?

Heaven is often understood as the last resting place for the righteous on Earth. Through our viewing of popular media, we may expect that Heaven is a white void filled with nothing but clouds, harps, and angels. But nowhere is this vision of Heaven found in Jewish wisdom literature. Indeed, the normative interpretation of Heaven in the Jewish tradition is not something we can picture as simple as Hollywood can design, but of another state of being altogether.

The great Talmudic sage Rava provides a litany of questions that are asked before one is accepted into Heaven. These questions are not what one might expect:

> Rava said: After departing from this world, when a person is brought to judgment for the life he lived in this world, they say to him in the order of that verse: Did you conduct business faithfully? Did you designate times for Torah study? Did you engage in procreation? Did you await salvation? Did you engage in the dialectics of wisdom or understand one matter from another?"[153]

---

[152] Genesis 28:17.
[153] BT Shabbat 31a.

What a powerful statement about the nature of religious life: that a question about business ethics would take primacy before one was to walk into eternal paradise! If we can extrapolate anything from these questions, it's that Heaven itself, in the thought of the rabbis, may not most centrally be a concept that primarily is about theological belief, ritual observance, or prayer, but that it's rather focally about day-to-day ethics. Whether or not one believes in it, let's embrace the power of spiritual imagination to entertain such an idea.

Interestingly enough, Heaven is not primarily an end-of-life moment in Jewish thought. Rather, Jewish literature discusses the Gates of Heaven as a prayer moment as well. Each time we pray, we stand at the Gates of Heaven. But, as the Talmud puts it, we have a problem:[154]

> From the day that the Temple was destroyed, the gates of prayer have been sealed, as the verse says, "Even as I cry out and plead, God shuts out my prayer."[155]

But let us not despair, for the Talmud also instructs: "[D]espite the fact that the gates of prayer were locked with the destruction of the Temple, the gates of tears were not locked."[156]

We have the opportunity, through emotional awakening and tears from deep existential arousal, to open the gates of tears and stand before the Holy One.

Even as we consider what might be asked of us when we die, we might also think about what the first question is that *we* would have for God? What is it that we yearn to know? Each day, with courage, we can think about approaching Heaven. What is my life ultimately about? What are the questions that guide me? "Make an opening for Me like the eye of a needle, and I will open wide for you the Gates of Heaven."[157]

The entrance of Heaven, that metaphysical barrier to the road to humanity's redemption, should always have a place in our minds and souls. While it might be too overwhelming to focus on the "entryway" with every action we take, it would be wise for us to take to heart the need to live ethically and to question ourselves before each of our actions. By doing so, we have not only the ability to restrain our basest impulses, but also the opportunity to reflect before we act.

We might ask ourselves each day the questions we suspect we might ultimately be asked: "Were you kind?" "Did you take care of the planet?" "Were you

---

[154] BT Berakhot 32b.
[155] Lamentations 3:8.
[156] BT Bava Metzia 59a.
[157] Song of Songs Rabbah 5:3.

compassionate?" "Are you ready for Me?"—implying that the goal of life is to prepare for the ultimate spiritual encounter! For me, for a long time, the question has been: "Did you give more than you took?" I find the question so overwhelming and paralyzing at times and so inspiring and empowering at other times. But the questions need not be interrogative and judgmental. They could also, for some, be compassionate and empathetic, such as: "How are you doing after that wild ride of life?" or "Did you love yourself and act gently with yourself?"

Of course, in this life we will never know with certainty what is to come in the next life. But engaging in the thought experiment about Heaven can provide an important challenge for us to live each day consistently with our deepest commitments. Death will come all too soon for all of us, and each day is a chance to prepare to live our best lives, with love, joy, reflection, and awe.

May we have the will and the vision to see the Gates of Heaven one day so that the world we live in now will have the potential to be redeemed, just as *we* have the ability to be redeemed in the days to come.

The other lens through which we might approach the Jewish historical question of Heaven vs. Earth is the prism of messianism.

Jewish Messianism, which we can understand as an interest in arriving at some sort of final societal perfection at the end of days, is in some way in evidence everywhere in modernity, including Zionist (both religious and otherwise), Chabad, and secular Jewish movements (and even in the thinking of secular Jewish thinkers such as Karl Marx, Rosa Luxemburg, and Leon Trotsky and other Bolsheviks). It seems we cannot take the messianic impulse out of the Jew.

Today, this messianic impulse unfortunately has very dangerous expressions. More and more, we see messianism leading to extremism and also to the watering down of core Jewish values; the notion of the coming of Mashiach has not only become disproportionately important in Jewish thought, but also has often acted as a justification for a lack of responsibility. The concept of Mashiach becomes a religious excuse, a crutch, a shortcut. When it is our collective version of the Tooth Fairy, we risk remaining children religiously, constantly expecting a supernatural intervention that will instantaneously change all of nature and save us from ourselves. We interpret prophetic hyperbole too literally.

But there is, of course, a very different model at the foundation of Jewish thought.

In the Gemara,[158] Rabbi Yehoshua ben Levi wrestles with the question of when and how messianism works, and asks Eliyahu HaNavi (Elijah the Prophet) when the Messiah will come. Eliyahu replies that he should go ask the Mashiach himself,

---
[158] BT Sanhedrin 98a.

who is sitting at the entrance to the city of Rome. Rabbi Yehoshua then asks Eliyahu HaNavi how he will recognize the Mashiach at the gates of Rome. Eliyahu replies profoundly that he will be sitting amidst the poor and sick, putting bandages on them one by one.

The Messiah exists on the periphery of society (the gates of Rome) and is a healer! In the conclusion of the story, Rabbi Yehoshua runs and indeed finds the Mashiach and asks him when he will reveal himself. The Mashiach replies, "Today!" Rabbi Yehoshua, confused, goes back to Eliyahu questioning what the Mashiach meant by "today." Eliyahu replies, quoting Psalms, that it is today "if you will hear His voice."

The Gemara is teaching us that Mashiach, if not literally then at least conceptually, is here already. Messianic possibility is always right in front of us in a very real way.

The Rambam explains[159] that at the pinnacle of human progress, nature will remain as it is, but there will be universal benefit to all humankind. That messianic change will not be via miracles. Mashiach is not a miracle worker. Rather, he brings about change through natural means. It is through the good deeds of Jews[160] that the road to the messianic era will be paved. He explains that there will be no more jealousy—all will feel they have sufficient resources due to the human transformation of society. There may be an enthroned king; Rambam calls this the Philosopher King (the one who fully contemplates and clings to God). But in the naturalistic view (as compared with the apocalyptic view), getting to a better place stems from us, not from this miraculous intervening redeemer. For the Rambam, the vehicle is *halakhah* (Jewish law), and he explains that the purpose of *halachah* is to create a just society.[161]

The 20th-century philosopher Yeshayahu Leibovitz explained further, based on his read of the Rambam, that Mashiach is not a person or event; rather it is a process. We are always waiting. It never actually comes about fully, but we must always be on that journey. The idea is, what we call in math, "asymptotic" (a line that continually approaches a given curve but does not meet it at any finite distance).

While the messianic impulse can be very dangerous, it can also be very positive, perhaps one of the most important Jewish values—to keep our optimism and idealism intact and to work to improve the world—where we progress but we never quite reach perfection. We improve ourselves and the world through our human

---

[159] Mishneh Torah, Hilchot Melachim (Laws of Kings).
[160] Rambam's Mishneh Torah exists in two versions: the one that had been the standard copy for many centuries, and the one in which censored excerpts have been reintroduced. In the uncensored version, Rambam suggests that Christians and Muslims also help pave the way for the arrival of Mashiach.
[161] Guide for the Perplexed 3:27.

toil. The Talmudic sage Rabbi Yochanan ben Zakkai explains that if you are in the midst of planting a tree, then even if the Messiah comes, what do you do? You keep planting your tree.[162] That we are a part of redemption does not exempt us from the work we continually need to do to advance it. "The *mitzvot* of the Torah will never be nullified, not even in the future days (i.e., the messianic age]."[163]

We have made too many mistakes throughout history, thinking that the Messiah is a person or an event. We know them as Bar Kochba, Abulafia, Shabbatai Zvi, Jacob Frank, and even some Hasidic rebbes. We even know them as the founding of the State of Israel. It was Christian influence that helped develop and perpetuate the idea of the single divine/messianic human. The Jewish notion, preceding that, suggested that all people are imbued with *tzelem Elokim* (divinity).[164]

At the end of the day, I would like to suggest that we are all Mashiach—we are the ones we have been waiting for.

The Baal Shem Tov, the founder of *Hasidut*, taught that one does not look outside one's soul to bring about redemption: "All our prayers for redemption are essentially bound to be prayers for the redemption of the individual." He taught that each of us must turn inward and seek redemption through seeking transcendence in all our actions and transactions.

While there are, of course, important things to learn from the Reform movement, I personally believe that it was a mistake to remove messianism from the liturgy, as that movement has done—we repair the world through activism but also through the moral components of all the *mitzvot*. Rav Kook emphasizes the messianic potential of our ethical actions and teachings.[165]

As Martin Buber said, "There is no definite magic action that is effective for redemption; only the hallowing of all actions without distinction possesses redemptive power. Only out of the redemption of the everyday does the Day of Redemption grow."

As passionate Jews, we are hopeful—we believe in progress. Mashiach is the name of the value of our doing something that is truly magnificent. It reminds us that we must keep the highest optimism about the human potential to achieve on the highest level.

So, we have raised the stakes. The Gemara[166] states, as we mentioned above, that when we ascend and stand at the end of our lives before Heaven, one of the

---

[162] Avot d'Rebbe Natan.
[163] JT, Megillah.
[164] *Tzelem Elokim* literally means "divine image."
[165] Talelei Orot, *Essay on Reasons for the Commandments.*
[166] BT Shabbat 31a.

main questions asked of us will be whether we yearned for redemption. Did we continue to believe in a better world and commit our lives to furthering that vision?

Yearning requires intentionality. We must ask ourselves: What is the redemption we are working to bring about? How is our *davening* helping us to get there? How are we helping to create a more just society? How are we preparing our children to bring their contribution to the redemption? How are we intertwining our *tikkun atzmi, tikkun bayit, tikkun kahal, and tikkun olam* (repair of self, family, community, and world)?

This is a formidable work, the biggest project that God gave the Jewish people and humanity. Perhaps the suggestion in the Talmud[167] that every Jew keeping Shabbat would bring the Mashiach means that if we were all to taste perfection together, we would be able to unite to collectively fulfill our mission. Perhaps the goal of Shabbat is to pause and taste a little bit of the perfection, the messianism that we never fully reach.

---

[167] BT Shabbat 118b.

DEBATE 9.

Rationalist-Monotheism vs. Mystic-Monotheism: On the Unity of God

There are so many different theologies of who and what and where God is. One could be an agnostic, claiming there is some prime force but suggesting we have no clue at all what that force is. One could go a step further and be an atheist, suggesting there is no god or force. One, of course, could be a polytheist, suggesting there are multiple gods. Among the polytheists, there can be henotheists, who argue that each unique god represents a different nation or region of the world. Other polytheists suggest that multiple gods rule over the entirety of the world. Another type of polytheism is dualism, where there are two separate gods, such as in Zoroastrianism, with a god of light and good (Ormuzd) and a god of darkness and evil (Ahriman). In Gnosticism, there are also two gods: one beyond this world and one who created this world. In Trinitarianism, the branch of Christianity whose adherents believe in the trinity, there are three beings within the godhead.

Any notion of multiple gods is rejected by the rabbis.

> Heretics asked Rav Simlai: What about that which is written: "El, Elohim, Hashem; El, Elohim, Hashem, He knows,"[168] which implies a plurality of deities? He said to them: It is not written here, "they know" rather, "He knows" in the singular. His disciples said to him: Teacher, those heretics you were able to push away with a reed, but what do you propose to answer us? He said to them: All three of them are together the name of the one God, as one would say, Basilius Augustus Caesar. Again, they asked about that which is written: "El, Elohim, Hashem spoke and He called the world into being."[169] He said: Is it written, "they spoke and they called? It only says, "He spoke and He called." His disciples said to him: Teacher, you could push away those heretics with a reed, but what will you answer us? He said to them: All three of them are actually the name of the One God, in the same way a person would call a builder a craftsman, a constructor, and an architect.[170]

---
[168] Joshua 22:22.
[169] Psalms 50:1.
[170] JT Berakhot 9:1.

Hasdai Crescas[171] writes:

> [The trinity] is opposed to the Jewish religion, for God is One in perfect simplicity and He alone is infinite in power. He embraces all perfections; to Him alone belong power, wisdom and will and all other eternal qualities. He has no partner and is in no way composite. He exists necessarily, that is to say, He is self-sufficient and owes not His existence to another. The refutation of the doctrine of the trinity is as follows. If, as the Christians say, the son born of the father is like the father, then the father, too, must have been born of another. But if so then He is an effect (i.e., not a cause) and has been created by another and has no necessary existence. The same applies to the holy ghost... It is also impossible to believe that the father has all perfections for if this were so, why should it have been necessary for him to give birth to the son who is god like him?.... A further proof that the son is not as perfect as the father and that the father cannot have given all his power to the son is the following. The father had the power of begetting a son while the son does not give birth. If this is because the son cannot give birth, then he is not perfect. If, on the other hand, it is because he does not wish to give birth, then the power he has is set at naught...[172]

On the opposite end of polytheism there is monotheism, suggesting that there is only one God. All of traditional Jewish theology is committed to monotheism, the only debate being about what monotheism means and entails. According to deists, it is true that God created the world, but God is so far beyond the world and removed from any involvement in this world. According to theists, on the other hand, yes, God is separate from, and beyond, this world, but at the same time God is involved with this world, both through imminence and transcendence. A panentheist would go even further, arguing that everything in this world is God, although God is beyond this world too (as opposed to a pantheist, who would say God is everything in this world but nothing beyond this world). A good example of pantheism could be illustrated through the ideas of Spinoza:

---

[171] Hasdai Crescas was a 14th-century Spanish Jewish philosopher. His rationalist approach was influenced, in part, by Rambam (Maimonides).
[172] Hasdai Crescas, *Sefer Bittul Ikrei HaNotzerim*.

Nothing exists but God

"God is one, that is, only one substance can be granted in the universe." [I.14]

"Whatsoever is, is in God, and without God nothing can be, or be conceived." [I.15]

"God is the indwelling and not the transient cause of all things. All things which are, are in God. Besides God there can be no substance, that is, nothing in itself external to God." [I.17]

Learning to see God in all things

He who clearly and distinctly understands himself and his emotions loves God, and so much the more in proportion as he more understands himself and his emotions. [v.15]

Our mind, in so far as it knows itself and the body under the form of eternity, has to that extent necessarily a knowledge of God, and knows that it is in God, and is conceived through God. [v.30]

Nature does not work with an end in view

Nature does not work with an end in view. For the eternal and infinite Being, which we call God or Nature, acts by the same necessity as that whereby it exists. . . Therefore, as he does not exist for the sake of an end, so neither does he act for the sake of an end; of his existence and of his action there is neither origin nor end.[173]

Here is a critique of the idea presented by Spinoza:

> He acknowledges God and confesses Him to be the maker and founder of the universe. But he declares that the form, appearance, and order of the world are evidently as necessary as the Nature of God and the eternal truths, which he holds are established apart from the decision of God. Therefore, he also expressly declares that all things come to pass by invincible necessity and inevitable fate. . . He does this in accordance with his principles. For what room can there be for a last judgment? Or what expectation of reward or of punishment, when all things are attributed to fate, and all things declared to emanate from God with inevitable necessity, or rather, when he declares that this whole universe is God? For I fear that our author is not very far removed from this opinion; at least there is not much difference between declaring that all things emanate necessarily from the nature of God and that the universe itself is God. . . I

---

[173] Benedict Spinoza, *Ethics*, translated by R. H. Elwes (Mineola: Dover Publications, 2018), Part IV, Preface.

think, therefore, that I have not strayed far from the truth, or done any injury to the author, if I denounce him as teaching pure Atheism with hidden and disguised arguments.[174]

The Rambam (Maimonides) makes a clear case for how he understands this point in Jewish theology:

> 1) It is the most basic of basic principles and a support for wisdom to know that there is something [namely God] that existed before anything else did, and that He created everything that there is. Everything in the skies, on the ground and in between exists only because of the fact that He created them.
> 2) Let it be known that if the Creator did not exist, then nothing else would, for nothing can exist independently of the Creator.
> 3) Let it further be known that if everything ceased to exist, the Creator alone would exist and would not have ceased to exist like everything else had. All things in creation are dependent upon the Creator for their continued existence, but He does not need any of them [for His continued existence]. Therefore, the reality of His existence is not like the reality of the existence of any creation.
> 4) One of the Prophets said, "But the Lord is the true God,"[175] meaning that only God is everlasting and that nothing else is. This is what the Torah has said: "There is none else beside Him,"[176] namely, that there is nothing in existence that is everlasting, except for God.[177]

Rabbi Schneur Zalman of Liady, the Alter Rebbe,[178] rails against deism:

> Here lies the answer to the heretics and here is uncovered the root of their error, in which they deny God's providence over particulars and the miracles and wonders recorded in scripture. Their false imagination leads them into error, for they compare

---

[174] Lambert Van Velthuysen of Utrecht (1622-1685), *Critique of Spinoza*. To be sure, this harsh critique of Spinoza, especially equating Spinoza's view with atheism, is based on Van Velthuysen's reading. Another reader may not come to such a strong conclusion.
[175] Jeremiah 10:10.
[176] Deuteronomy 4:35.
[177] Rambam, *Yad Hahazakah*, Laws of the Principles of Torah 1:1-4
[178] The Alter Rebbe, literally meaning the "older" or "first" rabbi, was the founder of the Chabad Lubavitch Hasidic sect.

the work of the Lord, creator of heaven and earth, to the works of man and his artifices. These stupid persons compare the work of heaven and earth to a vessel which emerges from the hand of the artificer. Once the vessel has been fashioned it no longer requires its maker. Even when the maker has completed his world and goes about his own business the vessel retains the form and appearance it had when it was fashioned. Their eyes are too blind to notice the important distinction between the works of man and his artifices—in which "something" is made from "something," the form alone being changed from a piece of silver into a vessel—and the creation of heaven and earth, which is the creation of "something" out of "nothingness." This latter is an even greater marvel than the division of the Red Sea, for instance, when the Lord caused a strong east wind to blow all through the night, until the waters were divided to stand as a heap and a wall. If the Lord had stopped the wind for but a moment, the waters, undoubtedly, would have begun to flow again in their normal, natural way and would no longer have stood upright like a wall. Although this nature implanted in the waters is also "something" created out of "nothing," for all that a stone wall does is stand upright without the help of the wind, this is not true of the nature of water. It follows a fortiori that with regard to creation ex nihilo—higher than nature and a much greater marvel than the division of the Red Sea—it is certain that the creature would revert to the stage of nothingness and negation, God forbid, if the creator's power were to be removed from it. It is essential, therefore, for the power of the Worker to be in His work constantly if the work is to be kept in existence.[179]

Rabbi Louis Jacobs explained this viewpoint of panentheism as found in Jewish mysticism and Hasidic thought:

> This idea of Hasidism... was dubbed heretical by the opponents of the movement who believed it to be a radical departure from traditional theism. To suggest that God is in all things or that all things are in God is to blur the distinction between God and His creation and between good and evil. That God's glory fills

---
[179] Shneur Zalman of Liadi, *Tanya*: Shaar HaYichud vehaEmunah, chapter 2.

the earth was taken to mean, by the opponents of Hasidism, that His providence is over all, not that He is found, as it were, in material things. But the Hasidic teachers did not hesitate to teach that from the point of view of God, as it were, there is no world, and that the purpose of man's worship is to pierce the veils of illusion until he sees only the divine in all things.[180]

It is easy to get confused between panentheism and pantheism. To make sure it is clear, here is how one scholar differentiated between Spinoza and the Alter Rebbe:

1. For Spinoza, God and Nature are one and the same, but for Schneur Zalman, God is transcendent as well as immanent.

2. For Spinoza, there is no creation of the world by God, but for Schneur Zalman, the Jewish view of *creation ex nihilo* stands.

3. For Spinoza, the universe is eternal, but for Schneur Zalman, the world is temporal and God alone is eternal.

4. For Spinoza, it is impossible to attribute will to God, but for Schneur Zalman, it is God's will which has created the world, i.e., which endows the world with the appearance of reality.

5. For Spinoza, God does not work *through* nature but *is* nature, but for Schneur Zalman, God is revealed *through* nature.[181]

So, when Jews recite the Shema, and we recite that God is *echad* (one), what do we mean by that? For some, this means there is one God and there is no other. "*Ein od milvado!*" ("There is none beside the one God!") For others, this means that God is one, i.e., God has no multiplicity. For others, still, this means that there is nothing but God. A new read of *Ein od milvado!*

In our debates of theism vs. atheism, some religious people label everything beyond their own viewpoint as "heretical" or "idolatrous." Others take a more tolerant view, while yet others go one step further and take a pluralistic view. The pluralist claims the other views are also true or at least have validity. For the soft pluralist, truth is complex, and so we hold some doubt and understand that there is more truth than we ourselves can hold within one religious tradition and one

---

[180] Louis Jacobs, *Principles of the Jewish Faith* (Eugene: Wipf & Stock Publishers, 2008), 115.
[181] M. Teitelbaum, *HaRav MiLiady*, Part II, 105.

spiritual experience. For the hard pluralist, everyone's ideas must necessarily be true. The tolerant religious person doesn't go as far, and claims that others' views are false, but that we should be respectful toward them. Is God worth fighting for? Is our vision of theology worth fighting for? Is someone else's viewpoint, whether religious or secular or however different from our own, worth fighting against?

Many Jews deemed Christianity to be idolatrous,[182] due to the multiplicity of gods. However, other Jewish scholars sought to differentiate Judaism from Christianity while also honoring that Christianity was not polytheistic or idolatrous. For example, the contemporary British scholar and theoretician Rabbi Dr. Alon Goshen-Gottstein writes:

> It is an entirely normative principle in Judaism that the monotheism expected of gentiles by the Noahide laws is of a less absolute kind than that expected of Jews. In the Middle Ages, many authorities indeed recognized Christian doctrine (even the doctrine of the Trinity) as basically monotheistic belief. One can readily understand how the doctrine of a triune Godhead could contaminate Christianity's claim to be monotheistic. However, Christianity was generally not considered polytheistic or idolatrous, though Maimonides—who did not live in Christendom—dissented from the widespread rabbinic agreement on this point. The concept of the Trinity was represented in the church as a mystery or paradox because it apparently contradicted a central component of their faith in the one God. Thus the Trinity, even though it is an essential feature of Christian theology and not merely one of folk religion, could be taken by Jewish scholars as a supplement to, rather than a replacement for, the idea of God as one. By Jewish standards as applied to Jews, Trinitarianism is not monotheism. But by the standards of the Noahide laws, the doctrine of the Trinity is not an idolatrous belief to which Judaism can express an objection."[183]

It's worth noting that Jewish concerns over Islam being idolatrous do not exist. Muslims are definitely monotheist and are even more opposed to concrete religious symbolism than traditional Judaism is.

---

[182] Ramban (Nahmanides), for example, in the famous Disputation of Barcelona, argued against Christianity. Although he received a reward from King James I for his successful defense of Judaism, Ramban ultimately left Spain as a result of the debate (the Dominicans claimed victory) and emigrated to Israel (then Palestine).

[183] Rabbi Dr. Alon Goshen-Gottstein, *Jewish Theology and World Religions* (Portland: Liverpool University Press, 2012), 286.

Rabbi Jonathan Sacks goes even further, arguing that Jewish theology is not only adamantly monotheist but also separate from other forms of monotheism:

> Not only is Judaism structurally different from the other monotheistic faiths, it is also different from the other great attempt to understand the human condition: philosophy, the invention of ancient Greece. The Greek idea is of truth as system. The Jewish idea is of truth as story. The philosophical quest has at most times been the search for truth that is timeless and universal. For Judaism, this systematically omits the most important features of the human situation, time and perspective. Time is the medium through which we learn, in which we make the long, slow journey from violence to justice, oppression to freedom, hierarchy to equality. Perspective is the dimension through which we discover that there are points of view different from, and not reducible to, our own.[184]

In the end, we can be humbled that each of us, individually and alone, knows very little. Even collectively, we know very little about the spiritual mysteries beyond. But part of that humility is also not rejecting ideas that we've inherited and honoring our tradition, and at the same time, respecting others' traditions in their search for understanding. We can debate the nature of God but, in the end, we must do so with deep humility.

Today, we have expanded in all new realms of theology (feminist, queer, liberation, etc.) and we can continue to seek and grow by learning from our past theologians even as we expand our inclusion. The Maor V'Shemesh asked why we repeat "Elokei" in the Amidah's first blessing when we say "Elokei Avraham, Elokei Yitzhak, v'Elokei Yaakov." Shouldn't we just say Elokei Avraham, Yitzhak, v'Yaakov? He answers his question saying that each had their own God, so to speak. One is singular but the manifestations we experience are multiple. Sometimes we need to become an "atheist" by the killing of the "god" that we no longer believe to be true to embrace a deeper theology that resonates much more deeply. Plato taught that our embrace of monotheism is a moral pursuit. If there are multiple gods there are multiple truths. If there is one God, there is one truth. May we continue to ensure that our personal theology is not only meaningful but that it challenges us to live by the deepest moral truths that we have come to know.

---

[184] Rabbi Jonathan Sacks, *A Letter in the Scroll* (New York: Free Press, 2004), 99.

DEBATE 10.

The Mussar Movement vs. the Hasidic Movement

Two of the most profound movements to emerge out of religious Judaism at the birth of the modern era were the Hasidic movement and the Mussar movement.

It seems clear that the Hasidic movement remains extremely popular. Membership continues to grow within the Hasidic community, and the learning of Hasidic ideas and the implementing of its practices are influential far beyond the community. But the Mussar movement, on the other hand, seems to not have enjoyed such staying power, perhaps even becoming a relic of the past. The ideas are still alive, but there are no longer strictly Mussar ideological groups or major institutions.

Why is this the case? Here are a few differences between the two movements that may play a role:

1. The first major difference may be about the different understandings of human nature. A major part of many Mussar ideologies is that we must overcome our desire for pleasure and for selfishness. We are at war with a part of the self. For a major segment of Hasidic thinkers, on the other hand, it is not a war but rather a channeling of energy. One channels one's desire for pleasure toward a deeper spiritual level, rather than trying to squash it. The Baal Shem Tov, the founder of Hasidism, for example, emphasizes spiritual bliss; Rebbe Nachman, another Hasidic giant, stresses deep joy in the service of God.

2. A second major difference could be about the relationship between the self and the community. For the Mussar teachers, the primary focus is on the self and the individual's growth. Surely there is a *va'ad* (a place for group reflection), but the spiritual work is about the individual's journey. For Hasidut, on the other hand, the community is primary in virtually every facet of life.

3. A third major difference could be on the bar for excellence. The Mussar movement had very high standards for growth and a high bar for excellence. The Hasidic movement, on the other hand, loves stories about innocent children who don't know how to pray. Whereas the Hasidic

story emphasizes the simple pious Jew,[185] the Mussar movement celebrates the elite virtuous leaders.[186]

4. A fourth major difference could be on the level of consciousness. For Mussar, the work is all on the conscious, moral, intellectual, and behavioral level. For the Hasidic movement, the work goes far beyond the conscious realm. There is a deeper aspiration to journey into the mystical and the subconscious.

Of course, there are exceptions within these four identified differences, but these may be some of the central factors regarding why Hasidut[187] "won" and the Mussar movement "lost."[188] But such a measure of success is only on the plane of numbers. From a different measure, we might suggest that the Mussar movement won in that it is a move from strict Talmud learning to the focus on Jewish values and Jewish character. One might argue, that while most American Jews don't identify themselves as Mussar practitioners, they do emphasize Jewish values over Jewish law, and they do emphasize Jewish character over Jewish learning. Now that is not directly because of the Mussar movement, we can say, but it may not be absent of the movement's influence either. It also seems safe to assume that more American Jews think about Jewish values than about Jewish mystical practice.

We have shown some possible differences in ideologies between these two schools of thought. But to be sure, there are also enormous similarities between the movements as well. Both seek to awaken the heart to our service. Rabbi Yisrael Salanter, the founder of the Mussar movement, writes about the need for our emotional engagement:

> So that one become accustomed to this [Mussar] wisdom, whose ways branch into two, the first being to inflame the souls through the purification of thought, through these sublime studies [the study of Mussar]; to learn with lips on fire, with correct apprehension, depicting each idea in a broad manner, and bringing it close through familiar imaginings, until the heart gets excited, whether to a great or small extent. And thereby it

---

[185] Indeed, the Chabad Lubavitch sect of Hasidism has made its main mission the inclusion of all Jews of all stripes, dispatching emissaries to the remotest parts of the world and establishing a campus presence in many a university.
[186] Consider Rabbi Yisrael Salanter's consistent emphasis on "spiritual perfection." See Rabbi Chaim Ephraim Zaitchik, *Sparks of Mussar* (New York: Feldheim Publishers, 2017), 13.
[187] Hasidut is the Hebrew term for Hasidism. (The "ut" suffix in Hebrew is equivalent to the "ism" suffix in English).
[188] The terms "won" and "lost" are being used loosely here, and refer to the abovementioned popularity of Hasidut vs. the paucity of the Mussar movement.

will be empowered to prepare the limbs, to actualize every good deed on its behalf, whether by desire or by strength of will.[189]

For the Baal Shem Tov and his followers, we need to go deep to the place of a broken heart. This theme comes up again and again. Consider this story.

> One time, the Baal Shem Tov of blessed memory commanded Rabbi Zev Kitzes of blessed memory that he should learn the kavanot [special mystical intentions] of each shofar blast, because he would be the one to blow shofar on Rosh Hashana. Rabbi Zev learned the kavanot and wrote them down on a piece of paper to look at when the shofar was being blown. He then put the paper in his pocket. When it came time for shofar, he began to look for the paper, but he was not able to find it. He looked to and fro, and realized that he did not know [the appropriate] mystical intentions. He became very upset. He cried out with a broken heart, and the shofar was blown without the kavanot. After this, the Baal Shem Tov said to him, "In the King's palace there are many rooms and chambers and different keys for each door. But an axe has the capability of all the keys. An axe can open the lock of any door. So, it is true with the kavanot. Each heavenly gate has a different kavanah. But a broken heart can open them all. When a person breaks their heart before God, it is possible for them to enter through all the gates in the palace of the King of Kings, the Holy One be Blessed.[190]

So how do we achieve such emotional engagement? For Rav Salanter, the pathway is through repetition and mantra:

> And therefore, it is appropriate to repeat Mussar sayings many times over. And specifically, when one comes across a saying of the sages or some other words of Mussar by which they feel they would be affected and that would penetrate into the chambers of their heart, they should review and repeat it with deep affect many, many times, until it becomes engraved upon the tablets of their heart, and as frontlets between their eyes. Then, upon

---
[189] Israel Salanter, *Ohr Yisrael* 2.
[190] Moshe Chaim Kalman, "Stories of the Baal Shem Tov," *Or Yesharim*.

> his going outside, and going to rest upon his bed, this teaching will ring in their ears like a bell, and will not depart from their memory.[191]

With all of this, the goal is to weaken our physical desires. Through our anticipation, and preparation, we can overcome our desires. Rabbi Salanter explains further:

> ... to have foresight, to look out from the get-go before the days of evil come, to prepare counsel and a plan, of how to conduct oneself and others, and to diminish the matter to make the experience easier, until awe grows greater than desire. For this is the entirety of the person, to strengthen awe and weaken desire with virtue and wisdom...[192]

For the Baal Shem Tov, on the other hand, we don't want to deny our body or our desire. Consider this teaching:

> It is written: "When you will see the donkey of your enemy collapsing under its burden, and you are inclined to refrain from aiding him, you shall nevertheless aid him" (Exodus 23:5). The Baal Shem Tov applied this instruction to the body and the material self (*chamor*, "donkey," also means "materiality"). Initially, the Torah is saying, you may see your body as your enemy, resisting your soul's objectives, collapsing under the "burden" of the mitzvot. You may therefore be inclined to fight the body by denying its needs and mortifying it. Says the Torah: You must aid your soul's "enemy." Purify the body, and refine it, but do not break it.[193]

For the Hasid, the Torah is reinterpreted, again and again, to be about inner life. For the Mussar practitioner, one embraces mindfulness (deeper sensitivities on the hyper-conscious level). For the practitioner of Hasidut, one embraces mindlessness (a letting go over mind to give more power to the soul).

Thankfully, for Jews who want to go deeper in their learning and practice, there are so many avenues to pursue. We need not view the Hasidic path and Mussar

---

[191] Israel Salanter, *Shaarei Ohr* 9.
[192] Israel Salanter, *Ohr Yisrael* 2.
[193] "Thirty-Six Aphorisms of the Baal Shem Tov," Chabad.org, last accessed 2023, https://www.chabad.org/library/article_cdo/aid/3073/jewish/36-Aphorisms-of-the-Baal-Shem-Tov.htm.

path as being at odds with one another. We can view them as complementary paths. Rav Kook, after all, was a Hasid, but he also wrote works of Mussar.

While there was, and still is, a battle between the rationalist and mystical camps, we can move beyond that battle. May we strive to do so as we each, individually and communally, find the appropriate avenue by which to deepen our learning, practice, and service.

Moral Philosophy

Debate II.

Einstein, Freud, & Marx vs. The Sages: Are We Free to Shape the World?

Those familiar with Jewish theology take free will for granted. After all, how could life (not to mention religious life) have any purpose if our choices are predetermined and we are not actually free to make meaningful choices? The question of freedom is not only about the individual's capacity of free will but also about the freedom of the human collective in the face of opposing forces.

It turns out that the three best cases for determinism were made by Jews. Freud argued that humans are determined by their early childhood experiences. Marx argued that people are determined by their socio-economic status. And Einstein argued that people are determined by the laws of physics, building off the work of an earlier Jew, Spinoza, who argued that people are determined by their inner dispositions (what we could today call our genes or DNA). Of course, they were right, at least partially. Marx was correct that one's socio-economic status is highly predictive of one's future lifestyle choices (and options for choices). Freud was correct that one's early childhood experiences are highly correlated with one's future. Einstein and Spinoza were correct that empirical data can be used to show causation, especially with regard to human DNA. And yet, is that the end of the story?

In the Torah, we learn of our opportunity to choose:

> See, I set before you this day life and prosperity, death and adversity. For I command you this day, to love the Lord your God, to walk in [God's] ways, and to keep [God's] commandments... Choose life—if you and your offspring would live.[194]

Maimonides is forcefully adamant that humans are free:

> Do not believe the thought expressed by foolish nations and many unwise Jews that when God creates a person, God decrees whether they will be righteous or evil. This is not the case. Rather, each person has the capability to choose to become righteous like Moshe Rabbeinu (Moses our Teacher) or evil like Yeravam (the biblical Israelite king), wise or foolish, merciful or cruel... and similarly regarding any other attribute.[195]

---
[194] Deuteronomy 30:15-19. Modified for gender neutrality.
[195] Rambam, Hilchot Teshuvah (Laws of Repentance) 5:1.

The consequences and responsibilities of having free will are enormous. Rabbi Eliyahu Dessler, a 20th-century *Mussar*[196] teacher, wrote:

> Each decision that one makes impacts on all situations in every day of their life, whether to a small or great extent, whether beneficial or detrimental. And one's decisions affect not only oneself. For example, the decisions one makes regarding one's children's education have repercussions for all future generations. Each person influences their environment. Therefore, the impact of one's decisions affects one's environment as well as one's generation, even the entire world, for all future generations.[197]

Can a person be held responsible, in a court of law, for something that was beyond their free will to choose or not choose? How do we understand mitigating factors in criminal justice? If one was abused and thus more likely to be abusive, should their punishment be less when they abuse another?

And yet, the Talmudic sages do also show limits to free will. Consider the Talmudic teaching: "Everything is in the hands of Heaven, except for fear of Heaven."[198] Rashi here teaches:

> Everything that is placed on a person is decreed by God. For instance, [whether the person is] tall, short, poor, rich, smart, dull, light, or dark is all decreed by Heaven. But [whether a person is] righteous or evil is not decreed by Heaven, but is entrusted to the individual's choice. A person has two paths in front of them, and they need to choose to fear Heaven.[199]

Rashi here is asserting that while one's *physical* attributes are predetermined by their inner disposition, his/her *spiritual* and *emotional* attributes are not. God created the world and gave humans the gift of freedom by engaging in *tsimtsum* (Divine retraction). God gave up some control in order for humans to have control, similar to how a parent educates a child as they grow older.

Rabbi Eliyahu Dessler further taught:

---

[196] *Mussar* literally means "teachings" or "traditions," and refers to an approach to Judaism, indeed a movement, which focuses on ethics and character development.
[197] Michtav M'Eliyahu, Vol. I, 115.
[198] BT Berakhot 33b.
[199] Rashi's commentary on BT Berakhot 33b.

> Decisions of free choice are limited to the meeting ground between the positive and negative forces within an individual. For example, many people might be negligent in speaking derogatorily about others, only because they are accustomed to it and are oblivious to its severity. The very same people however would never consider stealing or murder, because their education has ingrained in them not to do so, to the extent that they have no inclination to do such things.[200]

Rabbi Dessler teaches of a "bechira point." We are not free to choose an evil that we are far from, nor are we free to choose a heroic act too far from our grasp. Our freedom point is where our current moral internal battle lies.

But assuming for a moment that an impulse toward evil is indeed placed inside of us, how can we be free to choose? We are told: "I created an evil inclination, which is the wound, and I created Torah as its antidote."[201] Rabbi Moshe Chaim Luzzatto (Ramchal), of 18th-century Italy, explained:

> As we have discussed, humans are the creature created for the purpose of being drawn close to God. One is placed between perfection and deficiency, with the power to earn perfection. Humans must earn this perfection, however, through their own free will and desire.[202]

Furthermore, it seems that at times free will is suspended. For example, Pharoah's heart was hardened by God.[203] Rashi comments there:

> Since Pharaoh has acted wickedly and brazenly against Me and it is revealed before Me that the idol-worshipping nations have no intention to improve their behavior, it is better that his heart be hardened in order to increase My [miraculous] signs and have [Israel] recognize My strength . . .
> Nevertheless, during the first five plagues [God did not harden Pharaoh's heart] for it is not stated, "And God hardened

---

[200] Michtav M'Eliyahu I, 113.
[201] BT Kiddushin 30b.
[202] Moshe Chaim Luzzatto, *Derech Hashem*, 1:3:1, 45.
[203] Exodus 7:3.

Pharaoh's heart," rather "Pharaoh's heart became hardened"[204] [because of his own actions].[205]

Rambam (Maimonides) uses the Pharoah example to express a broader theology:

> A man may commit so great a sin or such numerous sins that justice requires of the true judge, as the penalty to be exacted from this particular sinner for the sins, committed by him voluntarily and of his own mind, that repentance shall be withheld from him and liberty to turn from his wickedness shall not be accorded him, so that he may die and perish in the sins which he committed.... Hence also, it is written in the Pentateuch, "And I will harden Pharaoh's heart."[206]

Furthermore, Proverbs says: "the mind of the king in the Lord's hand."[207] Rabbi Meir Leibush ben Yehiel (Malbim), of 19th-century Russia, taught on this verse:

> Even though an individual has the ability to exercise free will, this is not true of a king, for his decisions affect the welfare of the country. If the king would make a decision with negative consequences, the impact could be destructive to many people. Therefore, his heart is in God's hand, and regarding national matters, his free will is annulled.[208]

Ramchal writes:

> We have proven from the Scriptures and from our Sages' teachings that ultimately humankind will lose its free choice and evil will no longer exist, as the Talmud[209] states, "The verse says that transgression will disappear from the land." If so, the ultimate goal does not refer to [humans using free will and receiving] reward and punishment [for their actions], but rather to the world's general perfection. But [until that future time] God

---

[204] It would seem that according to Rashi, God only considered the idol-worshipping nations to be beyond hope after the first five plagues.
[205] Rashi's commentary on Exodus 7:3.
[206] Rambam, *Mishneh Torah*, Repentance 6:3, trans. Moses Hyamson, 1937-1949.
[207] Proverbs 21:1.
[208] Malbim's commentary on Proverbs 21:1.
[209] BT Berakhot 10a.

> combined the two issues (i.e., that God runs the world now with humans possessing free will and that God desires to reveal God's Divine Presence), in God's profound wisdom, in order to bring about the world's ultimate perfection.[210]

Then there are other rabbinic sources that seem to give complete control of the world over to God:

> Rabbi Chaninah said: A person does not even bang his finger below (in this world) without it being decreed above, as is written: "From God are the steps of man [211]...".[212]

The Talmudic rabbis also teach, on the other hand, that many matters are not only up to God but up to "mazal:"

> Rava said: Length of life, children, and sustenance do not depend on one's merit, but rather they depend upon fate.[213]

Some rabbis who embrace a maximalist approach to *hashgachah peratit* (Divine providence) attempt to make meaning of human existence. Rabbi Bachya ibn Pakuda (known by the name of his work Chovot HaLevavot) writes:

> Even when you are fully aware that effort is worthless without the decree of the Creator, nevertheless, a landowner must plow their land, clear it of thorns, plant it and irrigate it if they have water, and trust that the Creator will make it fruitful, protect it from mishaps, increase its yield, and bless it.
>
> But it is inappropriate to abandon the field and not work at cultivating it, but simply trust in God's decree to cause the earth to yield crops without being planted. Similarly, craftsmen, merchants, and hired workers are commanded to seek their livelihoods while maintaining their trust in God, for one's sustenance is under God's control, and God guarantees it to humans and provides it through whatever means it may be.[214]

---

[210] Moshe Chaim Luzzatto, Da'at Tevunot, chapter 44.
[211] Psalms 37:23.
[212] BT Chullin 7b.
[213] BT Moed Kattan 28a.
[214] Rabbi Bachya ibn Pakuda, Gate of Trust, Chapter 4:4.

In other words, Chovot HaLevavot is positing that success in one's endeavors is dependent upon both God and individual human effort. The Torah itself expresses this dual approach when warning about arrogance on the battlefield: "[A]nd you say to yourselves, 'My own power and the might of my own hand have won this wealth for me.' Remember that it is the Lord your God who gives you the power to get wealth."[215] People have the power to be successful in their endeavors, but that power comes from God.

Spiritually, we each have *bechirah chofshit* (free will) to act and choose our own destiny. Freedom is the constitutive means for all morality. That is to say, one can only be good if one can choose between good and evil. It is in the free choice that one attains one's humanity. Each human being is given the freedom to actualize their destiny. According to Rabbi Meir Simcha of Dvinsk (1843-1926), what it means for human beings to be created in the image of God is precisely that we have free will.[216] God is radically free and so humans are free, in God's image. And that freedom not only makes humans godly, but also makes humans human, i.e., not animals which do not have such freedom.

This gift is not, as previously stated, freedom from oppression, but rather the freedom to actualize one's purpose to make the world just and holy. Our commitment must be to *Ve'ahavta lerei'acha kamocha*, to love others like ourselves. This love is achieved, indeed enriched, through means such as *tzedek* (social justice, distributive justice), *mishpat* (human rights and procedural justice), *gemilut chasadim* (acts of love and kindness), and being *rodfei shalom* (pursuing peace and thereby creating a more trusting society).

And yet, in modernity, with the emergence of the social sciences, we learn that human behavior is both deeply complicated, yet also quite often predictable. In 1971, Dr. Philip Zimbardo, Professor Emeritus at Stanford University, conducted the famous Stanford Prison Experiment, in which students were assigned roles as either guards or prisoners.[217] Alarmingly, the intended 2-week study ended after only 6 days because of how quickly and wholly the students who were assigned the "guard" positions began acting in authoritative and violent manners. The "guards" inflicted such abuse that the disheartened "prisoners" were beginning to suffer from psychological damage, and the environment rapidly became toxic and dangerous. In his experiments and books, Dr. Zimbardo reminds us of the horrifying fact that, given the right situation, most good people can act in terrifying and evil ways:

---

[215] Deuteronomy 8:17, 18.
[216] Meshech Chochmah to Gen. 1:26, 31.
[217] The Stanford Prison Experiment: A Simulation on the Psychology of Imprisonment. http://www.prisonexorg/.

> Any deed that any human being has ever committed, however horrible, is possible for any of us—under the right or wrong situational circumstances. That knowledge does not excuse evil; rather, it democratizes it, sharing the blame among ordinary actors rather than declaring it the province only of deviants and despots—of Them but not Us.[218]

Professor Zimbardo has noted that at Abu Ghraib, American soldiers all too willingly adopted the sadistic guard model and behaved in a disgraceful and abusive manner that did damage to America's reputation and status around the world.[219] Zimbardo proves here that we should not believe that human behavior is entirely determined by circumstance, and at the same time we shouldn't be so naïve as to dismiss the enormous influence that one's context exacts on one's disposition and character.

Psychologists and sociologists have long tried to understand why seemingly good people commit crimes. Apart from unstable childhoods, the impulsive and peer-pressure-driven adolescent years, and varied demographic problems, there appears to be a need that motivation and opportunity must exist in order for people to commit crime.

Upon hearing disturbing tales of good people turning to evil, we might yield to despair about our human capabilities, but that would be a mistake. We who live in a post-industrial society have more power than ever before. We constantly fall in order to climb forward (*yeridah letzorech aliyah*), and as the falls are becoming more intense due to our immense technological capacity, so are the means to rise. In this cycle, we must remember that we possess the most powerful ability:

> Stone is hard, but iron cuts it. Iron is stiff, but fire melts it. Fire is powerful, but water extinguishes it. Water is heavy, but clouds carry it. Clouds are strong, but wind disperses them. Wind is strong, but the body resists it. The body is strong, but fear destroys it. Fear is strong, but wine averts it. Wine is strong, but sleep conquers it. Death is more powerful than any of these, but *tzedakah* redeems death.[220]

The most powerful weapon we possess is *tzedakah* (acts of righteousness). It is the way we defy the natural world (breaking from self-interest) and even death

---
[218] Philip Zimbardo, *The Lucifer Effect: Understanding How Good People Turn Evil* (Random House, 2008), 211.
[219] Ibid.
[220] Midrash Tanchuma.

(placing our souls in the realm of the eternal). The potential for spiritual and ethical actualization are all around us. We are reminded of the well-known and profound teaching of Reb Menachem Mendel of Kotzk:

> It is said that he once asked his disciples, "Where does God live?" They were bewildered. "How can the rabbi ask, 'Where does God live?' Where does God not live?" "No," said the rabbi, "God lives where we let God in."[221]

The age-old psychological debate about nature vs. nurture has been resolved with the concession that clearly human development is determined by both genetic factors and environmental influences—that is, considerations from outside ourselves—not to mention our own internal free will choices.

Researchers have increasingly focused on the potential influence of free will. This novel research is emerging from an exciting contemporary field of neuroscience called neuroplasticity, which observes how the mind's power alters the very structure and function of the brain in response to experience. Sharon Begley, the editor of the *Wall Street Journal* science section, writes: "Like sand on a beach, the brain bears the footprints of the decisions we have made, the skills we have learned, the actions we have taken." Today, neuroscientists can observe how repeated traumas etch neural pathways to turn grief into depression, how meditating monks can change the level of prefrontal activity by generating feelings of compassion, and how pianists can increase the shape of their motor cortex through sheer imagination.[222]

Until relatively recently in human development, analysis of free will could not rely much, if at all, on empirical analysis. In western civilization, for example, from the pagan philosopher Aristotle (pro) through the Reformation-era debate between the Protestant Martin Luther (con) and the Catholic theologian Erasmus[223] (pro), the debates used rhetoric and the then-current theological thinking as a way of understanding human development and free will.

The nature vs. nurture debate had profound implications for political philosophy and structure as well. Politically, monarchies and their noble supporters

---

[221] Martin Buber, *The Way of Man, According to the Teaching of Hasidism* (New York: Citadel Press, 1966).
[222] Medical practitioners have been observing neuroplasticity for many years in patients following a stroke. Often, when one functional cortex experiences damage during ischemia, a neighboring cortex will frequently activate, compensate for the impairment, and take over the function of the damaged region. Thus, after a stroke, some people may lose the ability to speak, but then, with training, their brain reorganization enables them to again achieve that ability. The cutting-edge current research provides an additional supplement to our knowledge of how the brain functions and copes with mental and physical injuries.
[223] "History of the Free Will Problem," *The Information Philosopher*, last accessed 2023, https://www.informationphilosopher.com/freedom/history/.

have supported the position that nature, rather than nurture, determines the type of person one is and can be. The noble class argued that they, by hereditary and innate qualities, provided a natural leadership and refinement to society, whereas the inherently ignorant and cruel peasants offered no discernible value to society, and that this was the inevitable order of the world. Not surprisingly, the nobility rarely elevated commoners to noble status.

Beginning with the Enlightenment, a counter-argument arose favoring the nurture position. John Locke, whose concept of "Natural Rights" was adopted most famously by Thomas Jefferson in the Declaration of Independence, wrote in his *Essay Concerning Human Understanding* that humans were born with a mind like a "white paper void of all characters"[224] (sometimes cited with the Latin *tabula rasa*, or "blank slate"), and that "experience" was what filled in one's character. Thus, Locke rejected the idea that humans had innate qualities, challenging the rationale of the nobility.

Even among scientists, the interconnected relationship between nature and nurture can no longer be ignored. One such example of scientific research's influence on the debate comes from the field of comparative genomics. When the genome of the common fruit fly was mapped, many scientists predicted that the human genome would be much more complex, since it was presumed that humans are of a far higher order of creature with infinitely greater mental capabilities. When the human genome was completed, many scientists were shocked and dismayed to learn that over 60 percent of the genes found in the fruit fly were also found in humans.[225] Since learning that fruit flies and humans use the same or similar genes to develop into adults, this research has become fertile territory for the nature vs. nurture debate. Professor Gerry Rubin of UC Berkeley, who worked on the genome processing, explains, "They [fruit flies] can become addicted to alcohol, cocaine and other drugs. They have a wake-sleep cycle like humans do. They have complicated rituals of behavior... in addition to sharing many of the biochemical pathways humans have." One particularly revealing breakthrough in the comparative genomic study concerned the discovery of BRCA1, or the "breast cancer gene." Professor Rubin writes, "It turned out that the molecules causing these problems in fruit flies were the same molecules that we know were responsible for causing cancer in humans." From this comparative genomic study, the importance of both nature and nurture is thus clear.[226]

---

[224] "John Locke: The Human mind as a 'tabula rasa,'" age-of-the-sage.org, last accessed 2013, https://www.age-of-the-sage.org/philosophy/john_locke_tabula_rasa.html.
[225] National Human Genome Research Institute, Comparative Genomics Fact Sheet, https://www.genome.gov/about-genomics/fact-sheets/Comparative-Genomics-Fact-Sheet
[226] Kevin Davies, "Nature vs. Nurture Revisited," *Nova*, April 16, 2001, https://www.pbs.org/wgbh/nova/article/nature-versus-nurture-revisited/.

Much evidence from scientific research suggests that human development, personality traits, and behavior come more from nurture than nature. Many philosophers take similar positions and ground their analysis in both physical science and philosophy. Consider the words of the philosopher and professor Thomas Nagel, who explains that we are not, in the materialist sense, simply brains on wheels that have evolved:

> ... So, if mind is a product of biological revolution—if organisms with mental life are not miraculous anomalies but an integral part of nature—then biology cannot be a purely physical science. The possibility opens up of a pervasive conception of the natural order very different from materialism—one that makes [the] mind central, rather than a side effect of physical law.... Both theism and evolutionary naturalism are attempts to understand ourselves from the outside, using very different resources. Theism offers a vicarious understanding, by assigning it to a transcendent mind whose purposes and understanding of the world we cannot ourselves fully share, but which makes it possible to believe that the world is intelligible, even if not to us. The form of this transcendent understanding is conceived by extrapolation from the natural psychological self-understanding that we have our own intentions.[227]

Harvard psychologist Professor Steven Pinker recently told me that he believes in free will, not as some miracle or soul-based phenomenon but rather based on the notion that the human brain is so complex that human behavior will never be entirely predictable. This minimalist scientific approach may be more appealing to those leaning toward determinism.

Much of Jewish tradition is adamant that humans are free to make choices and insists that these choices emerge from each person's unique nature. It also acknowledges that every individual has a unique internal psychology and spiritual influence. Consider this rabbinic teaching:

> They say that for the first thirteen years [of a person's life] the Evil Urge is greater than the Good Urge. There in his mother's womb, a person's Evil Urge grows with him. [After he emerges into the world,] he starts breaking the Sabbath, and nothing is there to stop him... After thirteen years, the Good Urge is

---
[227] Thomas Nagel, *Mind and Cosmos* (New York: Oxford University Press, 2012), 15, 23.

born. Then when he breaks the Sabbath, it says to him: Empty one! Isn't it written (Exodus 31:14), "One who breaks it will surely die"?[228]

We are so deeply influenced morally and spiritually in our youth before we are fully capable of making ethical decisions. Those "thirteen years" are invaluable. We should all seek to better understand ourselves and become more cognizant of how our uniquely complex development affected our character and the people we are today. We must also remain aware of how God has played such an important role in all of our lives and the spiritual light he has placed inside us. And we must approach our successes with humility. As the business saying goes: "Don't confuse brains with a bull market." Sometimes people find success because they existed at the right moment. So too, many fail for reasons that are not their own fault, such as a lack of opportunity or being a victim of circumstance.

In a dark world, we live by what Bertolt Brecht called "*Erst kommt das Fressen. Dann kommt die Moral*" (grub comes first, and ethics later). This idea is sometimes referred to as economic determinism, which means that many of us live according to physical needs and our natural instincts but never transcend to higher levels of awareness to live according to our values and principles. Instead, let us learn from science and Jewish teaching. Neuroplasticity teaches us that our minds are shaped by our experiences, so we should seek to create a society that will maximize our ability to keep our minds healthy and capable of making the right choices in life.

Most human beings appreciate stability. We appreciate it in our families and in our work lives. We like to observe developed routines. So too, ritual builds its spiritual power through its consistency and lack of change. In religion, continuity is valued above all.

Nonetheless, we know that the world is always changing and that we must adapt to it. Rabbi Abraham Isaac HaCohen Kook, the first Ashkenazic chief rabbi of pre-state Israel, teaches that the description of God as *chai vekayam* (living and established)[229] means that God is both changing and non-changing. God evolves and grows but also is rock-solid. This paradox is one for us to emulate in our own, smaller, way. We should ask ourselves which principles and values that we hold are non-negotiable, and which enable us to thrive through adaptation. Religious beliefs and practices fail when they shelter us from our changing world. They thrive when they prepare us to cope with the losses that are inevitable in change and help us evolve in the moment.

---

[228] Avot D'Rabbi Natan 16.

[229] This term is recited in the Modeh Ani prayer. *Modeh ani* literally means "I thank," and is the first prayer recited upon waking in the morning, in which one thanks God for returning one's soul (i.e., allowing them to live yet another day).

Another key factor in working for change is to believe that it's possible. Stanford University professor Carol Dweck identifies two different orientations toward change: a fixed mindset and a growth mindset. Those with fixed mindsets assume that our basic qualities, such as intelligence and talent, are fixed. Hard work may help us get ahead, but it doesn't improve our capabilities. Those with growth mindsets, on the other hand, believe that brains and talent are just a starting point, and that we can develop and improve our abilities. People with a growth mindset are better able to adapt and change when circumstances call for it.

History is filled with stories of both leaders who adapted to change and those who refused. Those who refused were engulfed by history. The biblical figure Joseph interpreted Pharaoh's dreams to mean that seven years of abundance would be followed by seven years of famine, and so the grain surplus was stored during the years of abundance and helped save Egypt during the famine.[230] Joseph could have become acquiescent, since Egyptians were used to regular flooding from the Nile that annually replenished the soil, seemingly guaranteeing a perpetual and plentiful food supply. However, he understood that eventually there would come a time of scarcity, and acted accordingly. On the other hand, the last king of Babylon, Belshazzar, ignored the literal "writing on the wall" and decided to celebrate what he thought would be a long, secure reign.[231] The result: a large force of Persians and Medes overthrew him and brought on the downfall of Babylon.

In our fast-changing and unpredictable world we must prepare for the new realities, both personally and collectively. Sometimes that means looking outside of our own "arks" to prepare, emotionally and practically, for the unknown changes awaiting us. Surely, the Covid-19 pandemic taught us that. To do so, we each need to reflect on our mindsets: Do I have a fixed mindset? Do I assume I'm hard-wired and can't improve my skills in order to adapt to change? Or do I have a growth mindset, one that helps me see the opportunities when change is called for?

Some suggest that God can be omniscient while humans can still have free will. Rabbi Aryeh Kaplan writes:

> Particularly ingenious is the approach of Rabbi Moshe Almosnino.[232] He explains that God is the Creator of time, and is therefore not in any way bound by it. Since God exists outside of time, His knowledge of the future is exactly the same as His knowledge of the past and present. Therefore, just as His

---

[230] Genesis 41:25-30.
[231] Daniel 5:25-28.
[232] 16th century, Ottoman Empire.

knowledge of the past and present does not interfere with man's free will, neither does His knowledge of the future.

Of course, all that Almosnino is doing here is demonstrating that God's omniscience does not interfere with free will. With a little thought, however, it becomes obvious that the paradox itself is not resolved by his approach. The paradox, as first expressed by Rabbi Akiva,[233] still remains, [as] "All is foreseen, yet free will is granted."[234]

So, who is right? Those who feel God is in control? Those who argue that nature is in control? Or those who argue that humans are in control? It is too easy and simplistic to just respond: all of the above. In the end, we can humbly embrace that this is yet another major intellectual conflict that we cannot resolve. Maimonides writes:

> Know that the resolution to this question [can be described as]: "Its measure is longer than the earth and broader than the sea.". . . Human knowledge cannot comprehend this concept in its entirety for just as it is beyond the potential of man to comprehend and conceive the essential nature of the Creator.[235]

Let us learn to discern and focus on our personality traits, community concerns, and global issues where we must strive harder (based on freedom) and on those where we must humbly relinquish control (based on trust that we are not completely free). We must learn to balance *hishtadlut* (effort) with *bitachon* (trust in walking a path of integrity in the face of that which we cannot control). Should we accept who we are (as determined) or accept who we can become (through our freedom)? That is one of the most important spiritual questions to get clarity on.

---

[233] Pirkei Avot 3:18.
[234] Aryeh Kaplan, *The Aryeh Kaplan Reader* (Brooklyn: Mesorah Publications, 1983), 132.
[235] Rambam, *Mishneh Torah*, Repentance 5:5, trans. by Eliyahu Touger, Moznaim Publishing.

DEBATE 12.

Ayn Rand vs. Karl Marx: On Wealth & Virtue

> There are four types of character in human beings: One that says: "mine is mine, and yours is yours": this is a commonplace type; and some say this is a sodom-type of character. [One that says:] "mine is yours and yours is mine": is an unlearned person (am haaretz); [One that says:] "mine is yours and yours is yours" is a pious person. [One that says:] "mine is mine, and yours is mine" is a wicked person."[236]

One of the hot-button topics in American politics today is taxation and, in particular, how it relates to the distribution of wealth. Income disparity continues to grow as the rich get richer and the poor get poorer. The gap is widening at a rapid rate. Far-right conservatives claim that it is like robbery to tax the wealthy and redistribute wealth; the far-left claims that the wealthy should be taxed far more than they are. Of course, there are countless other positions along the spectrum. While analogs to these debates can be traced throughout Jewish history, in modernity these two camps might best be represented by Karl Marx, the founder of Marxism, and Ayn Rand, a fierce advocate for unregulated capitalism, whose works can be read as suggesting that selfishness is indeed a virtue.

Ayn Rand, a Russian-American philosopher who was Jewish by birth if not by affiliation, lived from 1905-1982 and is best known for her two best-selling novels, *The Fountainhead* and *Atlas Shrugged*. She developed a branch of philosophy she called Objectivism in which she rejects religion and argues that reason is the only means of acquiring knowledge. She also rejects "ethical egoism," altruism, and any form of collectivism in favor of laissez-faire capitalism and individual rights. Furthermore, she rejects Libertarianism, although her ideas are very closely aligned with that movement.

In a very telling video, Ayn Rand says that the war is not between capitalism and communism since she views communism as pure evil and capitalism as the source of everything good. Rather the war is between capitalism and altruism. Altruism, she argues, means that people get their sense of worth through self-sacrifice and through giving to others. But capitalism means people get their sense of worth through their own capacity and determination.[237]

---

[236] Pirkei Avot 5:10 trans. Dr. Joshua Kulp.
[237] "Ayn Rand on Capitalism vs. Communism," Ayn Rand Institute on *YouTube*, January 29, 2015, https://www.youtube.com/watch?v=HQMDJPaGhzI.

Karl Marx was also born Jewish but, unlike Rand, was influenced by a very different culture in his homeland of Germany, and lived a century before Rand, from 1818-1883. Much of his political theory was developed in collaboration with another German thinker, Friedrich Engels. Perhaps Marx's most famous work was *The Communist Manifesto*, if not *Das Kapital*, published in 1848. He believed that progress emerges through class conflict. The Bourgeoisie (ruling class), for example, was in conflict with the Proletariat (working class) through the production and distribution of goods. Based on his philosophy of historical materialism, it was clear to him that such a class divide, based on all of its inequality, would inevitably self-destruct.

It is hard to compare Marx and Rand. Rand was primarily a novelist, who, through her works, espoused philosophical and political views; the political implications of Rand's novels are not always clear. Marx, on the other hand, was one of the most influential thinkers and movement builders in modern history, a philosopher and political theorist; his ideas are studied around the world.

Randian theory, though, has been on the rise. Conservatives in government consistently present budgets with steep cuts to food stamps (SNAP), Medicare, Medicaid, and Social Security, in contrast to huge tax cuts to the very wealthy and large corporations. These measures mirror, and sometimes have their roots in, the ideas of "objectivist" Ayn Rand,[238] whose works constantly exalted the individualistic millionaire while hurling invective at the poor and opposing any program to help them. Republican Paul Ryan, for example, tried to distance himself from accusations that he favors the Objectivist philosophy of Ayn Rand, but he stresses his religious differences only. While Rep. Ryan is a Catholic (Rand was born Jewish, and was an atheist), he repeatedly endorsed Rand's extreme views on pure capitalism, including an adversarial position toward the poor.

While Marx and Rand would have disagreed on almost everything, there is, perhaps, one point on which they may have agreed. It is a point that also puts them at odds with so much of Jewish thought. They are both opposed to *tzedakah* (charity) as understood by so many Jews, i.e., giving money to the poor and needy. Marx would oppose *tzedakah* because it perpetuates the wealth disparity, masking the real problem of systemic inequality. Philanthropy covers over class divides, confusing the responsibility of the rich and the rights of the poor. Marx rejects, even despises, humanitarian relief, since it makes the greedy look virtuous. Rand opposes *tzedakah* as a virtue for the opposite reason: individuals should not have to give up anything that is theirs. People may do so if they choose, but they need not. Here is a little taste of her perspective:

---

[238] Jonathan Chait, "Here's What Paul Ryan's Latest Answer About Ayn Rand Really Means," *New York Magazine*, September 12, 2014, https://nymag.com/intelligencer/2014/09/what-ryans-latest-answer-about-rand-means.html.

> My views on charity are very simple. I do not consider it a major virtue and, above all, I do not consider it a moral duty. There is nothing wrong in helping other people, if and when they are worthy of the help and you can afford to help them. I regard charity as a marginal issue. What I am fighting is the idea that charity is a moral duty and a primary virtue.[239]

Marx's and Rand's thinking is also similar in that they both espouse many inconsistent ideas. Marx articulates important critiques of capitalism but also sees the world in black and white. Either you are working toward revolution or you are perpetuating classism. For this reason, Marx rejects socialism as well. Yet, consider how Rand wrote ceaselessly about the great evils of government social services and still chose to accept social security payments herself.[240] She claimed in the "About the Author" section at the end of her book *Atlas Shrugged*, "I have always lived by the philosophy I present in my books—and it has worked for me, as it works for my characters."

Of course, in the Torah's worldview, a just society is built on *tzedakah*, both individual support and collective governmental support. The alternative is Sodom.[241] While both Marx and Rand present important perspectives worth reflecting upon, they also both overstate their cases. Rabbi Aharon Lichtenstein[242] famously argued that he believed Ayn Rand's thought was antithetical to Torah and that one should not read her books. To be fair, he would have denounced Marxism as well, although his critique would likely have been less fierce.

To Marx's credit, he seems to have had a distaste for a life built around making money, and he embraced a notion of progress that would lead to the redemption of humanity (a Hegelian dialectical form of secular messianism). There is something very noble about that, and this view can be located within Jewish ideals. But then he departed completely from Jewish values; he was through and through a materialist and believed that solving economic injustice would solve virtually all problems. He even embraced violence to get there. He rejected peoplehood and nationhood as a way to deepen human solidarity and expand culture, and he viewed them as another tool of the wealthy to enslave the masses. Marx might even be viewed as an antisemite, given his argument that humanity needs to

---

[239] "Playboy Interview: Ayn Rand," *Playboy*, https://rickbulow.com/Library/Books/Non-Fiction/AynRand/PlayboyInterview-AynRand_3-1964.pdf.
[240] "When Ayn Rand Collected Social Security & Medicare, After Years of Opposing Benefit Programs," *Open Culture*, December 27, 2016, https://www.openculture.com/2016/12/when-ayn-rand-collected-social-security-medicare.html.
[241] Ethics of Our Fathers (the tractate of the Mishnah dealing with ethics) 5:10 lists four views one may have regarding property; they are quoted at the beginning of this chapter, on page 91.
[242] Rabbi Lichtenstein (1933-2015) was the co-*rosh yeshiva* (rabbinic head) of Yeshivat Har Etzion, and obtained a PhD in English literature from Harvard University.

be emancipated from the Jews. He also argued that Jews must be checked and stopped (in general) since they were so central to the birth of capitalism and guilty of the poisoning all of civilization. One can easily make a Jewish case for socialism, but not for Marxism.

Back to the question related to economic fairness as it plays out in American political debate today: What might fair taxation look like? If one listened only to the avalanche of political ads during the 2012 election campaign, for example, one might believe that Americans were being crushed under the heaviest federal tax burden ever, and that raising taxes on the wealthy (the "job creators") was tantamount to national economic suicide. This view, bolstered by much of the record $4-$6 billion raised for the presidential and congressional campaigns,[243] was heavily supported by a small group of billionaires, perhaps topped by casino magnate Sheldon Adelson, who reportedly made contributions of a record $150 million himself.[244] In total, billions of dollars were spent, largely by people who claimed that they were forced to pay too much in federal taxes.

We can see this trend during the 1979-2005 period, which was unique for its lower taxes on the wealthy. Congressional Budget Office data indicate that among Americans:

1. The top one-hundredth of one percent of the population had an income growth of 384 percent, while their tax burden decreased by 11.4 percent.

2. Median income increased by 12 percent, while the tax burden for the middle quintile decreased by only 4.4 percent.[245]

In addition, from 2000-2007, the top 0.1 percent of American earners saw a 94 percent increase in income, compared with a 4 percent increase in income for the bottom 90 percent of earners. As former Secretary of Labor Robert Reich observed, citing 2011 data, poverty—especially among the young—is on the rise, and there are deliberate efforts to create even greater economic inequality:

1. 21 percent of American school-aged children lived in poor households, a 4 percent increase since 2007.

---

[243] Jennifer Liberto, "2012 election priciest to date: $4.2 billion tab and rising," *CNN*, November 5, 2012, https://money.cnn.com/2012/11/05/news/economy/campaign-finance/index.html.
[244] Peter Stone, "Sheldon Adelson Spent Far More On Campaign Than Previously Known," *Huffpost*, December 3, 2012, https://www.huffpost.com/entry/sheldon-adelson-2012-election_n_2223589.
[245] Kevin Perese, "Trends in the Distribution of Household Income," Congressional Budget Office, November 16, 2017, https://www.cbo.gov/publication/53320. https://www.cbo.gov/system/files/115th-congress-2017-2018/presentation/53320-presentation.pdf

2. Nearly one out of every four children lived in a family that had difficulty obtaining a sufficient food supply at some point during the year.

3. In spite of this, about 60 percent of all cuts in the proposed 2011 Republican budget targeted child food, nutrition, and school programs, food stamps, and Medicaid.[246]

In the past, this trend toward lower taxes for the wealthy and greater inequality of wealth led to a pattern of booms and busts. The worst economic downturn occurred after one such period, culminating in the stock market crash in 1929 and the ensuing Great Depression. The second worst economic downturn came in 2007 at the end of George W. Bush's second term, also following a period of tax cuts for the rich and great economic inequality. During his presidency, the stock market lost about 25 percent of its value, with the NASDAQ losing nearly half its value.[247] In contrast, President Bill Clinton, who raised income taxes for the highest earners, presided over a booming stock market, with the Dow Jones average climbing more than 7,000 points over his two terms.[248] Thus, we can infer from the above that raising taxes on the wealthy appears to aid economic growth, while cutting taxes for the rich only exacerbates income inequality and encourages reckless financial schemes that can lead to deep economic recession.

Looking back to a decade ago, although we need not necessarily look back that far, there is stark evidence of how lowering taxes for the wealthy tends to increase economic inequality. In one 3-month period in 2012, ExxonMobil's profits were $16 billion, the highest ever recorded by an American corporation. In spite of this, the oil industry receives an average of more than $15 billion in subsidies annually from the federal government.[249] On the other hand, most Americans continued to struggle. For example, the greatest number of jobs created was in retail sales, where the average annual salary was less than $21,000.[250] In addition, the number of those unemployed, working part-time but trying in vain to get full-time work, and those who gave up looking for work, reached more than 23 million.[251] In a

---

[246] Robert Reich, "Cliff Notes on the Three Real Perils Ahead," *Huffpost*, updated Feb. 4, 2013, https://www.huffpost.com/entry/cliff-notes-on-the-three_b_2246487?utm_hp_ref=daily-+brief%3Futm_source%3D-DailyBrief&amp%3Butm_campaign=120612&amp%3Butm_medium=email&amp%3Butm_content=BlogEntry&amp%3Butm=.

[247] Matt Egan et al., "From Reagan to Trump: Here's how stocks performed under each president," *CNN Business*, January 29, 2019, https://www.cnn.com/interactive/2019/business/stock-market-by-president/index.html.

[248] Ibid.

[249] Andy Kroll, "Will Big Oil Keep Its Subsidies in a Fiscal-Cliff Deal?" *Mother Jones*, December 12, 2012, https://www.motherjones.com/politics/2012/12/big-oil-subsidies-fiscal-cliff-deal-obama-congress/.

[250] Mary Dowd, "How to Write an Action Plan for a Sales Jobs," *Houston Chronicle*, 2022.

[251] "Monthly Latino Employment Report," *National Council of La Raza*, December 7, 2012, https://issuu.com/nclr/docs/employmentrpt120712/1.

callous gesture, the extended benefits period (the last 20 weeks) of unemployment insurance was cut off in the summer of 2012 due to congressional failure to renew the program, throwing millions of people off unemployment benefits. If Congress would fail to act by the end of 2012, it was argued, an additional 2 million Americans would lose their unemployment benefits.

The 2012 presidential election campaign offered Americans the opportunity to choose whether to continue the Bush tax policy or return to the Clinton-era policy of a slight increase on the tax rate of income above $250,000. Republican presidential nominee Mitt Romney stated that he paid a 14 percent rate on his income tax in the one year for which he released his returns. However, his effective tax rate was around 10 percent—far less than the rate of most middle-class Americans. In November of that year, the American people voted to re-elect President Barack Obama, thus voting, in effect, to raise taxes on the wealthy. As Americans, as Jews, and as activists for justice, we must continue to press Congress to carry out this policy.

The Jewish tradition has much to say about fairness in taxation, and consistently endorses the principle that those who benefit the most from society have the greatest obligation to pay for the support of the community. For example, the Torah states: "[D]o not harden your heart and shut your hand against your needy kinsman. Rather, you must open your hand and lend him sufficient for whatever he needs."[252] In addition, the Torah instructs farmers to go over their fields and vineyards only once, and not to reap the corner of their fields: "When you reap the harvest of your land, you shall not reap all the way to the edges of your field, or gather the gleanings of your harvest. You shall not pick your vineyard bare, or gather the fallen fruit of your vineyard; you shall leave them for the poor and the stranger."[253] According to the Mishnah, the community was expected to support a communal kitchen, burial society, and other needed infrastructure.[254] Later, more defined funds presided over by prominent members of the community were set up to assist the poor. In order to achieve this, citizens were taxed in proportion to their ability to pay. Thus, Jewish law has consistently upheld the idea that progressive taxation is necessary for the maintenance of the community.[255]

---

[252] Deuteronomy 15:7-8.
[253] Leviticus 19:9-10.
[254] BT Pei'ah 8:7.
[255] Rabbinic law can be read as such; however, it is worth noting that the Biblical law to pay *shekalim* was regressive. The biblical law of *machatzit hashekel* (a half-shekel coin), is regressive: A machatzit hashekel was to be donated by each adult Israelite (Exodus 30:11-16). The Torah is clear that all were to give this amount only, and "the wealthy may not give more and the poor may not give less." The proceeds served three functions: to be counted toward a census; to provide funds for the construction of the mishkan; and to atone for the donors. In fact, the machatzit hashekel donation is also referred to in the text as *kesef hakippurim* (money of atonement).

There are billionaires in America today who are not stereotypically greedy and selfish. Consider Warren Buffet's commitment to give away his billions in fortune:

> First, my pledge: More than 99% of my wealth will go to philanthropy during my lifetime or at death. Measured by dollars, this commitment is large. In a comparative sense, though, many individuals give more to others every day.... This pledge will leave my lifestyle untouched and that of my children as well. They have already received significant sums for their personal use and will receive more in the future. They live comfortable and productive lives. And I will continue to live in a manner that gives me everything that I could possibly want in life.... Were we to use more than 1% of my claim checks on ourselves, neither our happiness nor our well-being would be enhanced. In contrast, that remaining 99% can have a huge effect on the health and welfare of others. That reality sets an obvious course for me and my family: Keep all we can conceivably need and distribute the rest to society for its needs.[256]

As another example, in announcing their divorce, Bill and Melinda Gates stated their commitment to the work of their charitable foundation.[257] And the Gateses have been asking hundreds of the wealthiest Americans (billionaires or those who would be if not for charitable donations) to be part of The Giving Pledge, a commitment to give a minimum of half of their wealth to philanthropy either during their lifetime or at death. As of early 2014, more than 120 wealthy individuals and couples have accepted the pledge,[258] and now the list has expanded overseas to include some of the wealthiest people in the world. To facilitate the process, members gather annually to discuss their ongoing activities and learn ways to use their fortunes for good. The hope is that The Giving Pledge will provide crucial funds for education, the arts, scientific research, and other areas of concern, for the betterment of society.

This movement has historical antecedents. One such example was Andrew Carnegie (1835-1919), the steel magnate, who was perhaps the first modern mega-philanthropist. Even before he retired in 1900, he had written that any wealth that a person has beyond one's needs should be viewed as a fund to be

---

[256] Warren Buffett, "My philanthropic pledge," *CNN*, June 16, 2010, https://money.cnn.com/2010/06/15/news/newsmakers/Warren_Buffett_Pledge_Letter.fortune/index.htm.
[257] Nicholas Kulish, "What the Gates Divorce Means for the Bill and Melinda Gates Foundation," *The New York Times*, updated July 7, 2021.
[258] The Giving Pledge, http://givingpledge.org/.

expended for the good of the community. Carnegie put his fortune behind his idea and contributed about $350 million (its current value would be well into the billions) to charitable causes before his death.[259] He was especially fond of libraries that would enable people to read books and acquire knowledge free of charge. Carnegie and his posthumous corporation created more than 2,500 libraries,[260] and many generations of students owe much of the quality of their education to Carnegie and his spirit of philanthropy.

While some of the world's wealthiest happily engage in philanthropic efforts for the benefit of others, it should be acknowledged that it is not always easy to give up one's wealth. As we see from the Talmudic passage below, family dynamics have often made it challenging for philanthropists to actualize their giving. Consider the Talmudic story of King Munbaz:

> There was an incident involving King Munbaz, who liberally gave away his treasures and the treasures of his ancestors in the years of drought, distributing the money to the poor. His brothers and his father's household joined together against him to protest against his actions, and they said to him: Your ancestors stored up money in their treasuries and added to the treasures of their ancestors, and you are liberally distributing it all to the poor. King Munbaz said to them: Not so, my ancestors stored up below, whereas I am storing above."[261]

Many things come easily for the rich, and we should expect those who are so greatly blessed and privileged to give back to the community that enabled their success. With so much suffering, poverty, and sickness in the world that could be alleviated with just a fraction of the massive wealth that such a few enjoy, it is the ethical responsibility of the wealthy to aid the less fortunate. However, there are challenges to philanthropy that should be recognized and considered. Still, each person has a great amount to give back to society, regardless of their financial resources. We can give our time to social betterment organizations, give our old clothes to homeless shelters, donate blood to help the sick, or be a friend to the lonely, to name just a few things we can do. Almost all of us can push ourselves a bit further to give more, and we will only gain in the process.

---

[259] "Philanthropy of Andrew Carnegie," *Columbia University Libraries*, last accessed 2023, https://library.columbia.edu/libraries/rbml/units/carnegie/andrew.html.
[260] Ibid.
[261] BT Bava Batra 11a.

The *shemitah* (sabbatical) year[262] is one of the countless Torah-based vehicles that demonstrates a Jewish commitment to economic justice. Rabbi Zvi Hirsch Kalisher (1795-1874) writes:

> The wealthy man will learn not to look down upon the poor man, for the Torah said that in the seventh year everyone is equal. Both rich and poor have permission to enter gardens and fields and eat.[263]

Rebbe Nachman of Bratzlav (1772-1810) saw the deep desire for money as one of the hardest desires to overcome. He saw the emergence of capitalism as a dangerous force that could lead to violence and idolatry. "He would explain that the only true goal was to serve God all the days of one's life, spending one's time praying to God and singing His praise"[264] and said that "[w]ealth is not the goal of life at all... the only goal is the Creator, may God's name be blessed."[265] Rebbe Nachman went as far as to state that one should be ashamed of their wealth:

> ... money is the greatest shame. If someone wants to insult another, he says that the other has money. Money is so great a shame, that the more money a person has, the greater his shame... Now, it was revealed that wealth is the main thing of which to be ashamed."[266]

Jewish texts can be cherry-picked to argue for capitalism or socialism, of course. But the deeper truth is that Jewish thinkers have, for millennia, held very different views about economic justice based on their own ideologies, locations, and eras. What is clear from all the Jewish sources, however, is that selfishness is not a virtue. Each of us is responsible to take care of the other. On the other hand, dependence upon others is not a value either, and each person must therefore take personal responsibility not only for the other but, all the more so, for oneself.

Marx and Rand evoke such powerful emotions among ideologues today. We can understand why this would be true for Jews as well, since they were both Jews, and represent extremes as they represent the Jewish people. In our day, may we expand our learning, our generosity, and Jewish wisdom toward justice.

---

[262] The Torah designates every seventh year as *shemitah*, both for refraining from working land owned in Israel and for freeing of all debts. To prevent people from being discouraged from lending money due to the knowledge that the debt will be freed during the *shemitah* year, the *prozbul*, a document which effectively exempts one from freeing a debt owed him/her, was created by the Talmudic sage Hillel.
[263] Sefer HaBrit, Behar s.v. Derech HaSheni, U'Sefarta Lecha.
[264] Rabbi Aryeh Kaplan's translation of Sippurei Rav Nachman 280.
[265] Ibid., 297.
[266] Ibid., 349-350.

Debate 13.

The Angels vs. God:
Should Humans Have Been Created?

As we saw in our first debate, Hillel and Shammai argue about whether it is ultimately good or not that humans were created.

> For two and a half years, Beit Shammai and Beit Hillel disagreed. These say: It would have been preferable had man not been created than to have been created. And those said: It is preferable for man to have been created than had he not been created. Ultimately, they were counted and concluded: It would have been preferable had man not been created than to have been created. However, now that he has been created, he should examine his actions that he has performed and seek to correct them.[267]

In a similar vein, at the conclusion of the *vidui* (confession), a prayer well-known from the Yom Kippur *machzor* (the High Holiday prayer book) and used in prayer at other times as well, we recite:

> My God, before I was created, I was not worthy; now that I was created it is as if I were not created. I am dust in my life,[268] all the more-so in my death. I am before You as a vessel filled with shame and embarrassment.

This quote from the liturgy can be viewed not only as self-flagellation, but also as a reformulation of the debate between Hillel and Shammai. Perhaps when we say *vidui* we are asking ourselves: "Now that I have sinned, now that I cannot live up to what God expects of me (and what I should expect from myself), would it have been better had I not been created in the first place?"

And what exactly are Beit Shammai and Beit Hillel debating here? Whether there is more pain or joy in human experience? Whether humans give more to or take more from the world? Whether humans are more virtuous or more wicked at their core? We can never know for sure, but each facet is worth considering. And the conclusion is fascinating. We can't know with any degree of certainty which would be better, but we can know what we must do: *teshuvah* (a word

---

[267] BT Eruvin 13b.
[268] Perhaps a reference to Genesis 3:19, "For you are dust and to dust you will return."

which literally means to return, but which has come to refer to the process of self-reflection and growth)!

After all, according to the Talmudic rabbis, *teshuvah* was one of the concepts that existed before this world, as it were, was created:

> Seven phenomena were created before the world was created, and they are: Torah, and repentance, and the Garden of Eden, and Gehenna, and the Throne of Glory, and the Temple, and the name of Messiah.[269]

Rabbi Adin Steinsaltz adds here:

> The implication of this remarkable statement is that *teshuvah* is a universal, primordial phenomenon.... It is embedded in the root structure of the world.... Before we were created, we were given the possibility of changing the course of our lives.[270]

The rabbis explain that humans were literally born already with a consciousness, indeed an essence, in need of repair:

> "[And God created man dust] from the earth:"[271] R' Berechiah and R' Chelbo in the name of R' Shmuel bar Nachman said: He was created from the place of his atonement, as it says, "Make Me an Altar of earth."[272] God said: "Let Me make him from the place of his atonement, and hopefully, he will endure."[273]

What an amazing idea that humans were created from *kaparah* (a concrete place of atonement). In the postmodern era of deconstruction, we understand that there are multiple socially constructed worlds and many theories of reality and truth. One might ask if one's social identity is natural or essential to themselves or purely a social construct. Thinkers and activists go in both directions today. Many Black thinkers have said, "I'm born Black," arguing for race as something essential to them, not merely social. Many gay activists, on the other hand, say that their sexual orientation is how they were born, not a choice or a construct but essential to who they are. Judith Butler, on the other hand, argues that not only

---

[269] BT Pesachim 54a.
[270] Kol Haneshamah Machzor, 8.
[271] Genesis 2:7.
[272] Exodus 20:21.
[273] Midrash Genesis Rabba 14:8.

is gender a social construct but one's sex is, too. Ontologically, we cannot deny matter but as soon as we embrace theory construction and start giving names and identities, or assigning value, to such matter we are in the realm of construction.

Humans could only survive because God decided to create a world built not only on justice but also on mercy. Rashi writes:

> [A]t first God intended to create it (the world) to be placed under the attribute (rule) of strict justice, but He realised that the world could not thus endure and therefore gave precedence to Divine Mercy allying it with Divine Justice. It is to this that what is written in (Genesis 2:4) alludes—"In the day that the Lord God made earth and heaven".[274]

We are told that the angels were rather jealous, and perhaps infuriated, as it were, when humans were created in the image of God. Thereby, the angels debated with God:

> When the Holy One desired to create humanity, as it is said "Let us make humanity in Our image,"[275] God wanted to make humans above the celestial beings.... The angels came to accuse humanity, saying, "What is humanity that You should remember it, and the child of humanity that You should be mindful of it,"[276] for they will sin before you in the future. The Holy One said to them, "If you were brought down [to earth] below, you would have sinned much more than them."[277]

How fascinating that God sides with humanity over the angels. How can it be that angels would sin more than humans? It is normally explained that animals do not have free will but only obey their basic instinct. Angels are also not free but only obey their Divine commands. But humans, on the other hand, have both the basic instinct and the Divine command, as well as the freedom to choose one or the other. It remains unclear how angels would have failed more than humans, but God is clear in imparting to the angels that the humans are doing better.

So, let us first examine the question from a vantage point of self-interest. On average, do humans experience more joy or suffering? Of course, there are some who are born into a life of misery and there are others who live a life of luxury.

---

[274] Rashi on Genesis 1:1:3 trans. M. Rosenbaum and A.M. Silbermann, London, 1929-1934.
[275] Genesis 1:26.
[276] Psalms 8:5.
[277] Zohar, Genesis (I 25a-b).

But, on average, what is the human condition? Again, we cannot know for sure. But we do know that while some global problems are getting worse, we are also experiencing significant global progress in healthcare, technology, access to education, and cooperation to prevent warfare. Of course, we still must recognize that debates about access to healthcare are frequent and heated, technological advancements have led to much strife, the content of education is a topic of much contention, and war happens all too frequently.

Harvard Professor Steven Pinker argues that we're witnessing a huge reduction in global violence, but, he warns, this trend could reverse itself if we don't manage it properly:

> Substantial reductions in violence have taken place, and it is important to understand them. Declines in violence are caused by political, economic, and ideological conditions that take hold in particular cultures at particular times. If the conditions reverse, violence could go right back up.[278]

Violence is, of course, only one form of human suffering among so many others. There are reasons to think that things could get a lot worse due to climate change and environmental destruction, the spread of pandemics, cyberwarfare, and many other major threats. Rabbi Dr. Yitz Greenberg wrote: "The Holocaust was an advance warning of the demonic potential in modern culture... the strain of evil is deeply embedded in the best potentials of modernity."[279]

At this moment, if you are born into destitute poverty in the global south without access to healthcare, clean water, proper food, education, or any social mobility, your pain is likely higher than your pleasure. If you're born into 21st-century America, relative wealth with access to healthcare, a home, clean water, a fridge full of food, a car, a job, and other luxuries, it is likely that your pleasures exceed your pains. In short, there is no simple answer to whether humans experience more happiness or suffering, more pleasure or pain, as human experience is highly relative, highly volatile, and constantly evolving as new solutions and challenges emerge.

And we should be sure not to measure pleasure and pain in purely hedonistic terms. Professor Peter Singer writes:

---

[278] Steven Pinker, *The Better Angels of Our Nature: Why Violence Has Declined* (New York: Penguin Publishing Group, 2012), 361.
[279] Yitz Greenberg, *Cloud of Smoke, Pillar of Fire* (CLAL, 1977), 37.

The way of thinking I have outlined is a form of utilitarianism, but not the version of utilitarianism defended by classical utilitarians like Jeremy Bentham, John Stuart Mill, and Henry Sidgwick. They held that we should always do what will maximize pleasure, or happiness, and minimize pain, or unhappiness. This is "hedonistic utilitarianism"—the term "hedonist" comes from the Greek word for pleasure. In contrast, the view we have reached is known as "preference utilitarianism" because it holds that we should do what, on balance, furthers the preferences of those affected. Some scholars thin[k] that Bentham and Mill may have used "pleasure" and "pain" in a broad sense that allowed them to include achieving what one desires as a "pleasure" and the reverse as a "pain." If this interpretation is correct, the difference between preference utilitarianism and the utilitarianism of Bentham and Mill disappears.[280]

But do humans take more from or give more to the world? Here it seems clear that, by and large, humans take far more than they give. We are the only ones who kill animals en masse for food even when we are not hungry. We are the only ones destroying the planet. We are the ones committing genocide.

It is easy to fall into a psychological trap where one believes that someone else's loss can still be my gain. We are different people and what matters, for some, is what *I* have. But Rabbi Moshe Cordovero (better known by his acronym, Ramak)[281] argued that the boundaries of the self and the other are morally blurred:

> In everyone there is actually a part of their fellow human, and therefore a person should want their fellow's happiness and honor as much as their own, because they [the other] really is themself, and that is why we were commanded "love your neighbor as yourself."[282]

Indeed, our pathway toward happiness may be alleviating suffering for the other.

> [Viktor Frankl] used to say, in the name of Kierkegaard, that the door to happiness opens outwards. By that he meant that the

---

[280] Peter Singer, *Practical Ethics 3rd Edition* (New York: Cambridge University Press, 2011), 13.
[281] Rabbi Moshe Cordovero was a 16th-century kabbalist.
[282] Alan Morinis, Every Day, Holy Day (Boston: Shambhala, 2010),114.

best cure for psychic pain was to care more about other people's pain. That too I learned from the survivors.[283]

Perhaps the Edenic sin of eating from the tree of knowledge of good and evil is that human beings came to see all morality as binary (good and evil). Now there were only absolutes but no paradox. Is it better that humans were created or not created? Perhaps this binary question forcing us toward a monolithic answer is itself flawed in our time. But even as we reject a binary perspective, we dare not become relativists or, worse, become completely confused about what is evil. As the prophet Isaiah warns: "Woe unto them that call evil good, And good evil; That change darkness into light, And light into darkness; That change bitter into sweet, And sweet into bitter!"[284]

---

[283] Norman Lamm, *Festivals of Faith* (New York: RIETS, Yeshiva University Press, 2011) 254.
[284] Isaiah 5:20, JPS 1917.

DEBATE 14.

Past vs. Future

Jewish tradition proposes that three lights illuminate the world:

1. *Or Bereishit* – the light of creation[285]
2. *Or Sinai* – the light of revelation
3. *Or Mashiach* – the light of redemption

Typically, mystics engage in *Or Bereishit*, the beginning, in a sense, of the intellectual history of time. Here we will instead discuss and turn our attention to the other two lights, the competing lights of *Or Sinai* and *Or Mashiach*: One light pulls us back in history to our first interaction with ideas, which in some sense preceded history, and one light pulls us forward to a time when time as we know it no longer exists.

I think that what is so meaningful about the Jewish religion is that while we keep creation and revelation burning brightly and strong, we are focused equally on redemption. Theologically, we are focused on cultivating, appreciating and using the light represented by *Or Bereishit* and *Or Sinai*. We then use these lights to ultimately move us toward *Or Mashiach*—a redeemed soul, a redeemed Torah, a redeemed society, and a redeemed God, so to speak.

For many Jews, the idea of modernity runs counter to our tradition, our livelihood, or even worse, our religion's very survival. However, to be modern does not have to mean that we are tied to the present—such a perspective is reactive and reveals a potentially short-sighted religiosity. To be modern means that we are situating ourselves at the point of shifting toward the future—at the forefront of social change and paradigm shifts guided by Torah and fueled by *Or Mashiach*.

Traditionally, many Jewish thinkers embraced the idea of *yeridat hadorot*,[286] that humanity has been in descent since revelation, and that we have been rendered morally impotent. Yet even if this idea is embraced, there is still some virtue in being a small and impotent, yet still elevated, people (i.e., "dwarves on the shoulders of giants").

Religion and its tradition, when viewed as being situated in the past, can give birth to a comfortable religious stagnancy and instill an exclusionary spirit in its adherents. This enables someone to simply retreat from modernity into the ghetto. The Reverend Dr. Martin Luther King Jr. once taught, "The ultimate measure of a man is not where he stands in moments of comfort and convenience, but where

---

[285] Also known as *Or Ganuz* (the hidden light of creation)
[286] The term *yeridat hadorot* literally means "the descension of generations."

he stands at times of challenge and controversy." In a similar vein, Oliver Wendell Holmes, the great Supreme Court Justice, once admonished a young colleague that "it is required [that you] share the passion and action of [your] time at the peril of being judged not to have ever lived." We must leave our comfort zone to engage with the world in the context of our time and also to strive for a better future.

In the fifth century BCE, Protagoras led the philosophical transition from a focus on the universe toward one of human values. This monumental shift in philosophical thinking and understanding helped set the intellectual stage for important philosophers such as Socrates and Plato to explore eternal truths including virtue, justice, and the nature of human experience. Protagoras was responsible for a paradigm shift that proved crucial for the development of intellectual history and character development. Since the Era of the Enlightenment, however, we seem to have swung too far toward individualism, thereby neglecting the import of collectivism and our responsibility—even as individuals—to society and to the world in general. Today, we must work to interweave the global and the local more deeply and meaningfully, to develop a focus on the meta-picture (the cosmos, universe, globe, nation, society) from the perspective of the individual.

In Carl Stern's interview with Rabbi Dr. Abraham Joshua Heschel, Rabbi Heschel said:

> I would say, let them remember that there is a meaning beyond absurdity. Let them be sure that every little deed counts, that every word has power, and that we can, everyone, do our share to redeem the world in spite of all absurdities and all the frustrations and all disappointments. And above all, remember that the meaning of life is to build a life as if it were a work of art. You're not a machine. And you are young. Start working on this great work of art called your own existence.[287]

When we focus on redemption, we are stirred to remember our true significance, that every little action we take has an effect that matters. One of the great tragedies of the human condition is that millions of people live honest and earnest lives filled with love and dedicated to the service of others, but pass from the world never having fully appreciated their own greatness and holiness. Many don't fit within our society's current definition of "hero," and many receive no accolades for doing what they simply considered to be the right thing. Societally, we can keep a high standard for excellence while concurrently supporting and honoring

---

[287] *NBC-TV* on Sunday, February 4, 1972.

those who contribute to the true betterment of our society by serving others. All of us are unique and blessed with ideas, gifts, skills, and feelings that we can use to contribute to making the world a better place, and the uniqueness that each of us exhibits means that our contribution is one that no one else can make!

Those blessed with the gifts of easy access to knowledge and mentorship must not abuse the power, or ignore the responsibility, that come with those gifts; rather, they must exercise a particularly engaged role in creating an ever more just society. Passivity in the face of immorality and injustice has played a terrible and significant role in the descent and impotence of humanity. As the American 20th-century philosopher Richard Rorty concluded:

> The Foucauldian academic left in contemporary America is exactly the sort of left that the oligarchy dreams of, a left whose members are so busy unmasking the present that they have no time to discuss what laws need to be passed in order to create a better future.[288]

Let us reject the academic Ivory Tower and use our knowledge to perfect God's creation as we seek out Or Mashiach.

> [I]t is stated: "God vindicates the righteous, God is furious every day"[289] . . . Explaining the cause of God's anger, it is taught in the name of Rabbi Meir: When the sun rises and the kings of the East and the West place their crowns on their heads and bow down to the sun, the Holy One, Blessed be He, immediately grows angry.[290]

In a world of lights, we miss the light. Either we can't see it or we misunderstand its source. But the light is all around us and it should fill us with gratitude to God and responsibility to humanity. We all have unique gifts to share that are made all the more powerful when we are illuminated with the Divine light. However, the prerequisite for reflecting Divine light is the understanding of the source of our energy and success; and to achieve this understanding requires that we strive with all our might to engage in this endeavor while maintaining the humility it so requires.

---

[288] Richard Rorty, *Achieving Our Country: Leftist Thought in Twentieth-Century America*, (Harvard University Press, 1999), 139.
[289] Psalms 7:12.
[290] BT Berakhot 7a.

Let us take to heart the understanding that we were endowed with *Or Bereishit* and blessed with *Or Sinai*, and that now it is our duty, through the spiritual and actual cultivation of the light that is within us all, to seek *Or Mashiach*. Judaism is unique in its situational balance between the past and the future, leading many among us to seek the comfort of the past and to resist the responsibility that comes with being a modern people. We must not act in such a fashion. We must embrace our identity as a people blessed with its incredible tradition, and use the knowledge, spiritual revelation, and ethical obligations that come from our past to make the world we inhabit in the present a more holy and just place not only for ourselves but for all forms of life. This is our duty—this is how we seek the future light of *Or Mashiach*.

Will we ever end poverty, hunger, and genocide? Is there hope that tomorrow will look brighter than today? The effort to achieve movement toward social justice is guided by a messianic vision that a world that is more just and free is possible. Can we, as Jews, as humanitarians, embrace this promise of progress?

Since the Holocaust, most philosophers have rejected the notion that the Enlightenment represented the beginning of an era of progress. Two thousand years earlier, the Talmudic rabbis warned of the diminution of progress, claiming that the generations are in a steady state of decline. The Talmud refers to one generation as being of humans, and to a later one, as of donkeys.[291] The Sages exempted no one, even calling the matriarch Sarah a monkey when compared to Eve.[292]

This decline is punctuated mainly by ignorance of Divine truth—the prophetic *ruach hakodesh* (holy inspiration) ceased to inspire humans with the deaths of Chagai, Zechariah, and Malachi[293]—but also by the loss of basic ability: "The earlier generations made their Torah permanent and their work occasional, and this, Torah study, and that, their work, were successful for them. However, the latter generations who made their work permanent and their Torah occasional, neither this nor that was successful for them."[294]

Although the Sages articulated their clear concern regarding spiritual and intellectual decline, this is not the whole story. Rabbi Avraham Yitzchak Kook subscribed to the Hegelian school of thought that embraced historical progress, and articulated his vision thus:

> "We should not immediately feel obliged to refute any idea that comes to contradict something in the Torah, but rather we should build the palace of Torah above it. In so doing we reach

---

[291] BT Shabbat 112b.
[292] BT Bava Batra 58a.
[293] BT Sanhedrin 11a.
[294] BT Berakhot 35b.

a more exalted level, and... the ideas are clarified. And thereafter, when we are not pressured by anything, we can confidently also fight on the Torah's behalf."[295]

Rabbi Kook further defended the idea of progress, suggesting, "An evolution marked by constant progress provides solid grounds for optimism."[296]

Other Jewish voices share this view that we need not merely long for the past. Rabbi Shlomo Almoli (16th century, Ottoman Empire), for one, argued that greater access to information makes it "plausible that the knowledge and understanding of the latter generations should exceed that of the former ones." The Midrash claimed that while we are, indeed, very far from the past sources of spiritual light, (Creation, Sinai, and the Temple), we stand closer to the anticipated "*Or Mashiach*" and are correspondingly more illuminated. Rabbi Tzidkiyahu ben Avraham Anau (13th century, Rome) argued in his noted work *Shibolei Haleket* that while we may have lost great scholars, inhabiting a world "like that of dwarves standing on the shoulders of giants, our view is much broader and deeper than previous generations."

In addition to the search for religious truth as a barometer of progress and decline, we must be concerned with the general human welfare which that truth illuminates. Today, we have more access to transportation, medication, and technology than ever before; we have a greater awareness of tragedy, and more resources to combat oppression and injustice. Eradicating poverty and hunger are now only a matter of human will.

For this reason, we must maintain hope in progress, in the possibility that we can create a more just world, where all children have access to quality education and all people have adequate food, shelter, and healthcare. We may have diminished access to more simple truths, but we have a greater potential than ever before to embrace the more challenging truths and responsibilities of our interconnected universe.

---

[295] *Iggerot haReayah* I, 163-164.
[296] Ibid., 369.

Debate 15.

A Purpose to Life vs. No Meaning to Life

One of the elementary, yet mysterious, dimensions of humanity is the desire to derive something called "meaning" from our existence. The exact nature of this term is nebulous. No less so is the answer to our puzzlement about why we're here. Surely, there must be a reason why we were all placed in this universe, given the opportunity to use our faculties to think, to breathe, and to dream, no? Life, the ultimate quandary, gives us a framework to search for something greater than the various mental, physical, neural, emotional, and philosophical pieces of ourselves that interact with each other within each of us, enabling us in turn to relate to the rest of the world as individuals and as a whole. We can perceive the task that each of us has as being to strive for what is true and what is good. We strive not merely for an understanding of what we perceive as metaphysical, but also—maybe even in the first instance—for an aspect of ourselves that approaches the realization of a worthwhile reality.

Let us suggest three primary options in the debate about the purpose of life:

1. There is no meaning to life. We are here randomly without any purpose. We should eat drink and be merry. Life is, therefore, about the pursuit of pleasure and happiness if it is about anything.

2. There is one purpose and we all share it—to recognize that the world is broken and needs us to repair it.

3. Each of us has our own unique purpose that we must discover and fulfill.

Stephen Hawking argued that "the human race is just a chemical scum on a moderate-size planet, orbiting round a very average star in the outer suburb of one among a billion galaxies."[297] This is possible. John Gray argued that "human life has no more meaning than that of slime mold."[298] Israeli historian, now read around the world, Yuval Noah Harari, concludes that "looking back, humanity will turn out to be just a ripple within the cosmic data flow."[299]

When living is devoid of truth, virtue, and responsibility, the human being often falters and is in a state of confusion, perhaps because we are each faced with a perpetual challenge of balancing these three potential answers to the question

---

[297] Raymond Tallis, "You chemical scum, you," *Reflections of a Metaphysical Flaneur* (New York: Routledge, 2014).
[298] Ibid.
[299] Yuval Noah Harari, *Homo Deus* (New York: Harvill Secker, 2016), 395.

about the meaning of life against each other. On one hand, we shouldn't only be attracted to what feels right and comfortable. We should also be attracted to that which, in a healthy and generative fashion, makes us *un*comfortable. It is hard to live in a community where a significant portion of communal life doesn't work well for us; we cultivate humility by remembering that communities are not our family rooms fashioned just as we wish. It's hard to leave our comfort zones and encounter people and ideologies outside of our immediate circle of familiarity, but by engaging in such encounters we learn what it means to be human.

It wouldn't be a stretch to say that we must work to ensure that the experiences we have in life contain some meaning, whether subtle or overt. When we go out into the vast world, it will be moments when that work is successful that actually matter. They touch us, they warm our souls, they spark inspiration. But perhaps even more so, we should strive for experiences that are transformative, challenging, and enlightening, even if they are, or perhaps more precisely, *particularly* if they are, difficult. Religion, philosophy, indeed, any life ideology, is empty of its meaning if it is derived only from purely transmutable elements—running from one stimulation to another: a moving film, a compelling book, an emotional sermon. These are merely transitory experiences if our minds and hearts are closed in the process. Transformation will not chase after us; rather, we must chase after self-growth as if we are addicted to inspiration. Experiences of consequence help us grow as beings of integrity. Such experiences allow us to see each other more deeply as people filled with an enlightened perspective, help us connect more deeply as relational beings.

And, to be sure, for all the power that these moments contain, it is vital that we never settle for their mere occurrence. We must see ourselves as being obligated to fill these moments with purpose. In fact, the *mitzvot* categorized as *bein adam laMakom*, between people and God, are viewed by the biblical prophets[300] as missing the mark if they are not imbued with purpose, with action, with improving the world. Shabbat is of little or no value if it does not serve as a springboard for the Jew to recall the Creation story, thereby being inspired to engage in further creation; it is of little or no value if it does not call to mind that we were slaves to Pharaoh in Egypt, and therefore must treat others equitably.

Hold on! you might say. Who could be against the idea that life itself has inherent meaning, and that perhaps one need not strive for more? The solipsistic dimensions of such a possibility couldn't be so stacked against the intangible enormity of ultimate significance, right?

I am, of course, not against meaning. The eminent psychiatrist and social thinker Viktor Frankl was correct, in my view, that meaning is what enables us

---

[300] See, for example, Isaiah 1:11-17.

to survive the steepest challenges that life presents us. "Ever more people today have the means to live," Frankl wrote in his book *The Unheard Cry for Meaning: Psychotherapy and Humanism*, "but no meaning to live for." Just because somebody acquires ways to sustain a certain comfortable lifestyle doesn't mean that anything significant can stem from it without a particular notion of a *joie de vivre* independent of material gain. A certain amount of ennui sets in when life is devoid of an appreciation of every opportune experience.

Toni Morrison, the great novelist and professor emerita at Princeton University, articulated this line of thinking in a 2011 speech she gave to a group of college graduates at Rutgers University. She said: "I urge you, please don't settle for happiness. It's not good enough. Of course, you deserve it. But if that is all you have in mind—happiness—I want to suggest to you that personal success devoid of meaningfulness, free of a steady commitment to social justice, that's more than a barren life, it is a trivial one. It's looking good instead of doing good."[301]

Indeed, this sentiment is what Frankl was aiming for in his seminal work *Man's Search for Meaning*. Writing in the years after surviving and bearing witness to the horrors of the Holocaust, Frankl took all his inner torment and projected his thoughts into a cogent social ethos. Frankl wrote: "What man actually needs is not a tensionless state but rather the striving and struggling for some goal worthy of him. What he needs is not the discharge of tension at any cost, but the call of a potential meaning waiting to be fulfilled by him." We are waging a constant war between the elements of our inner selves that cry out for unfettered, unbounded consequence. Some parts of us seek only to satiate the material, while others look to more lofty realms for validation.

Throughout the lamentably short time each of us will be present in this universe, we should be willing to sacrifice to cultivate virtue and not merely wonder where we might find meaning.[302] One should join a community even if one feels it to be most meaningful to be alone. One should also spend time alone even if one is only comfortable in a group; only then can they appreciate what it means for the other to feel alone. One should speak up if one is an introvert and one should step back if one is an extrovert who uses up all the oxygen in a room. The purpose of life, then, isn't merely happiness or superficial significance. Life is too short and valuable for that. Meaning is cheap if the reality upon which each of us is built as

---

[301] Toni Morrison commencement address. Rutgers University, May 15, 2011. https://www.rutgers.edu/news/new-tradition-begins-nearly-30000-attend-commencement-rutgers-stadium.

[302] The seminal kabbalistic work *Zohar* suggests that the reason, according to the strict reading of the biblical text, that man was at first created as both *zachar* and *nekeivah*, and only then separated, was to imbue in man the realization that he/she is only a part of a whole. The individual is not a complete entity when estranged from all others. The complete person is one who realizes he/she needs others, and in turn they need him, in order to survive. I am not my best self if I live my life only for myself.

an individual lacks a need to interact and improve the lives of others and a sense of moral foundation. We need to do so even when that work doesn't feel great or meaningful. Likewise, attaining a meaningful existence is unappreciated if done purely for its own sake. The tautology of "meaning is meaningless" without x or y in our life presents us with a fool's errand, not to mention a fool's philosophy. We should never just resolve to "find meaning," whatever that means. Instead, with every fiber of our respective beings, we need to create deeper meaning, to seek our spiritual relevance in both the empyrean echelon of existence and in our day-to-day lives that we perceive as mundane. This dual focus on both heaven and earth is the manna that sustains our outer lives and our inner worlds.

If we conclude that "meaning" is not enough, but that we also need purpose, then we can ask: What is the purpose of my life? The fundamental commitment of being a Jew is to answer the question, "*Ayeka*" (Where are you?), with "*Hineini*" (Here I am),[303] affirming a sense of responsibility and obligation to the other.

Different Jews feel different kinds of commitments. We can come together as one people not because we share the same understanding about the origin and nature of our obligations but because as Jews, indeed as human beings, we all feel obligated toward one another and the world at large. There are many different sources that we can consider as leading to obligation, but the great majority can be grouped into one or more of the following categories:

Traditional Jews: Obligation originates from the commands given at Mount Sinai, from an ultimate Authority rather than from the self.

Existential Jews: Obligation originates from an autonomous and voluntary affirmation of and subjection to Jewish law and values.

Narrative Jews: Obligation originates from a sense of continuity with the faith and lives of Jewish ancestors.

Conscience Jews: Obligation emerges in the moment of encountering another's (or a community's) plight and need for assistance, as well as from moral and spiritual intuition.

Gratitude Jews: Obligation stems from recognition of and gratitude for the gifts that have been provided in one's life.

Consequentialist Jews: Obligation results from the compulsion to ensure that the proper outcomes are achieved from one's actions.

Social Contract Jews: Obligation comes from a sense of collective responsibility that binds us together, and from affirming mutual obligations.

Of course, all of us can operate differently with multiple ways of being and few can be pigeonholed. Further, there are, of course, alternative ways to think

---

[303] *Ayeka* is the language used by God when confronting Adam and Eve after eating from the fruit of the Tree of Knowledge. *Hineini*, on the other hand, is the language used by Abraham when God called upon him to sacrifice his beloved son Isaac, both prior to and during the event, as well as by Jacob and Moses when called by God.

about why we feel obligated to live as we do. One might simply live by social conformity, or by national law, or according to desire, or by rejecting the notion of obligation altogether. These possibilities might be real, but seem to me to be departures from a Jewish approach to living intentionally and to feeling charged to improve the self and the world.

Many put each other into boxes based upon the perceived origin of the other's commitments, but we must recognize that there are many entry points into Jewish obligation. We should move to a more inclusive and pluralistic paradigm in which, even if we differ on the origin and nature of our commitments, we unite around our common sense of obligation. It is this ethical and spiritual impulse that we are "called" upon and that we are responsible for. This is a fundamental part of being a human being, but still more particularly of being a Jew.

In the modern era, Jews have expressed their sense of obligation in different ways. Theodor Herzl, the founder of modern Zionism, spent the last ten years of his life in an unceasing quest to find a homeland for the Jewish people. After pursuing his later-in-life dream for years, he wrote: "It goes without saying that the Jewish people can have no other goal than Palestine and that, whatever the fate of the proposition may be, our attitude toward the land of our fathers is and shall remain unchangeable."[304]

Lion Feuchtwanger, who grew up in an Orthodox family, expressed his sense of obligation through his novels. In *The Oppermanns*, first published in 1933, Feuchtwanger wrote a chillingly accurate prediction of what would happen to Germany's Jews based on only the first year of Nazi rule. One of the protagonists, Gustav Oppermann, a retailer of cheap furniture, has admittedly become "indifferent" to his contemporary society. However, as the political situation worsens, he feels uneasy, and dictates a card to himself with a paraphrase of Avot, *Ethics of Our Fathers*, 2:16: "It is upon us to begin the work; it is not upon us to complete it." Gustav at first flees from Germany, but eventually (like Feuchtwanger) realizes that his obligation is to document the Nazi atrocities to alert the world about this danger.

Elie Wiesel, through his experience in a concentration camp, devoted his life to educating the world about the Holocaust and to work toward preventing future instances of genocide. His words ring with Jewish values: "Our obligation is to give meaning to life and in doing so to overcome the passive, indifferent life."

Albert Einstein was one of the most noted scientists of the 20th century, but he was also noted for his humanistic philosophy, which often expressed Jewish values. His attitude toward obligation fits in well with this tradition: "Many times a day I realize how much my own outer and inner life is built upon the labors of

---

[304] It's worth noting, however, that even after becoming a Zionist, he didn't consistently advocate for Palestine specifically as the future homeland of the Jewish people.

my fellow men, both living and dead, and how earnestly I must exert myself in order to give in return as much as I have received."

In the religious sphere, many leading rabbis have become involved in modern social justice movements. Abraham Joshua Heschel, who famously marched with the Rev. Dr. Martin Luther King, Jr., for civil rights, expressed his moral obligation this way: "...[T]here is no limit to the concern one must feel for the suffering of human beings, that indifference to evil is worse than evil itself, that in a free society, some are guilty, but all are responsible." Conservative Rabbi Jill Jacobs, Executive Director of T'ruah: The Rabbinic Call for Human Rights, believes that Jews can work effectively for social justice within their congregations and other Jewish institutions:

> The Jewish obligation for social justice stems from four sources: the historical experience, the legal imperative, a vision of the world to come, and practical considerations about the place of Jews in a diverse society. These four sources should inspire Jews to do social justice work not only as individuals, but also within the specific context of Jewish communal institutions.[305]

Even Jews who convert to other religions often display a sense of obligation consistent with Jewish values. Simone Weil, who grew up in a secular Jewish home in France, had a philosophical trip through socialism and anarchism before converting to Christian mysticism. In the years before her early death, she focused her attention on the tremendous suffering of people during World War II: "It is an eternal obligation toward the human being not to let him suffer from hunger when one has a chance of coming to his assistance." Another secular Jewish phenomenon was that exemplified by the "red diaper" babies of the baby boomer generation. These were the children of Jewish parents (many in Brooklyn) who had been Communists during the Great Depression and World War II, when the Party was virtually the only political faction working for racial civil rights, unionization for unskilled workers, and opposition to fascism worldwide. Many of these children later took part in the civil rights and anti-Vietnam War movements, and also connected back to their Jewish roots.

We all exist within this *brit* (sacred covenant) of obligation and shared responsibility. Biblically, the *brit* was articulated in multiple contexts: for all people at the time of the Flood, but more intensely for Jews in the mutual divine-human

---

[305] Rabbi Jill Jacobs, *Where Justice Dwells: A Hands-On Guide to Doing Social Justice in Your Jewish Community* (Woodstock, Vermont: Jewish Lights Pub., 2011), 4.

commitments surrounding the initial encounters between Abraham and God, the experience of the Exodus, and Sinai Revelation. A covenant can be understood religiously, existentially, legally, emotionally, socially, etc., but all of these origins and viewpoints share a commitment to what "ought to be" and not just to what "is." We are not merely a descriptive but also a prescriptive people. To "be" Jewish means that "I must do." Judaism is oriented to value, which allows us to define the future that we commit to creating; to be a Jew means much more than being fact-oriented, which simply tells the story of our past and describes our present.

The foundation of our pluralism and our shared commitment to function creatively in the world can be in our embrace of a dream of a more redeemed self and a more fulfilled world. The multiplicity of narratives about our commitments need not and dare not inhibit—quite the contrary, it can and should enhance—our ability to create partnership and to thrive together.

And so, a plausible case could be made, from a scientific approach, that there is no inherent meaning to life and that life, from a cosmic perspective, is meaningless. But this is not a Jewish approach. Judaism embraces science but also goes spiritually and ethically beyond the descriptive realm of science. As Jews, we can embrace that life is meaningless (embrace the humility that we are little more than dust and ashes) but also simultaneously embrace that life is inherently meaningful (that the world was created for us). It is through this humility and this grand vision that we can "Only to do justice[,] And to love goodness, And to walk modestly with your God."[306]

---

[306] Micah 6:8.

Debate 16.

Prioritizing the Poor vs. Equity Toward All Parties

On the one hand, we need to be fair to all parties in a conflict. On the other hand, we know there are times when we are called to morally prioritize the most vulnerable.

In Jewish law, we are told that it is unjust to be biased and to be swayed by poverty, to favor the case of the poor over the rich—and certainly not that of the rich over the poor—in a dispute. Within the realm of a formal court's judgment this is crucial.[307] However, does this notion apply in other contexts, and does it still apply today, where the disparity of wealth between the poor and the rich has become so large that the poor often can no longer properly advocate for themselves?

The rabbis taught that in some cases, we should indeed prioritize the more vulnerable party over whoever may be right.

> Certain porters broke his barrel of wine after he had hired them to transport the barrels. He took their cloaks as payment for the lost wine. They came and told Rav. Rav said to Rabba bar bar Chanan: Give them their cloaks. Rabba bar bar Chanan said to him: Is this the halakha? Rav said to him: Yes, as it is written: "That you may walk in the way of good men" (Proverbs 2:20). Rabba bar bar Chanan gave them their cloaks. The porters said to Rav: We are poor people and we toiled all day and we are hungry and we have nothing. Rav said to Rabba bar bar Chanan: Go and give them their wages. Rabba bar bar Chanan said to him: Is this the halakha? Rav said to him: Yes, as it is written: "And keep the paths of the righteous" (Proverbs 2:20)."[308]

Interesting enough, if it were "the law," we would expect to have seen a very specific verse from the Torah quoted. Instead, we see vague, broad verses quoted from the book of *Mishlei* (Proverbs). This perhaps implies that the proper way to determine an appropriate mode of conduct may actually be above the letter of "the law." Beyond the specific commandments, we are called upon to be righteous in all ways possible. Here, for Rav, that means prioritizing the vulnerable over the more powerful, regardless of who is technically more correct, regardless of who would win in a court of law.

---

[307] Exodus 23:3,6.
[308] BT Bava Metzia 83a.

This notion of equality before the law is often a fallacy in today's America, since the poor have such a serious disadvantage in the courtroom. So many people without resources find themselves litigating cases, whether civil or criminal, in situations that put them up against resource-heavy individuals, corporations, and government entities. In too many cases, people with meritorious positions find themselves losing, or just giving up, because their relative poverty allows them to be ground down by their opponents and by the system.

Every individual should have the same fair opportunity before the law, as we must be committed to truth and justice. But this is too often not the reality today. Even if it were true, Judaism teaches that we must act *lifnim mishurat hadin* (above or beyond—literally, within—the letter of the law) to support the most vulnerable. Indeed, we learn that God created and destroyed many worlds that were built upon the foundation of *din* (judgment), and then God finally created this world built upon *rachamim* (mercy).[309] Our world cannot exist on pure judgment; rather, as fallible beings, we rely upon the grace, empathy, and kindness of God and people.

In turn, as humans created in the divine image, we should act with grace, empathy, and kindness toward others. In the *Shirat Hayam* (Song of the Sea) sung by Moshe and the Israelites upon safely crossing the Red Sea, Moshe praises God with the words "*zeh Keili v'anveihu*" ("This is my God and I will enshrine [God]").[310] The Talmud explains that one way to glorify God is to emulate Divine behavior: "Just as God is merciful, so must you be merciful. . ."[311]

We must be moved toward mercy for those who are suffering, and this must affect how we build society. Former President Obama explained the importance of empathy in jurisprudence when choosing Supreme Court justices: "I will seek someone who understands that justice isn't [only] about some abstract legal theory or footnote in a casebook; it is also about how our laws affect the daily realities of people's lives. I view the quality of empathy, of understanding and identifying with people's hopes and struggles, as an essential ingredient for arriving at just decisions and outcomes." Law is not only about principle; it is also about life. Law is not a mathematical calculation. It must include the subjective elements involved as well.

In a recent book entitled *Noise*, the authors explore just how wildly different results emerge in different courtrooms with very similar cases. There is too much subjectivity and room for "noise" to color fair results. On the other hand, we don't want non-human algorithms to resolve matters in our justice systems. How can

---

[309] Rashi to Genesis 1:1.
[310] Exodus 15:2, JPS 1985 translation, modified for gender neutrality.
[311] BT Sotah 14a.

we find the right balance between objectivity and subjectivity, between formalism and empathy?

Outside the courtroom, within the realm of Jewish grassroots activism, we learn that our primary responsibility may not only be to equality, but, at times, to prioritize our support for the vulnerable. After all, numerous Jewish teachings remind us that our primary responsibility is to protect and prioritize the most vulnerable individuals and parties: "God takes the side of the aggrieved and the victim."[312] When there is conflict, God simply cannot withhold support for the one suffering.

Rav Aaron Soloveichik[313] writes: "A Jew should always identify with the cause of defending the aggrieved, whosoever the aggrieved may be, just as the concept of *tzedek* is to be applied uniformly to all humans regardless of race or creed."[314] Seeking to put this perspective into practice, Rav Aaron was a strong supporter of the civil rights movement during the 1960s.[315] This is what it means to be Jewish, to prioritize the suffering in conflict.

This point is made time and time again by the Rabbis. The Talmud, based on the verse "Justice, justice shall you pursue,"[316] teaches that the disadvantaged should be given preference when all else is equal. The Rambam teaches that even if the disadvantaged arrive before the judges later than the others, they should be given precedence.[317]

Thus, in a court of law, all parties ideally are treated equally, as we are guided by the Jewish value of *din*. Today, however, justice unfortunately does not always seem to prevail. Perhaps we can find a legitimate way to tip the scales in big-picture terms by seeing that in activism we can favor the vulnerable, guided by the Jewish value of *chesed* (empathy, loving-kindness). In life, we must learn to balance all of our values: love, justice, mercy, etc. In justice, we do not choose only one guiding principle: As the 20th-century British philosopher Isaiah Berlin teaches, moral life consists of embracing a plurality of values.

We must always be absolutely committed to the truth and be sure that our justice system is fair for all parties. Yet we also, as changemakers, have a special and holy role to give voice to the voiceless and to support the unsupported in society. This is the role of Jewish activism. The Rabbis teach that "Even if a righteous

---

[312] Ecclesiastes 3:15.
[313] Rabbi Ahron Soloveichik (1917-2001) was the Rosh Yeshiva of Yeshivas Brisk, Chicago, IL. He was recognized as one of the eminent *poskim* (halachic decisors) of the 20th century.
[314] Rabbi Ahron Soloveichik, *Logic of the Heart, Logic of the Mind* (Genesis Jerusalem Press, 1991), 67.
[315] Rabbi Tzvi Sinensky, "Orthodoxy and the Civil Rights Movement" (*Philadelphia Jewish Exponent*, January 13, 2017).
[316] Deuteronomy 16:20.
[317] Sanhedrin 21:6, SA CM 15:2.

person attacks a wicked person, God still sides with the victim."[318] All people deserve our love and care, but we must follow the path of God and make our allegiances clear: we must stand with those who are destitute, oppressed, alienated, and suffering.

So, on the one hand, we know we must prioritize the most vulnerable. On the other hand, as we learn from the verse in Exodus, we must be fair to all parties and not pervert justice by merely siding with the most vulnerable in every conflict. I would suggest this distinction emerges when considering how we relate to others in the societal realm relative to the way we treat others in the personal realm. In the societal realm, all parties should be treated equally in matters of justice. In the personal realm, we can sensitize ourselves to the opportunity to go above the letter of the law in how we treat those more vulnerable than ourselves.

It would not be fair to prioritize a Black person over a White person in court simply because the Black person is statistically more likely to be poor and marginalized. On the other hand, we cannot ignore that courtroom bias is likely to lead to a better outcome for a White person. It would not be fair to support a claim from a Palestinian Muslim blindly over a claim from an Israeli Jew simply because the Palestinian individual is likely to be less privileged than an Israeli. On the other hand, we cannot ignore the Jewish bias that we, as Jews, might automatically believe the Israeli and discredit the Palestinian. It would not be fair to blindly believe the union over the corporate owners just because the workers make a lot less money than the owners. On the other hand, we know that without collective organizing, workers historically have been taken advantage of by the wealthiest individuals.

None of this is simple. Sometimes, with each choice of justice we can create a new form of injustice. If we only prioritize truth, we can deepen the disenfranchisement of the most disadvantaged. But if we show bias toward the more vulnerable, we can do injustice to the other party. Here we must make the case against hard ideology. We must wrestle with each case rather than impose some ideological approach upon every situation. This applies beyond the courtroom. Should the rich be taxed more? If they are, it is not necessarily fair to them? If they are not, it is not necessarily fair to the working class that can't meet their needs. Should large numbers of refugees be welcomed into the country? If so, they will benefit from services that even some taxpaying American citizens do not benefit from. If not, we will put lives at risk, people who are stateless and desperate. Will we embrace the claim that systemic racism is pervasive in the police force? If we do not, we will ignore racial injustices. If we do, will we go so far in defunding that it makes society less safe for all? When we hit hard times economically, will we

---
[318] Yalkut Shimoni.

place a moratorium on tenants paying rent? If we do not, how will we avoid mass evictions leading to homelessness for countless people? But if we do, how will it be fair to property owners who depend on rent to get by? If we wish to move the country to a more environmentally responsible place, a new green economy may create many new jobs but it may eliminate even more. If so, how is this fair to those who have dedicated their lives to certain industries? If not, how can we justify irreparably harming the planet just to maintain those particular jobs?

Throughout history, Jews were second class citizens, at best. We know what it's like to be denied fair access to justice systems. From our Torah and from our history we know we must advocate for those who can't always advocate for themselves.

These are messy matters. We must listen to the most vulnerable and we must also seek truth and justice. To do so, we must be introspective in recognizing and considering our biases, and must hold ourselves and others accountable to the highest levels of truth and justice.

Debate 17.

Judging Others Favorably vs. Judging for Justice

In the Torah, we learn that when we sit in judgment, we should do so "with righteousness."

> You shall not render an unfair decision: do not favor the poor or show deference to the rich; judge your kinsman fairly.[319]

Based on this verse, the Talmud teaches us to be *dan l'chaf zechut* (to give the benefit of the doubt to others):

> "But in righteousness shall you judge your colleague," [320] that you should judge another favorably.[321]

Rashi comments here:

> "Judge your fellow favorably"—This does not refer to judging litigants in court. Rather, it refers to someone who observes another person doing an action that could be interpreted as either a wrongdoing or as a neutral act. You should not suspect him of a wrongdoing; rather assume he is innocent.[322]

For the Sefer HaChinuch, this applies not only in the social realm but also in the courtroom. His view could be taken as a step beyond the idea of being "innocent until proven guilty." In his words,

> The commandment to judge with righteousness: . . .
> the judges were commanded to treat the parties to the dispute equally . . .
> And also included in this commandment is that it is fit for every person to judge his fellow favorably, and only to understand his deeds and his words favorably.[323]

---

[319] Leviticus 19:15.
[320] Ibid.
[321] BT Shavuot 30a.
[322] Rashi's commentary on BT Shavuot 30a.
[323] *Sefer HaChinukh*, 235, trans. R. Francis Nataf, Sefaria 2018.

To presume that someone is innocent until proven guilty is to recognize the importance of *hamotzi mechaveiro alav hara'aya*—literally, someone who wants to take from another, the proof is upon that person. That is, someone who wants to prove that someone else is guilty or liable—a plaintiff in a civil case or the prosecution in a criminal matter—bears a burden of proof. To view someone's actions always in a positive light adds another layer of favorable treatment.

For some commentators, there is an interesting intersection between justice and love.

> If one truly loves another as a father loves a son, he will very naturally have a positive outlook toward that person. He will see everything that person does in a positive light, and judge him positively.
>
> Thus, the mitzvah of judging positively is really an outgrowth of the mitzvah to "love your fellow as yourself." The extent to which one judges others positively is a good indicator of his love for others.[324]

For this *Mussar* teacher, judging favorably is about loving others. The spiritual shift required here is to move from just observing an action to inspiring oneself to assume that another person's actions are motivated by positive inclinations. Rabbi Shlomo Wolbe taught:

> Someone who judges others favorably really hopes that his fellow man is guiltless. He seeks ways of understanding the other's actions as good.
>
> This is the extent to which one must regard another person with a positive attitude, and wish to see his actions as issuing from a good source. We should search out another's positive qualities. This is the opposite of what most people usually do, which is to immediately notice another person's shortcomings and ignore his strong points.[325]

This idea of judging others favorably has precedent in the Mishnaic tractate Pirkei Avot (Ethics of the Fathers).

---

[324] Rabbi Dovid Kronglass, *Sichot Chochmah U'Mussar*, Vol. I (Feldheim, 2021), 82.
[325] Rabbi Shlomo Wolbe, *Alei Shur*, Vol. II (Jerusalem: Bais Hamussar), 207.

Joshua ben Perahiah used to say: appoint for thyself a teacher, and acquire for thyself a companion and judge all men with the scale weighted in his favor.[326]

The Rambam (Maimonides) comments here:

> "Judge every person favorably"—This refers to someone whom you do not know, and therefore cannot tell if he is a *tzaddik* [an upright person] or *rasha* [habitual wrongdoer].
>
> In such a case, if you see him doing something or saying something that could be interpreted in two ways, one good and one bad, you should give him the benefit of the doubt and assume the action was good ... This approach is praiseworthy.[327]

The Rambam is addressing three categories. Someone we know to be righteous; we should view their deeds positively. Someone we know to be wicked; we should obviously view their deeds skeptically and suspiciously. But, when it comes to the third category, someone we do not know, that is where we need to make this leap toward "the benefit of the doubt."

On the other hand, we have another teaching from Pirkei Avot on this matter:

> "Do not judge your fellow ... until you have reached [their] place."[328]

This source does not seem to distinguish between the righteous and the wicked. Rather, we are not positioned to be judgmental at all since everyone is different, in a different place, at a different time, with different genes, a different background, and in a unique scenario. A man and woman cannot judge each other? A White person and Black person cannot judge each other? A child and adult cannot judge each other? A rich person and poor person cannot judge each other? Any one person cannot judge any other? Human perspectives and experiences are so radically diverse[329] that we might never be able to fully understand one another, and therefore should try to refrain from judging each other.[330]

---

[326] Pirkei Avot 1:6, trans. Dr. Joshua Kulp.
[327] The Rambam's commentary on Pirkei Avot 1:6.
[328] Pirkei Avot 2:4 trans. Dr. Joshua Kulp, modified for gender neutrality.
[329] When trying to console another, it is not uncommon to hear one saying, "I know what you're going through." In truth, as well-meaning as the friend may be, they cannot truly know what the other is going through. There are simply too many variables for two seemingly equal experiences to actually be equal.
[330] Of course, a judge and jury are called upon to do just that, but every precaution should and must be taken to judge favorably and honestly.

Rabbi Ovadia of Bartenura[331] limits this to specific challenges:

> If you see your fellow come to a test and fail, do not judge him unfavorably until a test like it comes to you and you overcome [it].[332]

Rabbi Yehoshua Leib Diskin offers a brilliant psychological insight here about how judging others favorably is not only more empathetic toward others but holds *us* accountable in our own behavior as well.

> [Consider the following:] A town has ten Jewish people living in it. If one person commits a transgression, he breaks down the fence of embarrassment, which had prevented people from sinning until now. If a second person sins, he does not need to break this barrier, and he does not need as much brazenness, because the second person is only sinning in front of eight others, and he has [the other sinner as] his accomplice. If a third person sins, he [requires] even less brazenness. Following this principle, the fifth person does not need any brazenness at all...
>
> ...In telling us to "judge every person positively" (Pirkei Avot 1:6) the Sages are giving us wise advice. This advice is in order that we should not break down the internal barriers of embarrassment that hold us back from transgressions. [How so?] When we view every person as being righteous, then we will hold ourselves back from transgressing [since we will think that no one else is transgressing, so how could we be the first?!] However, when one sees the negative in every person, then he is likely to stumble [since he will think others are transgressing, and therefore it becomes more acceptable in his mind to transgress].[333]

For the Sefer HaChinuch, there is a related but different goal here: to build community.

> Also about that which we said that every person is obligated to judge his fellow favorably—that it is included in the

---
[331] Rabbi Ovadia of Bartenura is best known for his commentary to the Mishnah. He is also known by his acronym, Ra'av.
[332] Bartenura on Pirkei Avot 2:4 (Sefaria Community Translation, 2023).
[333] Rabbi Yehoshua Leib Diskin (Maharil Diskin), *Teshuvot Maharil*, end of Vol. I.

> commandment—is a cause for there to be peace and amity among people. And [so] it comes out that the essence of the whole intent of the commandment is to help in the civilization of people with righteousness of judgment, and to bring peace among them with the removal of suspicion of one man towards another.[334]

By judging favorably, we develop social trust, foster positivity, and build a more peaceful coexistence.

For the Rambam, this should be a priority for a learned person who will be serving as a public model.

> A scholar should not shout like an animal when he speaks with people. Neither should he raise his voice. Rather, he should speak calmly with everyone...
> He should make sure to take the initiative to greet everyone first, so that he is pleasant to be around. He should judge people positively, and speak favorably about others, never speaking negatively of them. He should love and pursue peace ... In general, he should always speak words of wisdom and loving-kindness.[335]

Another theological layer informs how we should treat others. The Talmud teaches:

> And you, just as you judged favorably, so may God judge you favorably.[336]

The way we judge will determine the way God judges us. The Ba'al Shem Tov takes this approach to another whole level:

> We have a tradition that no verdict is ever passed on a person until he himself issues that verdict. How so? The person is shown someone else doing what he himself is guilty of, and his reaction to that person's flaw is what determines the judgment of his own misdeeds.[337]

---
[334] *Sefer HaChinukh*, 235, trans. R. Francis Nataf, Sefaria 2018.
[335] Rambam, *Yad Hachazakah*, Hilchot Dei'ot (Laws of Conduct) 5:7.
[336] BT Shabbat 127b. Also see Chafetz Chaim, *Shmirat HaLashon*, Sha'ar HaTevunah, Chapter 4.
[337] *Ba'al Shem Tov Al HaTorah*, Vayikra 19:15.

For the Ba'al Shem Tov,[338] every moment and activity, as well as its interpretation, is about both others and us. It is all intertwined. Everything comes back to our interpretation and to our personal reality (i.e., the way we judge external events affects us internally).

For Rabbi Moshe Cordovero, this is less about self-interest and self-protection; rather, it's about Divine emulation. God restricts Divine harsh judgement, and so should we. God is merciful, and we should be, too.[339]

So, a very strong case can be made for not being judgmental. Clearly, it is an important spiritual way to live. On the other hand, we are called upon to be advocates for justice, to be discerning about good vs. evil, and to speak out against evil. We are to learn how to identify the righteous from the wicked, and we are bidden to associate with the righteous and to distance ourselves from the wicked. We are to speak out to advocate for the downtrodden and to avoid crossing moral boundaries. We must assess and judge fairly but also critically. Only if we can judge injustice done by others and learn from it can we truly be aware of the hazards of being judgmental.

So how do we hold a spiritual consciousness of being non-judgmental alongside a social justice consciousness of being a public ambassador for what is just and to provide a public critique of what is unjust? The answer to this seeming paradox is that we must slow down and not bandwagon on rapid social shaming or support campaigns without facts. It means we must not equate not liking someone with them being evil. It means that we cannot and must not confuse ideological diversity with a stark categorization of people as good and evil. Perhaps we can be suspicious of those whose attitudes and actions harm others, but at the same time we must try to give them the benefit of the doubt.

There is a lot at stake here: how we are to judge others fairly; our own spiritual health; the way we ourselves will be judged; and how we can sustain communities and society. We will need to take stock of our defense mechanisms that fear our own judgment and thus channel that fear by turning our judgment upon others. In addition to healing ourselves with less judgment, we can heal our relationships by ensuring others feel less judged. This intellectual and spiritual work is some of the most challenging, yet most elevating, we will encounter. We must make it our endeavor. We must rise to the occasion.

---

[338] The Ba'al Shem Tov, to whom the perspective underlying the modern Hasidic movement is attributed, literally meaning "one of a good name," is also known by his acronym, Besht.
[339] Rabbi Moshe Cordovero, *Tomer Devorah* Ch. 1, Eighth Attribute.

Israel

DEBATE 18.

Yitz Greenberg vs. Meir Kahane: On Sovereignty and Contemporary Jewish Political Power

Rabbi Dr. Yitz (Irving) Greenberg and Rabbi Meir Kahane could be described as mirror images of each other, which is to say that they emerge from the same world, yet come to reverse conclusions. And those opposing conclusions play out more broadly in the tug-of-war between extremism and a more measured type of thinking that allows for serious debate to be paired with respect.

Rabbi Meir Kahane (1932-1990) was born in America, was ordained as an Orthodox rabbi, and ultimately moved to Israel. He was an ultra-nationalist politician who served one term in the Israeli Knesset (1984). He was a founder of the far-right, militant, Jewish Defense League (1968) and the founder of the Kach party in Israel (1971). In 1988, this party was banned from entering elections.[340]

In 1971 he was convicted on criminal charges in the U.S. for conspiracy to manufacture explosives, for which he received a suspended sentence of five years.[341] He was also convicted in Israel for ostensibly planning an act of terrorism in a plot to blow up the Libyan embassy in Brussels in retaliation for the eleven Israeli athletes tragically murdered at the 1972 Munich summer Olympics.

Kahane claimed that his militarism constituted Torah-true Judaism and was required by *halachah*. He was wildly prolific and active in the press, and argued that there would inevitably be a "Holocaust" in America which would necessitate mass aliyah. He argued for annexation by Israel of all Palestinian lands (those in the West Bank and in Gaza) and believed that the State of Israel should enforce halachic observance by its citizens.

One example of his extremism, based on an interpretation of Maimonides,[342] was his suggestion that any gentiles living in the land of Israel should either embrace limited rights or leave (either willingly with some compensation or forcefully without compensation). He also wanted Israel to forbid intermarriages between Jews and Arabs, and fought for other forms of segregation.[343] Kahane was assassinated in 1990 in a New York City hotel by El Sayyid Nosair (an Egyptian-born U.S. citizen). He continues to inspire a movement of far-right Jewish militants to this day.

---

[340] Morris Kaplan. "Kahane Gets 5-Year Suspended Sentence in Bomb Plot." *New York Times*, July 24, 1971.
[341] Ibid.
[342] Mishneh Torah, Laws of Kings, Ch. 6. Extrapolating from Maimonides' rulings about the legal system during the time of kingship in Israel is tenuous at best, as Israel is no longer governed by such a system. It is not possible to know if Maimonides himself would apply his writings about biblical Israel to even his own time, let alone ours.
[343] Joel Brinkley. "Israel Bans Kahane Party from Election." *New York Times*, October 6, 1988.

Born in 1933, Rabbi Dr. Yitz Greenberg's preeminence in Torah thought is but a minor aspect of his larger role in shaping contemporary Jewish attitudes toward the entire world. From the time he was ordained at Beth Joseph (Novardok) Rabbinical Seminary (New York City) and earned a PhD in American history at Harvard University in the 1950s, to his tenure as a professional working to stimulate the development and application of new ideas within the Jewish community in an array of significant capacities,[344] Greenberg has been a tireless proponent of a more engaged and tolerant Judaism. In his understanding, pluralism is the Jewish ideal in which narrow particularism is eschewed as a remnant from earlier, more precarious times.

Undoubtedly, Greenberg is one of the most significant moral voices in our time. I'm quite fortunate to benefit from him being a close personal mentor of mine. His years of service in the rabbinate, as an author, lecturer, and as an organizational leader and activist for a multitude of spiritual causes, have been responsible for spreading Jewish values across the spectrum of other religious traditions and cultures. Rav Yitz is this generation's consummate bridge builder; he constructs bridges within the Jewish community, as well as between different faiths and over the vast gulf that separates tradition and modernity. While committed to Orthodoxy, Rav Yitz has made great contributions across all walks of Jewish life, always remaining rooted within a forward-looking halachic framework of observance. He is that rare pedagogue who has demonstrated the relevance of a modern Judaism while assembling and nurturing the vibrant Jewish institutional landscape that we know today.

So, at first glance these two figures are quite similar: straight, White men born in America in 1932 and 1933; Orthodox rabbis; Zionists committed to Torah; both deeply influenced by the Holocaust and its aftermath. Indeed, they even grew up together, with a relationship that Greenberg described in the following terms: "Meir Kahane and I started out as good friends. During our high school years, we were classmates and joint performers in weekly skits that we often wrote together."[345]

And yet, as we just noted, Kahane was a radical particularist, while Greenberg was and is a committed universalist and pluralist. This departure sets the stage for a showdown between these two, which took place in 1988 in a public debate at the Hebrew Institute of Riverdale.

The debate was moderated by Modern Orthodox Rabbi Avi Weiss. Weiss was more aligned with Kahane in that he was right of center on Israel. But Weiss was more aligned with Greenberg in regard to building a pluralistic state.

---

[344] Greenberg now serves as a Senior Scholar at the Hadar Institute.
[345] Irving Greenberg "(Orthodo)-X Men, On Screen and Off," *The Forward*, June 13, 2003, https://forward.com/opinion/7470/orthodo-x-men-on-screen-and-off/.

In this debate, Kahane is passionate while Greenberg is dry and exacting. Kahane appeals emotionally to fear of annihilation, while Greenberg thinks the argument can be won on the merit of moral persuasion.

Here is a snippet to give you a taste of their remarks in regard to democracy in Israel and the rights of Arab Israelis living in the land.

Kahane:

> Halachah. I'm a man of halachah. The halachah is clear that the non-Jew does not have [the] status of a Jew. Democracy is not Judaism. It may be painful to the modern Orthodox. Of course, it's painful. It's too bad. But it's halachah. Should I read to you the Rambam? The halachah is clear...
>
> But more important, long before the Arabs are a majority, what happens when they become a third of the population and they join together in a coalition government with the extreme left? Is that what you want? Is that what you want? Who is a Jew [d]ecided by one third of an Arab Knesset[?] And above all there is halachah here and if there is one Arab in the country who is not willing to accept the status that was given to him by the halachah... or are we not ordained rabbis?....
>
> The Palestinians believe that there should be no Israel. That is the problem. We sit and play games and games with them, and worse, with ourselves. The Arabs are not, I repeat for the second time, are not, leaving the Territories. They are coming back in droves. Unemployment now is rife in Kuwait, in Saudi, in Oman, and in Abu Dhabi. They are returning. They never left. They left their families behind and send them checks constantly. There are Arabs from America who are not coming back. I saw them when I was on reserve duty for a month. Now, to live in this delusion, "if we give this back and we give that back," that somehow, we will realize that time is not on our side. Time is on their side. As long as we have Jews who split the community. As long as we have Jews who condemn the policy of the government of Israel. As long as we have Jews who march with the Palestinians, then time is on their side. I'm not afraid of the Arabs. I'm afraid of such Jews as this one here who with no meaning is a danger to the existence of Israel.

Greenberg:

In short, the overwhelming consensus of responsible rabbis of any halachic standing, or learning, or menshlichkeit, is that these laws do not apply to Arabs or to Christians or non-Jews who are not idolaters, and therefore [Kahane] is using this [argument] totally out of context in order to make the halachah appear to be cruel, atrocity ridden, antagonistic to gentiles. The truth is, I would say, the opposite, that there should be no limits to Arab rights because, in fact, democracy gives them a chance to grow and become integrated into society and to commit themselves to that society. Democracy is the best fulfillment of the vision of the Jewish covenant...

There is an indigenous Arab population [in] the West Bank and Gaza. It's 1,342,000 and growing. If we add them to the Israeli Arab population, that changes... the balance from 82/16 to 65/35. The highest birthrates in the Arab world are in the West Bank and Gaza because the women there are in rural situations and are in poverty, and their absolute births would make Arab births outnumber the Jews. And for that reason alone, that is the only potential plausible theory of imbalance demographically. But the deeper reason is even deeper than that. Our dream is realized. We came back to the land of Israel; we paid in full for it. But there is a population there; and they are human beings. It's true they are exploited by the PLO and Israel. But they have roots, attachment, hopes, and lives. They didn't have a Palestinian nationalism twenty-five years ago but now they do. In part because of [the] exposure of Israel and our model of self-respect and dignity and self-rule. If I can make room for them, I should. If I can make room for their dignity, the answer is yes. And the greatest [chance for] respect and peace comes when there is self-rule and self-responsibility. Now our commitment to their dignity and their freedom cannot be to commit suicide. It is no mitzvah to destroy ourselves, and therefore we will long for peace; and if there is a new leadership that is prepared to make peace they are going to change. It's up to them to convince, to convince us, the Jewish people.[346]

---

[346] One place, among many, to read parts of this debate is in *The New Jewish Canon* (Brookline: Academic Studies Press, 2020), 34-36, where I found this particular transcription. Even better, you can watch the full debate on YouTube: https://www.youtube.com/watch?v=_tOcf3EPocQ.

The entirety of this debate is fascinating and heated, yet this bit gives enough of a sense of how Rabbis Greenberg and Kahane interpret Jewish law and how they understand Jewish sovereignty. Indeed, the two perspectives represented by Greenberg and Kahane are still very much in evidence today. Right-wing Zionists frequently use rhetoric of fear to show how insecure Israel is and the drastic measures that must be taken to survive. Liberal Zionists frequently use rhetoric of peace to show how urgent it is to preserve this rare Jewish experiment in building a modern democracy under Jewish sovereignty. I'm sure there are aspects of both sides that speak to most modern Jews. We can reject Kahane's racism, xenophobia, and ultra-nationalism, and yet still see merit in a muscular Zionism. Kahane rejected that there was a Palestinian "people" and even rejected peace: "In my plan, there will be no peace. When Messiah comes there will be peace. Until then, survival, survival, survival." Professor Shaul Magid critiques Greenberg for not being forceful enough with Kahane.

> Greenberg could have deflected the halakhic conversation by claiming that Kahane's idea of transfer was not an attempt to transform the state into a theocracy, which was antithetical to the entire Zionist project. He did not make that argument, and I think he missed an important, even crucial, opportunity. Indeed, Kahane openly said that he supported democracy in Israel only for Jews and not for Arabs.[347]

Interestingly enough, at the time of the above-quoted debate, Greenberg would have been considered a polar opposite of Kahane: the former liberal and the latter conservative. By today's new standards, Greenberg would be considered a centrist, even right of center by many. Left-wing Zionism has moved further left, in ways that have made Greenberg very uncomfortable and that he has denounced. Greenberg rejects most of former President Trump's positions and rhetoric, yet has still expressed public gratitude to him for his support of Israel, in ways that American Jewish liberal organizations and leaders would never, or very rarely, do.

Many in the space perceived by some as the far left in American Jewish life have declared themselves post-Zionist, even anti-Zionist. But just because a few op-eds emerge each month declaring Liberal Zionism to be dead doesn't make it so. We should resist the tempting urge to bandwagon and fall into the dangerous extremes of either far-right ultra-nationalism or the far left's demonizing and boycotting of Israel. We can adamantly defend the Jewish people's right to a state and celebrate the enormous successes of that holy enterprise while also being fervently opposed to the many seemingly horrible policies championed by so

---
[347] Ibid., 38.

many Israeli leaders of late. I know it may seem like this middle ground is dead since its proponents get silenced by the extremes, but the future of the Jewish people (not just its survival but also its soul) depends on this nuance.

Personally, I'm very uncomfortable with the far-left perspective on Israel, as it often fails to adequately appreciate Israel's security, Israel's global reputation, the Jewish historical narrative, or the extent of pervasive antisemitism. And I'm very uncomfortable with the far right because that side often fails to adequately appreciate peace, gentile life, or the Palestinian narrative. I remain a passionate Religious Zionist (finding deep religious meaning in the Jewish return to the land and return to sovereignty) and I remain passionate about reconciliation (grassroots bottom-up relationship/trust building) and a two-state solution (political top-down agreement). I've remained hopeful that eventually a heroic Israeli leader and a heroic Palestinian leader will emerge (each with real clout in their communities) who could make a deal happen. I fear that the Trump-Netanyahu collaboration may have caused irreparable harm to a peace process on various levels (increasing the settler population, destroying any remaining bridge-building enterprises, fostering a new fundamentalist confidence, breaking down attempts at empathy across party lines, etc.). We need to ensure that the new administration in the United States is held accountable to Trump's statements against settlement expansion and we also need to oppose a new flat-out rejection of a two-state peace solution that is necessary to save lives, enhance dignity, and ensure the right to self-determination. I know some feel a two-state solution is a thing of the past, but I don't believe we can responsibly give up on this dream. The alternatives are too dangerous (existentially and morally). I am in the camp that sees it as the only option for Jewish survival and for Jewish ethics.

If we don't prioritize reconciliation between Jewish Israelis and Arab Israelis (and other Palestinians), the radical fundamentalists will, God forbid, destroy the State of Israel. We have no option but to work for a two-state solution and to work toward reconciliation. It may seem naive to some to return to such work, but it is more naive to think that we can maintain the status quo and come out alive. That means that we can't have everything we want. It means that we must take the moral high road. It means that we must prioritize survival over land.[348]

The right and the left both live in denial. The right says that if we annex Palestinian territories then all will be resolved and we'll have security and peace. The left says that if we just give back land to Palestinian control then we'll have security and peace. Of course, both are oversimplistic and will not achieve the results they claim.

---

[348] Shortly after the Six-Day War, when the Western Wall and the Temple Mount were recaptured, Rabbi Joseph B. Soloveitchik stated at a public lecture (at Yeshiva University, September 1967), that if at some point in the future it is determined by the military and political officials that these holy sites must be returned, then it is our obligation, as citizens, to accept that decision.

It is hard to survive, and we should feel the gravitas of this weight upon us in our advocacy. We can find inspiration from past generations. A very frail, old man in a wheelchair with bloody bandages along his face was sitting behind me in shul one Rosh Hashanah. At the end of the service, he grabbed my hand and pulled my face close to his and fervently said: "I'm a Holocaust survivor and I'm entitled to give you a bracha (blessing)." It was a beautiful bracha to remember and cherish, and I gratefully replied "Amen!" Sensing a spiritual fire within this humble man, I asked: "Might you share with me your wisdom of survival? What has sustained you?" He paused for a few moments and then whispered: "When I was in the concentration camps, I always reminded myself that things could always be worse. Things can always be worse!"

When we face difficult challenges in the coming years, may we always remember his wisdom: "Things could be worse!" Can we learn to complain less and channel the energy of our self-absorption more toward helping others?[349]

In the Greenberg-Kahane debate, Rabbi Greenberg modeled for us how to make the important effort to keep the dialogue alive even when we confront others who are deemed extremists. We must denounce extremists rather than give them a pass, downplaying their influence.

We can also sharpen our ideas through such dialogue. I was invited to do something like this during the Pesach of 2020 when I was asked to spend the week at a venue that would have given me the opportunity to debate conservative (although not necessarily extremist) thinkers Dennis Prager and Ben Shapiro for the week.[350] While this experience was cancelled at the last minute due to the Covid-19 pandemic, I was prepared to be dismissed and shamed in order to have the privilege of putting out an alternative narrative to what was likely to be a right-wing Orthodox audience.

And, so, there is a lot to learn from the Greenberg-Kahane debate. It is worth watching the full video or reading the full transcript. In the meantime, we see that that very debate is still, almost exactly, completely relevant and alive today.

Greenberg and Kahane were friends as teenagers. But this debate was the last time they appeared publicly together. We must ultimately walk away from some relationships.

---

[349] Disclaimer: this reminder is for one's own spiritual growth, not for counseling others. When dealing with others, it's best not to ever minimize their suffering, but to reply only with empathy.
[350] Shira Hanau, "A Seder With a Side of Political Debate," *NY Jewish Week*, February 19, 2020. https://www.jta.org/2020/02/19/ny/a-seder-with-a-side-of-political-debate.

DEBATE 19.

Israel vs. the Diaspora: What is the Center?

For decades, modern Jews were taught that the two most formative events that define the contemporary Jewish experience are the Holocaust and the founding of the State of Israel. That trauma and that glory remain formative, but they can no longer be exclusive and central if we're serious about fostering thriving Jewish life throughout the world, including where so much of contemporary Jewry is found: in the Diaspora. Indeed, we must focus on the here and now. Since the moment many of us took our first breaths, we've been taught that our priority should be supporting Israel, as that is the playing field for Jewish life; those of us outside Israel are merely on the sidelines. It is as if those who live inside Israel are the book and everyone outside the borders are the footnotes. It may be the case, however, that the opposite is true. Israel may become—by reality and necessity—less significant and central to the success of global Jewish life.

Israel is vitally important for what it has achieved for the Jewish people and for what it has contributed to the broader world. The potential is even greater with the hopes that the State of Israel can constitute a center from which the Jewish Nation might fully become an *ohr lagoyim* (a unique light to the other nations) representing our cherished eternal values. With all of this work to build the Jewish state over the decades, however, have we neglected the needs of the Diaspora?

Don't mistake my intentions: I am a passionate Religious Zionist who will visit, donate, support, love, struggle with, and challenge policies of Israel all of my life. I (or my kids, in any event) may even move there one day. But I think we need to question whether the propaganda was wrong and that Diaspora Jewry's primary role is not to support Israel through blind advocacy and fundraising. Rather, the primary role of our Diaspora communities is to build vibrant Jewish life here. Now. The souls here and now matter. Their values and visions matter. Here, we interact with great respect with other cultures, bring Jewish values into the public marketplace in healthy ways, and have a full spectrum of pluralistic ways to engage with Jewish life. There is no doubt we have enormous challenges here in American Jewish life: rising antisemitism, low affiliation rates, and political challenges (among many others). But, for many, those challenges are far less alienating than the state-mandated religious coercion, violent conflict, and sectorial infighting for which today's Israel is so well known. Indeed, even many Israelis seeking a pluralistic vibrant Jewish life that is authentically rooted while also being universalistic, inclusive, social justice-oriented, and innovative are often attracted to American Jewish life.

American Jews have been taught to make Israel so primary that, sadly, nationalism is slowly replacing religion. Has Judaism, for many, been replaced by a new religion: Israelism? Heated arguments are no longer about God, *halachah*, denominations, innovation, or Jewish values as much as they are about Israel policies. One's Israel politics is what decides if they are in or out of social circles. A rabbi told me that worse than declaring from the bimah that he was an atheist would be to fail to attend an AIPAC policy conference, or to attend but to fail to stand and clap at each moment his congregation's delegation does so. On the other hand, some who identify as Zionists at times find themselves marginalized in Jewish progressive circles precisely because of their commitment to Israel—viewed, perhaps inaccurately, as being at the expense of other global Jewish concerns.

Obviously, we should invest in Israel in strategic ways. But if we're wise, we'll focus on building our local community here first. The identity of this community will be defined by prioritizing our own Jewish learning and incorporating Zionism secondarily. There are those, including Natan Sharansky—former chairman of the Jewish Agency—who make clear that Israel is no longer the home for non-Orthodox religious Jews in the Diaspora. Given the rapid growth of the ultra-Orthodox population, the near-abandonment of a peace process, attempts to expel African asylum seekers, the long-time rejection of egalitarian prayer spaces, the Israeli government's policies being at odds with American Jewish liberals (i.e., the vast majority of American Jews), it is lamentably easy to see a critical sector of the community becoming disengaged with Jewish life itself. If Israel was once the greatest tool for American Jewish engagement, it may now be one of the least effective (with some exceptions) and often the greatest force for alienating young American Jews.

Why is this the case? First, the ultra-Orthodox population in Israel is expected to boom over the coming decades, and if they maintain a grip on Israeli politics, they can be sure to secure religious fundamentalism as the dominant religious force. Even while so many in that sector reject work, social integration, service, and women's leadership and education, they are empowered when they maintain a powerful role within political coalitions. Second, with over half a million settlers living beyond the green line (and rapidly growing), a peace deal becomes only vanishingly possible with a very dangerous and unsettling status quo. Third, Israel as a political entity alienates many when it is seen as lacking interest in cultivating a pluralistic ethos and as rejecting and discrediting the many varied approaches to Jewish life which are dominant in the Diaspora.

Jews the world over share the wish that we had not been exiled for two millennia. But we were. Jews evolved to be a flourishing people of the Diaspora, having developed alongside other cultures seeking mutual respect and solidarity (even if that respect hasn't always been returned). More than being a people of the past looking to return to past models, we are a people of the future seeking to solve global moral problems of the coming centuries. Many will be driven by the dream to return to the homeland after two millennia and can't understand why anyone would remain in "the antisemitic galut" when they could help shape the longed-for Jewish state. Others disdain "the new shtetl" of Israel which often places nationalism as primary, and they seek to cultivate a cosmopolitanism in this rare new era where antisemitism is alive but far eclipsed by the forces of universalism, tolerance, and pluralism. To be sure, just as the far-right obsession with nationalism may be a distortion of Judaism, so too the far-left rejection of nationalism is also a distortion, one might argue. Further, it is inconsistent to reject nationalism on an ideological basis but then support the Palestinian call for nationalism.

When we pray for *kibbutz galuyot* (the ingathering of exiles), I believe we are referring to those in danger, not those thriving. Israel can be, and should be, a refuge for those Jews who live in antisemitic cultures, but living in Israel is not the answer for all of global Jewry. Jews in the Diaspora should play a role not just of advocacy and fundraising for the State of Israel, but also to learn and to teach, to bring light and to receive light, as proud Diaspora Jews. And the issues about which we choose to advocate should not be limited and predictable. We must diversify our ethical interests to represent the fullness of Jewish values.

As a traditional rabbi who embraces the eternal truth of the Torah, and as a religious Zionist who believes God compassionately returned us to our land, I nonetheless believe there are crucial moral and theological limits that need to be recognized regarding religious Zionist identity. Torah must have more weight than only religious Zionism in forming our ideologies. The Hasidic masterwork, the *Tanya*, teaches that there is a special virtue in the worship of God outside of Israel that does not exist in the service of God in the Land of Israel, because the resting of the Divine spirit that is to be placed in the light that follows from the darkness is greater than the light that comes from within the light. It's not that the majority of Jewish wealth sustaining the Jewish community is in the Diaspora, as true as that may be; rather, that spiritual light can be experienced uniquely here, too. Rebbe Nachman taught that wherever we bring our spiritual energy, we are "in Israel." For millennia, Israel has been not only material but also conceptual and spiritual. God is omnipresent, and the spiritually refined can find God in all places.

One serious question that David Ben-Gurion,[351] Israel's first prime minister, faced just before the creation of the State of Israel was whether ultra-Orthodox Jews would recognize a secular state. In order to win their support, he offered to nationally recognize the Sabbath, observe kashrut in state institutions, allow autonomy for religious schools, and apply religious law to marriage and personal

---

[351] It is interesting to note that David Ben-Gurion was born David Green. He, like many others then and since, Hebraicized his family name.

status. But Ben-Gurion may have underestimated what effect this would have over the succeeding decades. Over time, the majority Jewish secular population has undergone a profound shift, due to immigration and the territory seized in the Six-Day War where some ultra-Orthodox populations are booming.

Echoing Ben-Gurion's sentiments, former Israeli President Reuven Rivlin, in his July 2015 speech at the 15th Annual Herzliya Conference, announced that a "new Israeli order" of "four principal tribes" had emerged, comprising significant numbers of ultra-Orthodox [Haredi], national-religious [modern Orthodox], secular Jewish, and Arab populations.[352] Rivlin stated that "there is no longer a clear majority, nor clear minority groups," and that each are "essentially different from each other." He pointed out that each tribe has its own schools and media that create "huge gaps" in society. He hoped that providing a sense of "security," "shared responsibility," "equity and equality," and "the creation of a shared Israeli character" would provide a solution to Israelis living together in society.

One consequence of ceding religious control to the ultra-Orthodox is that civil marriages within Israel are not recognized by the Chief Rabbinate; many Israelis either do not qualify or do not believe in marrying according to ultra-Orthodox rules, so they feel compelled to go outside Israel (e.g., Cyprus) to have a legal marriage. Even immigrants who wish to marry, who provide proof of Jewish identity by obtaining a letter from a rabbi, are often rejected. In 2016, the Chief Rabbinate rejected letters from 160 rabbis, many of them recognized as Orthodox in their own communities, in 24 countries, thus denying these people the right to marry in Israel. To share a more recent problematic example, Sephardic Chief Rabbi Yitzhak Yosef brought shame to the community when he called Black people monkeys. To the majority of Jews today, the Chief Rabbinate, which to them represents Israel's broader religious culture, has lost its moral authority.

We have seen the scourge of racism, antisemitism, and similar bigotry afoot in America. Intolerance of a somewhat different kind has been curdling in Israel. The Israeli government's policy regarding egalitarian prayer at the Kotel—the Western Wall—in Jerusalem illustrates an increasing divide between official Israeli and American Jewish groups. The Chief Rabbinate, which controls religious policy at the Kotel, has consistently opposed the active participation of women (and non-Orthodox practices) at the Kotel. Since 1988, a group of Jewish women from various denominations and nations, who go by the name Women of the Wall, has attempted to conduct prayer services at the Kotel, and have been physically and verbally harassed by ultra-Orthodox adults and children, and often arrested for their efforts. One egregious example of this harassment occurred in July 2013

---

[352] It is instructive, and perhaps seems counterintuitive, that Ben-Gurion, who advocated for institutionalized religious practice, was himself a secular Jew. Rivlin, on the other hand, who as president emphasized the need to cater to all segments of Israeli society, is an Orthodox Jew.

when more than 350 women were forced to pray near a public bathroom while ultra-Orthodox opponents were not prevented from throwing eggs at them and blowing whistles to disrupt the prayers.

After years of resistance, Israel's Attorney General supported Women of the Wall's contentions that they were victims of discrimination and unjust exclusion, and it seemed that the government would finally act. There appeared to be an agreement in January 2016, when the Israeli cabinet passed a resolution agreeing to set up an egalitarian space at the Kotel. However, Prime Minister Benjamin Netanyahu failed to follow up, and after intense lobbying from ultra-Orthodox forces (including the rabbi of the Kotel Rabbi Shmuel Rabinowitz), reneged on the agreement in June 2017, saying that "several difficulties arose," while disingenuously indicating he still wanted a settlement. Rabbi Rick Jacobs, President of the Union for Reform Judaism (URJ), replied that Netanyahu's reversal "would be a slap in the face to the vast majority of world Jewry."[353]

In November 2017, to celebrate the ordination of four Union of Reform Judaism rabbis, a group of URJ leaders (including Rabbi Jacobs, Rabbi Joshua M. Davidson, Senior Rabbi at Temple Emanu-El in New York City and member of the Board of Governors of the Hebrew Union College-Jewish Institute of Religion (HUC-JIR), Rabbi Naamah Kelman-Ezrahi, Dean of HUC-IR, Gilad Kariv, Executive Director of the Reform Movement in Israel, and Anat Hoffman, leader of Women of the Wall and executive director of the Israel Religious Action Center) bearing eight Torah scrolls were accosted first by security personnel at the security checkpoint to the Western Wall complex for a quarter of an hour (where Rabbi Jacobs was threatened with mace by a security guard), and then in the plaza by ultra-Orthodox men who tackled several of those bearing Torah scrolls.

Rabbi Rabinowitz, as administrator of the Western Wall, has long opposed egalitarian worship, calling Women of the Wall's attempts to pray a "plague" and an incitement to "civil war," and has refused to comment on the assault of URJ rabbis. A Supreme Court ruling questioning why security personnel did not protect the non-Orthodox has gone unanswered. Rabbi Davidson denounced the ultra-Orthodox abuse of power: "The impunity with which the ultra-Orthodox in Israel too often assault the religious liberties of the non-Orthodox should be intolerable in a democratic state. But empowered by the stranglehold of Israel's religious parties on its coalition government, the Chief Rabbinate rules as if without a care." Hoffman feared that the violence will increase: "We are sitting ducks."

In the Diaspora, each community's first priority should be to make their own local community robust and engaging; unity of a Jewish spirit is essential, but

---

[353] It is correct that the majority of all Jews worldwide who affiliate with a denomination identify as Reform. In Israel, however, Reform Judaism makes up a very small percentage of the Jewish denominations.

shouldn't be equated with the notion that all Jewish communities must interact with the rest of the world in the same way. The dream of Zionism—a protective state for a persecuted people, as many adherents to Modern Zionism would put it—shouldn't be transformed into an excuse for reactionary myopia. Should disproportionate amounts of resources be channeled toward Jewish nationalism rather than toward fulfilling our Jewish mandate to reduce suffering in the world on a global scale in keeping with our charge to work to end oppression in recognition of the oppression that we have faced as Jews? We must be clear that in prioritizing the Diaspora, we are not, God forbid, abandoning Israel, but rather that we see greater potential in our era to actualize the mission of the Torah in the Diaspora where there is a more open, pluralistic, and progressive ethos for Jewish values to develop within and among us.

What we are witnessing today is a great ideological divide between elements of the Israeli leadership and the Jewish voice in the Diaspora. Indeed, this divide puts Israel's security at risk and puts American Jewish identity at risk. There is enormous power, wealth, and creativity in the United States that cannot yet be actualized when it is sidetracked to focus, so often exclusively, on investing in Israel as the center. We would benefit from embracing our Diaspora potential rather than merely exporting our Judaism to the Israeli playing field of Jewish life while we rest on the sidelines. Israeli culture seems to be becoming more interested in the lucrative technology field and less in the intellectual challenges and growth possibilities in Jewish thought. Israelis engaged in advanced Jewish Studies programs who are looking to work in academia are moving to America to find jobs. Such brain drain indicates that America is becoming a more alluring home for those seeking a spiritual and intellectual playing field when it comes to Jewish thought. Assimilation is only one part of the story. The other part is that innovative Jewish social entrepreneurs in America are creatively and robustly reimagining Jewish life.

The Diaspora, of course, includes far more than just American Jewry, but that is undeniably the largest community. Most of the six million (or more) Jews in America want to be here. No aliyah campaign, or minor, albeit serious, antisemitism campaigns, will persuade them to make a mass exodus. They are here to stay and their identity and future are indispensable. The most recent estimates of Jewish denominations among American Jews are about 35 percent Reform, 30 percent no denomination, 18 percent Conservative, 10 percent Orthodox (modern and ultra-Orthodox), and 6 percent among smaller denominations. This is a liberal Jewish community that increasingly does not find a home in Israel. Should America be the new center for global Jewish life, displacing the perception of Israel as the center? I'm not sure. But the American Jewish leadership and philanthropists would certainly be wise to take liberal American Jewry, and its bright future, very seriously, just as Israel takes its future very seriously. When American Jews prioritize making the world a better place and consistently feel shame about the Israeli government's policies, are we really going to tell them that they're bad Jews who don't get it?

We must, of course, engage in American-Israeli dialogue, as we have so much to learn from one another, but we must also be respectfully honest about the growing divide in our Jewish values and ideologies.

Now is the time for Jews everywhere to take heed of the words of David Ben-Gurion, who expressed in a 1950 letter that "... the Jews of the United States... owe no political allegiance to Israel.... We, the people of Israel, have no desire and no intention to interfere in any way with the internal affairs of Jewish communities abroad. The government and the people of Israel fully respect the right and integrity of the Jewish communities in other countries to develop their indigenous social, economic, and cultural institutions in accord with their own needs and aspirations."

Jews, no matter where they are, have something special to contribute to the world, regardless of where they live. For those who continue to find Zionism to be the most meaningful dimension of their Jewish identity, we need not discourage them on their journey. Rather, we can hope that they will continue to shape Israel morally and spiritually. And for those who find Zionism and their relationship to Israel to be more draining and alienating than uplifting, we can urge them not to bail on that engagement, thereby fostering a big tent, and at the same time urge them to build a positive Jewish identity in ways that are most meaningful for them. We are blessed to have a Jewish state, but we are also blessed to have learned how to survive—even thrive—outside of it during our thousands of years in exile. These two complex interwoven truths can coexist. This is yet another layer of the pluralistic ethos we must embrace.

The value of living in Israel is clear. It is our ancestral homeland and deeply tied to our history and our destiny. However, it is also clear that there is a deep value to living in the Diaspora, based both on our history and on our global mission. Living in caravans in a small settlement town during my years learning in Israel, my dream was always to settle the land. As a religious Zionist, I feel that living in Israel is a tremendous and miraculous opportunity, and that all Jews can and must consider making this life transition. Indeed, the *halachic* obligation of *yishuv ha'aretz*, the religious obligation to settle the Land of Israel, is a matter of significance and cannot be underestimated. I would like to suggest, however, that in addition to this well-known imperative, there is also a crucial duty, in many instances, to reside in the Diaspora.

The Rambam, following the BT, allows for limited exceptions to the *mitzvah* to reside in the Land, including studying or teaching Torah, searching for a marriage partner, living in safety, or in the case of economic hardship, to earn a living. The Jerusalem Talmud, however, suggests that there is no prohibition against leaving Israel at all, even if one is already living there.[354]

In fact, some of the great 20th-century rabbinic authorities have argued that one is not obligated to reside in Israel today: Rav Yehudah Amital, the late Rosh Yeshiva[355] and Israeli leader, once said, "In America there are many great Torah scholars, Rav Joseph Soloveitchik, Rabbi Moshe Feinstein, the Lubavitcher Rebbe, the Satmar Rebbe and others. Is it possible that not one of them knows the *halachah*?"

While Israel remains the destiny of the Jewish people, we also must not abandon the Diaspora. The Torah demands that we, as a nation, commit to pursuing justice; as warriors against injustice, it behooves us to be stationed everywhere around the globe. This work as an *ohr lagoyim*, a light unto the nations, is our raison d'être.

It is in the Diaspora where we can fulfill the Torah's charge to combat global poverty, injustice, and oppression wherever these negative forces may be found. While Israel has been known to do inspiring humanitarian work, a nation-state's primary concern must be the welfare and security of its own citizens. We must be concerned with Israel's security as well, but our responsibility is also broader. I've met thousands of other young Jewish leaders who have intertwined their religious Zionist identities with identities as global citizens.

Further, though Jewish thought can and should remain distinct from that of other cultures, and obviously, other religions, the Jewish intellectual tradition has always benefitted, and continues to benefit, from development in conjunction with a diverse array of neighboring societies. Taking a cue from Muslim scholars such as Al Farabi and Avicenna, Rambam integrated Jewish thought and Greek philosophy without the need to sacrifice our *halachah* or identity. In addition, today in America, as in the "Golden Age" of medieval Spain and earlier, in the days of the Talmudic academies of Babylonia, we see a great concentration of stellar Jewish academic programs and yeshivot.

The Mishnaic sage Rabbi Nehorai goes so far as to suggest, "[G]o as a [voluntary] exile to a place of Torah and say not that it will come after you, for [it is] your fellow [student]s who will make it permanent in your hand."[356] This can and should raise Diaspora self-esteem, as it mandates that one must reside where they can develop their best intellectual and spiritual achievements.

---

[354] The exact limitations and parameters of this statement in the Jerusalem Talmud are debated and beyond the scope of this chapter.
[355] Rav Amital was the founder of Yeshivat Har Etzion (known colloquially as the Gush), as well as the founder of the left-leaning (now defunct) Meimad political party.
[356] Pirkei Avot 4:14, trans. Dr. Joshua Kulp.

Diaspora Jews are not watching the game from the Israel sidelines. Some of the most significant Jewish contributions have and will continue to be made in the Diaspora, where Jews can play a leading role in fighting injustice, alleviating poverty, advocating for Israel and Jewish interests, and learning from people of other faiths. While the modern State of Israel is one of the greatest blessings the Jews have received—and it cannot be neglected—we must also be sure to actualize all the values of our Jewish tradition.

Aliyah to Israel is on the rise. A total of 17,880 immigrants arrived in Israel in 5770 (2009-2010) as compared to 15,180 in 5769 (2008-2009)—an increase of 18 percent. In more recent years the totals have topped 20,000 and even more. There is no need for the demographic prophecies of gloom that if we don't make Aliyah immediately Israel will fumble, and that the Diaspora provides no hope for the Jewish future. Neither argument paints an accurate picture, nor does either reflect the faith to survive that has driven Jews for millennia.

Many have argued for *shelilat hagolah*,[357] the idea that one cannot sustain a Jewish life outside of Israel. One should be cautious of those who suggest that one can only live fully as a Jew in Israel. While there are particularistic *mitzvot* that can only be performed in Israel,[358] there are also universal *mitzvot* that can only properly be achieved with the cooperation of Jews in the Diaspora. Ultimately, after considering the needs of one's own family, one should not feel shame in choosing to reside in London, Paris, or Chicago, but rather should proudly accept the responsibilities of supporting Israel while at the same time serving as a global ambassador for the Jewish people.

Just as Jewish history shows that Jews were not ultimately safe in the Diaspora, so too Jewish history shows that Jews were not ultimately safe in the land of Israel either. We can hold some humility that we do not truly know what will enable the Jewish people to survive and thrive. But our conversation should not be primarily fear-driven, but rather life-affirming. We wish to live meaningful, fruitful lives all over the world, based on our own needs, and to respect one another in those choices. We can make those choices individually (what we need as individuals and as families) and collectively (what we believe is best for the Jewish people). The debate should always be guided by Ahavat Yisrael (a love for our fellow Jew). It may be that we need not debate at all, since in a post-Covid world where technological access to participation has expanded so much that decentralization is the new reality. There is no center as we become more interconnected. Our resiliency has never been in our rootedness to a location but rather in our ability to move and adapt as needed.

---

[357] *Shelilat hagolah* literally means "negation of the Diaspora."
[358] *Shemitah*, the sabbatical year, is a prime example of an entire category of *mitzvot* referred to as *mitzvot hateluyot ba'Artetz*, those that pertain specifically to the agriculture of Israel.

Debate 20.

No State, One State, or Two States: Herzl vs. Wise, Art Green vs. Peter Beinart

It may seem obvious to us today that Orthodox Jews would have been pro-Zionist[359] one hundred years ago, but that was far from true. It may also seem obvious to us that Reform Jews would have been pro-Zionist one hundred years ago, but that also was far from true. The bulk of Zionists, in the late 19th and early 20th centuries, were found among secular Jews.

We know about Theodor Herzl's famous 1897 address[360] in Basel, Switzerland. But do we know about Rabbi Stephen S. Wise's opposition? At the 1897 Reform rabbinic conference, Wise supported a resolution that emphatically denounced Zionism: "Resolved, that we totally disapprove of any attempt for the establishment of a Jewish State. Such attempts show a misunderstanding of Israel's Mission ... We affirm that the object of Judaism is not political nor national, but spiritual." Further, in the Pittsburgh Platform of 1875, which was considered the first significant statement of the American Reform Movement, we find these unequivocal words: "We consider ourselves no longer a nation, but a religious community, and therefore expect neither a return to Palestine... nor the restoration of any laws concerning the Jewish state."

The American Reform movement wanted to make clear that there were no dual loyalties. We were to be fully American and seeking America as our home. Jewish nationalism, in their view, would compromise such a commitment. Further, part of the reason for calling synagogues "temples" was to make clear that they were replacing any desire to return to a central Temple in a central location (Jerusalem).

For the Orthodox, the opposition was very different. A future Jewish state, they argued, needed to be built by Torah Jews, not secular Jews, and thus it would need to wait until the messianic era. We should focus, instead, on learning Torah and observing the *mitzvot*, and not be distracted by state-building.

Fast forward to the mid-20th century, the years leading up to and following 1948, and Orthodox Jews, at least the more modern ones, tend to be some of the most fervent Zionists. Many Orthodox synagogues in America recite the Prayer for the Welfare of the State of Israel on Shabbat morning; many synagogues and schools celebrate Yom Ha'Atzma'ut (Israel's Independence Day) and sing Hatikvah at functions such as the annual dinner. And in Israel, there are many *yeshivot hesder* (yeshivah programs that combine the study of Torah and serving in the

---

[359] For the purposes of this essay, we are defining a Zionist as one who is pro-modern State of Israel, and Zionism as the movement supporting the creation of, and maintaining of, the State of Israel.

[360] Theodor Herzl organized the congress of Zionists at which he delivered his address. He later became the first president of the WZO (World Zionist Organization), an outgrowth of his congress.

IDF). There is even a division of the army called Nahal Haredi, for young men who hail from a more Ultra-Orthodox background. The story in the Reform movement is a bit more complicated as the movement has moved left on its relationship to Israel; it is still of a Zionist orientation, but far more critical of the enterprise.

It might seem clear that the Zionist agenda and goal was achieved. After all, there is a Jewish state. Yet the debates rage on regarding the conflict:

1. Should we maintain status quo and deny Palestinian nationalism?

2. Should we work toward a two-state solution where Israeli Jews and Palestinians can, for the most part, live separately, each with their own sovereignty?

3. Should we try to build one state, living together in harmony and co-governing?

4. Is there a middle ground, with a confederation where we can co-govern and cooperate with one land but with two states on that one land?

Peter Beinart was known as a leading articulator for liberal Zionism for some years. Recently, however, he pivoted from being a two-state visionary to a one-state visionary. Rabbi Dr. Art Green, who remains committed to a two-state solution, responded publicly to Beinart. Green agrees with many of Beinart's critiques but ultimately rejects his abandonment of the two-state solution.[361] Green offers three primary critiques of Beinart's one-state solution:

1. **Jews need a Refuge**: "I do not believe that a bi-national state, shared with Arabs still wounded by the real suffering of their own refugees, could be counted on to be there when Jews need it."

2. **Jews need Defense**: "I fully agree with the critique of the Israeli army's conduct toward civilians in the West Bank, and I am sympathetic to some of the claims about excesses in Gaza. I am appalled by the government's ongoing whitewash of obvious violations of human rights by members of the Israeli army. But I am not ready to give up on the country's vital need and right to defend itself."

---

[361] Rabbi Art Green, "Art Green Responds to Peter Beinart's Abandonment of the "2 State Solution," *Tikkun*, July 16, 2020, https://www.tikkun.org/2-state-solution-response/.

3. **The value of Jewish culture**: "The third point, the culture of Israel, is personally just as vital to me. What has been created, thanks to the Jewish state—including its financial support—in the realms of Hebrew literature, Jewish scholarship, fine arts, and lots more, has enriched and transformed Jewish life in myriad ways. This cultural aspect of Zionism, to which we are both committed, has been an incredible success... I simply do not believe that a Palestinian Minister of Culture in this single state you propose would have the same commitment to it."

Green ultimately supports the founding of a confederation after the establishment of two states. Of course, all of this will take time, and the ultimate goal cannot be to live with walls but to learn to partner, cooperate, and coexist even while each separate state advances its own religious and cultural goals.

For other Jews today, any talk of peace, be it one state, two states, or a confederation, is only naïve. There are no peace partners, they would argue, so all we can do practically for now is maintain the status quo. But this view also poses an extreme danger to the Jews:

- Israel may lose its claim to democracy if it controls the Palestinian population.
- Anti-Israel sentiment around the world may continue to rise at an even more rapid rate.
- Many threats in the region continue to exist, and it is unclear that Israel can withstand them indefinitely.

We must never abandon hope for peace. We must also never abandon our commitment to Jewish security. For Herzl, Jews needed a state. For Wise, Jews did not. For secular pioneers, Jews needed a state. For many among the Orthodox, Jews did not.

Of course, Rav Kook in Israel and Rabbi Soloveitchik in America, as well as other pre-state Israel Orthodox rabbis, were early founders of Religious Zionism.

While Rav Kook held a passion for Religious Zionism, he also was a visionary for peace:

"As we return to capture our land," he wrote, "we do so not by might or the sword but the path of peace, paying in full for every footstep of our land, even if our right to the earth of our holy land never lapsed," whether wrested from Israel by cash or by the sword. "We want to fulfill the mitzvah of love thy neighbor[362] not only toward individuals but also toward nations so that none of the gentile nations will bear any claim or resentment against us."[363]

In addition to the non-Zionists, there are also the anti-Zionist Jews. We think of these as all being very young far-left American Jews. But they can be found among the ultra-Orthodox as well (the Neturei Karta[364] sect is but one example). One well-known rabbi, perhaps jokingly, tried to re-interpret Neturei Karta.

> Rabbi Yitzhak Ze'ev ("Velvel") ha-Levi Soloveitchik of Brisk, who lived in Jerusalem, once heard a member of Neturei Karta curse the State of Israel, to which he responded, "This man is a Zionist." How so? "In Poland or in Russia would he thus curse the authorities? Would he act like this in America?" Since he acts differently here, then he must necessarily find a different essence in the Jewish state, a unique experience. "He must therefore be a Zionist."[365]

Another group of anti-Zionists among the Orthodox today are the fringe hilltop youth settlers engaged in acts of terror. They reportedly want to see the end of the State of Israel with a Kingdom of Israel replacing it. But the path to peace, in my view, is achieved through bridge-building, not bridge-burning. Denying gas as a heat source would not be a valid security measure but just outright discrimination and racism. Statements like this remind me that even though I'm fervently religious and adamantly Zionist, I struggle more and more to identify with the camp of "Religious Zionists,"[366] (*dati leumi*) as long as some in that camp move toward extremes.

I will always be religious and I'll always be a Zionist, but I don't know that I'll always affiliate with the political faction of Religious Zionism. Zionism is not

---

[362] Leviticus 19:18.
[363] Rabbi Dr. Yehudah Mirsky, *Rav Kook: Mystic in a Time of Revolution* (New Haven: Yale, Jewish Lives series, 2019), 201.
[364] Interestingly enough, the name *Neturei Karta* literally means "those who guard the land." Their view is that creating an independent Jewish homeland is forbidden until the messianic era. Earlier we mentioned that there are those religious Jews who feel that practically speaking we cannot create a Torah-based state in our day; Neturei Karta goes one step further and claims that it is forbidden to do so by *halachah* (Jewish law).
[365] Aviezer Ravitzky, *Messianism, Zionism and Jewish Religious Radicalism* (Chicago: University of Chicago Press, 1996) 155.
[366] "Rav Levanon: One May Not Sell Gas to Arab Motorists," *The Yeshiva World*, November 13, 2014, http://www.theyeshivaworld.com/news/headlines-breaking-stories/271104/rav-levanon-one-may-not-sell-gas-to-arab-motorists.html.

an ideological commitment to a current reality but an aspiring dream, a protest calling for a national and global moral revolution. We need partners who share our dreams.

I am a proud and passionate Zionist for many reasons, but the main reason is because I believe we finally have the holy opportunity to bring the Torah's most cherished ethical values to fruition through the vehicle of a state. When Israel continues to offer humanitarian relief around the world, I believe we are taking yet another step to bring this spiritual vision to actualization! When Israel can enable millions of Jews to live safely within its borders and to learn Torah, it is a dream from past millennia.

For me, there are so many different lenses through which to experience Israel:

1. A biblical homeland
2. A post-Holocaust refuge
3. A religious-Zionist ideology
4. A Jewish social justice opportunity
5. A playing field to foster Jewish peoplehood and Jewish culture
6. A personal place where my family, friends, and teachers live
7. A spiritual playground
8. A home from my own personal religious narrative
9. A messianic yearning
10. An idea of political debate

It is hard to have a monolithic relationship to a place so rich and so complicated. There is no debate more sensitive and more fury-driven among Jews today than the debates about Israel. More passionate than debating God, *halachah* (Jewish law), denominations, ethics, or even secular politics, it is the debates surrounding Israel that make every Jew's blood boil.

How can we lower the temperature? How can we talk, debate, and learn once again? We can find a way to do so, and we must.

Contemporary Moral Issues

DEBATE 21.

Local vs. Global, Particular vs. Universal

> It isn't enough to talk about peace. One must believe in it.
> And it isn't enough to believe in it. One must work at it.
> —Eleanor Roosevelt

We have a unique challenge today to balance a local presence with one that is global. It is not easy to remain connected to the global Jewish conversation while also investing time and energy in Judaism at the local level. And while meta-connections provide gratifications and expectations that local Judaism rarely actualizes—that is, if I'm part of an exciting national and global conversation about the priorities of the Jewish people, why would I continue spending time concerning myself with purely local matters (which can sometimes be erroneously thought of as minor matters)? Our local *shuls*, schools, and neighborhoods continue to be the hubs of Jewish life.

Perhaps experiences of the global and the local scales can inform one another. And that interplay can be facilitated by considering a rabbinic teaching in the *midrash* about the role that "borrowing" played in creation:

> The day borrows from the night, and the night from the day. The moon borrows from the stars, and the stars from the moon. Knowledge borrows from comprehension and comprehension from knowledge. The heavens borrow from the earth and the earth from the heavens. Thus, it is also with human beings, with a single difference: all these others borrow without ending up in court.[367]

Day does not end where night begins. Rather they merge and learn from one another. Their very essences are too intertwined to separate. But humans sometimes forget that although they exist as individuals, their individual and collective experiences rely on each other for meaning.

Global and local discourses are, thus, interdependent; the two realms can and must borrow from one another. Today, our global relationships and meta-discourses (which we often experience by means of social media) are both important—indeed, perhaps essential—and yet each can preclude important and holy opportunities that manifest themselves in the other right before our eyes. On the one hand, it is easy to love our neighbor (commanded by the Torah only once),

---
[367] Midrash Shemot Rabbah, 31:15.

but it is very hard to love a stranger (commanded by the Torah 36 times).[368] We must still work to cultivate our local relationships, but it is the foreign and often distant relationships that expose our true character. The local determines our fate, the distant our destiny. The parochial evokes nostalgic contact, while the less familiar inspires the dream. The Torah is adamant that we must go beyond the local and familiar and enter relationships of giving and healing beyond our four walls.

As Rabbi Jonathan Sacks explains, neither tribalism nor universalism alone works:

> Tribalism denies rights to the outsider. Universalism grants rights if and only if the outsider converts. Tribalism turns the concept of a chosen people into that of a master race. Universalism turns the truth of a single culture into the measure of all humanity. The results are often tragic, and always an affront to human dignity.[369]

In tribalism, we retreat to the familiar, and in universalism we try to bring others into our expanding tribe. An alternative is a merging of the two—to love and cherish our local uniqueness but also to value and engage with the diverse peoples and ideas that a global approach introduces to us. We should insist that tribalism "borrow" from universalism and vice versa.

As we learn in the Book of Job, we can experience the closeness of a friend who sits with us in a time of loss, even when the friend's feelings are articulated in words of rebuke and challenge, even when the friend gives us advice that we don't want to hear about achieving a closeness to God in a lonely and dark world. And in that world, alongside the stretch of a global community, we can find warmth within locality. We must strive to use our attempts to achieve a closeness with God to make the world a smaller, more familial place; we are bidden to embrace the lonely and the isolated, just as the Torah commands. When I walk in complex or dangerous environments, I remind myself of the presence of the Divine, and particularly its compassionate and loving elements, walking with me. We can gain the necessary courage to tread in new and sometimes dark places if we carry the lights of spiritual intimacy with us. Those lights are not only from God but from local relationships that we know are supporting us as we enter into unfamiliar territory and strive to make a difference.

---

[368] The commandment to love a stranger, or *ger*, technically concerns itself with a convert to Judaism. Nevertheless, the same mitzvah to love the *ger* applies, of course, to all strangers, i.e., individuals and communities we do not necessarily know and with whom we do not otherwise associate.

[369] Rabbi Jonathon Sacks, *A Letter in the Scroll* (New York: The Free Press, 2004), 93.

We must be spiritually prepared to interact with each other on both the local and global levels. That means that while we must know how to engage in an intimate one-to-one conversation, we must also know how to remember that local one-to-one when we're a "one" interacting with a huge range of additional "ones" who themselves interact with each other and with us as part of a vastly more complex and diverse discourse. The micro-voice is a spiritual voice within our global deliberations. We should never forget the individual when we consider the system. But the additional consideration of the whole and of its many parts should lead to active participation in the work of that whole and the meaning-making of its parts. It is a necessary spiritual practice to go from the proverbial balcony to the dance floor. We simultaneously shift from observing to interacting and back again.

Social media hits us with a flood of information (at least some of which is likely true), emotion (or a reasonable facsimile thereof), and encounter (of at least a two-dimensional kind) while also leaving us empty of concrete relationships. Personal encounters, on the other hand, form strong bonds but cannot fully provide us with the perspective to appreciate the bigger reality. The local and the global inform one another. We are spiritually in both places at once. The individual narrative and global trends are intertwined. The local rootedness of our individual communities sustains us, while our interaction with those far away drives us forward on many levels.

Achieving a healthy balance between the near and the far requires both reverence for the vastness of the ecosystem surrounding us and humility flowing from our awareness of its complexity. We must feel simultaneously empowered to engage and yet remain aware of our limitations. Our community leadership must empower this courage and model this humility. There are individual limits that we must all learn for ourselves but also collective limits which our communal leadership must help us respect and uphold.

There is one *midrash* in particular that has inspired how I think of my own local/global spiritual practice:

> God gathered the dust [of the first human] from the four corners of the world ... Why from the four corners of the earth? So that if one comes from the east to the west and arrives at the end of their life as they near departing from the world, it will not be said to them, "This land is not the dust of your body, it's of mine. Go back to where you were created." Rather, every place that a person walks, from there they were created and from there they will return.[370]

---

[370] Yalkut Shimoni, Genesis 1:13.

In the 21st century, perhaps more than ever before, we belong everywhere ("every place that a person walks, from there she was created"). We are all made up of the same stuff and share equal dignity. On the other hand, each of us has our own uniqueness marked by the disparate sources of our respective personal makeups and individual relationships. I think of my particularism informed by my work and deep local relationships when I venture beyond my local borders (physically or virtually). Too often, highly interconnected individuals dismiss the value of local presence. And too often, individuals remain too locally rooted and become stagnant in a small sphere of ideas. The above *midrash* teaches us that there is a cost to us all when we don't dance between both. We are committed beyond one sphere as that is what our age enables and therefore requires of us. As we grow as individuals and train the next generation, we must commit ourselves to love our unique colors while also blending into the earth-tone universal terrain.

Supporting Israel, helping the Jewish poor, funding Jewish day schools; there are an infinite number of Jewish concerns and needs today, some of which can't be viewed as anything but local, while others bridge the gap between local and more global. How can one justify giving time to even broader, universalistic, and not just Jewish, social justice issues?

Rabbi Abraham Isaac HaCohen Kook, the first Ashkenazic Chief Rabbi of pre-state Israel, wrote:

> There are some righteous individuals who are very great and powerful, who cannot limit themselves to *Keneset Yisrael* (the Jewish community) alone, and they are always concerned for the good of the entire world. . . . These *tzaddikim* (righteous people) cannot be nationalists in the external sense of the term because they cannot stand any hatred, or iniquity, or limitation of good and mercy, and they are good to all, as the attributes of the Holy Blessed One, for God is good to all. God's compassion is over all of God's works.[371]

There are some who will mostly give their holy energy to their family, and others who will prioritize building the Jewish community and Israel with all of their might. These are wonderful and necessary endeavors. But Rav Kook, as a pluralist very attuned to the diversity and complexity of souls, taught that there are others who cannot remain parochial but need to go out beyond the Jewish community and that these are righteous individuals.

---

[371] Orot HaKodesh 3:349.

Sadly, I have met too many Jewish social justice leaders who feel marginalized and think of themselves as "bad Jews." The opposite is true! Those dedicating themselves to supporting the poor, sick, beaten, and alienated are model Jews! Abraham was "chosen" precisely because he was committed to *"tzedakah u'mishpat"* (pursuing righteousness and justice).

Lurianic *kabbalah* teaches that our role in this world is to find hidden sparks, to liberate them from their evil *kelipot* (shells), and to elevate them. Social justice activists who go out to support the most vulnerable are doing just this.

Rabbi Joseph Soloveitchik wrote:

> There is nothing so physically and spiritually destructive as diverting one's attention from this world. And, by contrast, how courageous is *halakhic* man who does not flee from this world, who does not seek to escape to some pure, supernal realm.[372]

Rabbi Elchanan Wasserman, one of the most prominent 20th-century pre-World War II Lithuanian rabbis, similarly wrote:

> For "among two hundred is to be found a hundred," [a common rabbinic idiom], meaning that in all *mitzvot* between humans and their fellow there is also a component between humans and God. Why then should they be lessened by being between humans and their fellow? And it is for this reason that the Rosh[373] saw mitzvot between humans and their fellow as being weightier, for they contain both elements.[374]

As we can discern from the above passage, to be religious is to emulate the compassionate ways of God. Thus, this is the most fundamental principle that underlies all of Torah study and that shows us that to engage in social justice activities is to heed the divine call:

> Rabbi Elazar quoted this verse: "He has told you, O man, what is good, and what the Lord requires of you: 'Only to do justice (literally, "to do *mishpat*"), to love goodness (*chesed*), and to

---

[372] Rabbi Joseph B. Soloveitchik, *Halakhic Man* (Philadelphia: Jewish Publication Society of America, 1991), 41.
[373] The Rosh, Rabbi Asher ben Yechiel, was a 13th-14th-century talmudist. Rosh is the Hebrew acronym for Rabeinu (our Rabbi) Asher.
[374] Rabbi Elchanan Wasserman, *Kovetz Maamarim*, ed. R. Eliezer Simchah Wasserman (Jerusalem: Yeshivat Ohr Elchanan, 1963), 42-43.

walk modestly with your God.'[375] What does this verse imply? "To do justice" means to act in accordance with the principles of justice. "To love goodness" means to let your actions be guided by principles of loving-kindness. "To walk modestly with your God" means to assist needy families at their funerals and weddings [by giving humbly, in private].[376]

The quest for a more just world is not relegated merely to interpersonal ethics and happenstance encounters. Rather, a life-affirming, dignity-affirming theology should be applied to all of the ways and venues in which we relate to society (government, the workplace, community, etc.). While Jews have a unique and holy mission in the world, we dare not look down upon gentiles or other faith groups in our pursuit of universal justice. Indeed, we must come out of our isolation, our false sense of being at the center, and emerge in a faith-rooted manner that is transformative for us, as well as for populations who experience oppression and injustice. To be sure, there are texts from Jewish tradition that imply that we have a higher obligation to Jews than to gentiles.[377] Yet there are also texts that instruct that we are equally obligated to all in their time of need.[378]

Nachmanides teaches that "We are commanded to save the lives of non-Jews and to save them from harm, that if they were drowning in a river or a stone fell upon them, that we must use all of our strength and be burdened with saving them, and if they were sick, we engage to heal them."[379]

As the *Mishnaic* sage Hillel HaZakein (Hillel the Elder) says, we must live the truth of the tension inherent in my need to advocate for myself and my responsibility to recognize that I cannot work only for my own interests.[380] And in contemporary times, Rabbi Yitz Greenberg writes: "Tzedakah means taking responsibility for life. One shares one's own possessions in order to take responsibility for the needs of others because life is indivisible. My life cannot be whole while others' lives are not."

We must take care of our Jewish family. Who else will do it? But we must also remember that as Jews, we are not only a tribal family but a global community as well. We are called to be an *Am Kadosh* (a holy nation) on so many levels, to bring repair to the self, to the home, to the community, to humanity, and to all the world.

---

[375] Micah 6:8.
[376] BT Sukkah 59b.
[377] BT Bava Metzia 71a.
[378] BT Gittin 61a.
[379] Sefer Hamitzvot, mitzvah 16.
[380] Pirkei Avot 1:14.

Debate 22.

Pro-Choice vs. Pro-Life

Try as we might to resolve the polarizing issue of abortion to everyone's satisfaction, whatever conclusion we reach will leave no one happy. We can't do any better than to see if we can find an approach that at least many people can see as consistent with their way of thinking. The issue is extremely complex, personal, and perhaps painful. The goal here is also not meant to pass judgment on anyone's leaning regarding a very volatile political issue in American society. Rather, I'd like to take the effort to launch a serious conversation about abortion rights in America. Rarely does the Torah merely affirm one side of a contemporary issue that is debated not only as a matter of public policy but also frequently as a partisan question. While there may be a dominant leaning, there are centuries of diverse Jewish positions that need to be considered when trying to articulate a Jewish approach to a debate that plays out in the clash among diverse sets of values and between opposing parties challenging each other in the American judicial system.

In the case of abortion, our subject at hand, Jewish law, which is the source of so much contemporary Jewish perspective, leans toward the modern pro-choice position, but also provides many powerful arguments for the pro-life perspective as well. (I have used the terms that each side uses for itself, for fair balance.)

The conversation begins in the Bible: If one kills a fetus, they are not charged with murder. Rather, feticide is a considered an act remediable by money damages.[381] Such a rule implies that a fetus is not yet a life per se, even it carries the potential for life. Yet, because the fact that a fetus is not granted the same legal value as a living child does not mean that the fetus lacks weighty significance. In the first forty days following conception, the fetus is considered by the Talmudic sages to merely be water, and as "the thigh of its mother."[382] After forty days, however, the fetus is described as a fully potential life which becomes an actual life upon birth.

At birth, of course, there is a full status change. "A child one day old... inherits and transmits; he who kills him is guilty of murder, and he counts to his father, to his mother and to all his relatives as a fully grown person."[383] *Halachic* authorities have declared that many abortions are forbidden by Jewish law, while disagreeing on the stage of pregnancy at which the procedure becomes forbidden. The value of potential life is so cherished that even the needless spilling of semen is forbidden.[384] (Even that rule, though, might mean less than it appears to on the question of the

---

[381] Exodus 21.
[382] Babylonian Talmud Yevamot 69b; Bava Kama 78b.
[383] BT Niddah 5:3.
[384] BT Niddah 13a-b.

need to protect potential life; considerable rabbinic authority supports the idea that sex has important positive non-procreative purposes.[385]) A fetus is viewed as a holy gift, a precious potential for life. Some Jewish legal authorities even view a fetus as life, although not a full life of equal value to a human post-birth.

It's no surprise, given the different ways to view the distinctions between potential life and actualized life, that there are various Jewish views regarding when and in which situations an abortion can be permitted.

The primary concern that Jewish law has with pro-life thinking is the way in which proponents often equate the value of the mother's life with the value of the fetus' life. The Catholic pro-life position that life starts at conception is generally viewed as foreign to Jewish thought.[386] Jewish law is unequivocal that saving the mother's life trumps that of the fetus:

> If a woman is in hard travail, one cuts up the child in her womb and brings it forth member by member, because her life comes before that of [the child]. But if the greater part has proceeded forth, one may not touch it, for one may not set aside one person's life for that of another.[387]

The Talmud comments further on the above:

> Rabbi Huna states: A minor who is pursuing another to kill him may be killed. Thus, he rules that a pursuer does not need warning [that he is committing a crime] and it makes no difference whether the person is an adult or a child. Rabbi Hisda asked Rabbi Huna: "If the fetus sticks out its head, one does not touch it since one does not substitute one life for another." Why? Is it not a pursuer? That case is different, since from heaven it is pursuing her.[388]

Maimonides codifies this rule one way, and Rashi another. Maimonides writes:

---

[385] R. Dov Linzer, "Two Approaches to Marital Sex," YCT Library, December 4, 2009, https://library.yctorah.org/2009/12/two-approaches-to-marital-sex/.
[386] Putting it another way, *halachah* is neither purely pro-life nor purely pro-choice. There are many cases when abortion is called for, even mandated, according to Jewish law. One such example is reducing the number of fetuses in a multiple pregnancy if one or more are endangering the survival of the others.
[387] BT Ohalot 6:7. The above means of abortion seems harsh by today's standards, but of course must be viewed through the lens of science and technology of that time.
[388] BT Sanhedrin 72b.

> This, indeed, is one of the negative mitzvot—not to take pity on the life of a rodef. On this basis, our Sages ruled that when complications arise and a pregnant woman cannot give birth, it is permitted to abort the fetus in her womb, whether with a knife or with drugs. For the fetus is considered a rodef of its mother. If the head of the fetus emerges, it should not be touched, because one life should not be sacrificed for another. Although the mother may die, this is the nature of the world.[389]

Maimonides is teaching here that a fetus is indeed a person, and abortion is murder, and is indeed only permitted to save the life of the mother. Rashi completely disagrees. While commenting on the Talmud above, he explains the rule this way:

> "It sticks out its head." The Talmud is speaking about a woman who is having difficulty giving birth and is in danger. The beginning section recounts that the midwife should stick in her hand, cut and remove the fetus limb by limb, since all the time that the fetus has not entered the air of the world, it is not alive, and may be killed to save the life of the mother; but once its head is out, one cannot touch it to kill it, since it is already born, and one may not choose one life over another.[390]

Most commentaries adopt Rashi's view and a minority accepts Maimonides'. So, abortion to save the life of the mother is always permitted and the life of the mother is more precious than the life of the fetus. On the other hand, abortion for reasons less than the physical or mental health of the mother is not at all favored by the Jewish tradition and considered murder by Maimonides. If one were to view the debate according to Jewish law and values, the infinite dignity of the mother always exceeds the value of the fetus in extreme situations, and abortion for financial comfort is never considered proper.

But there is a larger gray area in between. Many women suffer during pregnancy (physically and emotionally), and Jewish law demands that rabbinic authorities must respond emphatically and compassionately (within the boundaries of Jewish law) to address individual cases of distress. This issue is extremely sensitive and case-specific. Anyone who wishes to conform their conduct to *halachah* who is struggling with a particular case should approach a Jewish legal authority to talk through their particular issue.

---

[389] Rambam, *Mishneh Torah*, Murderer and the Preservation of Life 1:9, trans. Eliyahu Touger, Moznaim Publishing.
[390] Rashi's commentary on BT Sanhedrin 72b.

Considered from a utilitarian perspective we might inquire whether the fetus suffers. The question is not about the dignity of a human being but about the sentience of a being that can suffer.

It is also worth noting that one might make a different choice for oneself than for society. One might say I will be pro-life in my personal practice and not have an abortion but pro-choice in one's advocacy wanting women to have the access and choice. The flip side seems hypocritical though: choosing to have an abortion but advocating for a pro-life position denying other women of that same access. Couples considering marriage should consider getting tested for Jewish genetic diseases in order to find out if they are a likely match for a disease. This may be a factor in whether they should marry. Judaism does not accept eugenics that we should abort based upon imperfections in a child that do not produce the "perfect" child and so a couple has to decide if they're willing to go into a relationship with some higher risks.

Of course, as Americans we are guided in our decision-making not only by *halachah* but also by the terms of the secular laws that bind us. With the overturning of *Roe v. Wade* via *Dobbs v. Jackson Women's Health Org* in 2022, states have much more power than before to limit women's abortion access. This was not seen as a straightforward victory by most segments of the Jewish community.

In only one example of a Jewish organization asking the Court to uphold *Roe*, the National Council of Jewish Women had asked its supporters to sign a pledge which reads, in part, "I support abortion access and am outraged by the Supreme Court's decision to hear Dobbs v. Jackson Women's Health Organization.... Consistent with the Jewish value of *kavod ha'briot*, or respect and dignity for all human beings, I believe that everyone deserves access to the abortion care they need."[391]

Is Judaism pro-life? It's complicated, but, yes. Is Judaism pro-choice? When put in different terms, i.e., are there situations when abortion is permissible, even mandated? The answer to this is yes as well. Whichever side of the equation of pro-choice vs. pro-life one comes down on, one must be mindful of the overarching teaching and emphasis of the Talmud here, that both life itself and quality of life are paramount. At the same time, we should recognize that when we rely on our Jewish values to support our position on the question of abortion availability, we risk imposing our religious mores on other Jews and on still others who are not even Jewish.

---

[391] National Council of Jewish Women, Dobbs vs Jackson pledge, https://web.archive.org/web/20220126202536/https://www.ncjw.org/act/action/ncjw-pledge-dobbs-vs-jackson/.

Debate 23.

Gun Rights vs. Gun Control

The debate about gun rights vs. gun control is polarizing. The issue is becoming increasingly politicized. The conservative end is afraid they will lose their right to protect themselves. The liberal end is afraid of mass shootings and public gun violence. As is so often the case with a broad range of issues, Jewish sources support both sides of this debate. It is not hard to base a gun rights case on Jewish sources. After all, the Torah clearly values self-defense:

> If the thief is seized while tunneling, [i.e., under a wall for housebreaking] and he is beaten to death, there is no bloodguilt in his case.[392]

The Talmud teaches:

> What is the reason for this *halakha* concerning a burglar who breaks into a house? He explains: There is a presumption that a person does not restrain himself when faced with losing his money, and therefore this burglar must have said to himself: If I go in and the owner sees me, he will rise against me and not allow me to steal from him, and if he rises against me, I will kill him. And the Torah stated a principle: If someone comes to kill you, rise and kill him first.[393]

By any interpretation of the Torah, Jewish tradition (at least the biblical element) clearly allows for, and even requires, war at times. This is well summed up by the most famous passage in Ecclesiastes:

> A season is set for everything, a time for every experience under heaven: .... A time for loving and a time for hating; A time for war and a time for peace.[394]

---

[392] Exodus 22:1.
[393] Sanhedrin 72a. This principal is known as the law of a *rodeif*, literally meaning "pursuer." It is grounded in another principal which states that one's own life is as precious of that of another. While the above quoted verse is the source of the law of *rodeif*, it has many other applications as well. During the Holocaust, for example, if a baby's consistent cries would divulge the location of a family in hiding, it was ruled that it would be permitted to kill the baby to save the lives of the other family members. In addition, if, during a multiple pregnancy it is determined that a fetus will invariably hurt the chances of viability of the other fetuses, some *halachic* decisors have ruled that the fetus may be aborted to save the lives, even potential lives, of the other fetuses.
[394] Ecclesiastes 3:1-8.

This passage reflects a sensibility requiring us to save the lives of others, and that starts with ourselves.

Perhaps the most radical text[395] supporting, and even glorifying, the use of weapons, is a *midrash* in which God is revealed as adorned with weapons:

> "The Lord, the Warrior—Lord is [God's] name!."[396] R. Yehudah says: This is a verse "rich in many places." It teaches that the Holy One be blessed revealed God's self to [the Israelites] with all kinds of weapons. God revealed God's self to them as a warrior girded with a sword, viz.[397] "Gird Your sword upon Your thigh, O Hero. God revealed God's self to them as a rider, viz."[398] "And God mounted a cherub and flew. . . ."[399]

Then again, it is equally not difficult to make the opposite argument—that is, the case in favor of gun control—based on Jewish sources. The Torah requires that we take special precautions to ensure that our property can never cause harm to another:

> When you build a new house, you shall make a parapet for your roof, so that you do not bring bloodguilt on your house if anyone should fall from it.[400]

In our days, we can relate to this in regard to a homeowner's duty to put up a pool fence lest someone who can't swim accidentally falls in. The Talmud further elucidates:

> Rabbi Natan says: From where is it derived that one may not raise a vicious dog in his house, and that one may not set up an unstable ladder in his house? As it is stated: "You shall not bring blood into your house" (Deuteronomy 22:8), which means that one may not allow a hazardous situation to remain in his house.[401]

---

[395] There's a real difference between soldiers' weapons and homeowners' weapons, as well as between swords and guns, particularly assault weapons, creating a bit of a challenge for a reading of the warrior-God image as supporting gun rights.
[396] Exodus 15:3, modified from JPS 1985 for gender neutrality.
[397] Psalms 45:4.
[398] Psalms 18:11.
[399] Mekhilta d'Rabbi Yishmael 15:3:1.
[400] Deuteronomy 22:8.
[401] Bava Kamma 46a.

Protecting ourselves and others from harmful objects is codified in Jewish law. On one hand, then, gun ownership could be viewed as halachically permissible protection. But at the same time, isn't a gun, and even more so an unsecured gun, the quintessential dangerous item?

> Likewise, one has a positive duty to remove and guard oneself of any life-threatening obstacle, as it is said "beware and guard your soul." If one did not remove said obstacles, one has cancelled a positive commandment and transgressed "do not bring bloodguilt."[402]

The necessary precautions create obligations not only for a gun owner, but also for a society and a business collective on selling weapons:

> And furthermore, it is taught in a baraita:[403] One may not sell weapons to gentiles or the auxiliary equipment of weapons, and one may not sharpen weapons for them.[404]

Of course, this emerges not as a general anti-gentile teaching, God forbid, but rather within a particular historical context where it was taken for granted that gentiles would oppress Jews. Rashi explains that the reason for these prohibitions is to avoid having a gentile use a weapon to harm a Jew. In our day, this can be read not as an argument in favor of applying social group-based distinctions in deciding who may purchase weapons, but rather as pointing out the sense it makes to determine whether someone has an issue in their personal history that would disqualify them from being able to buy a gun.

We read in the Talmud that Rabbi Eliezer finds artistic, non-instrumental value in weapons, while the rabbis with whom he debates draw upon one of the most famous pacifist utopian prophetic teachings about how weapons are disgusting and are ultimately to be abolished. Thus, in discussing the laws of carrying in a public domain on Shabbat, the rabbis appear to really be philosophizing on how to define and categorize a weapon:

> A person may neither go out on Shabbat with a sword, nor with a bow, nor with a shield... nor with a spear. And if they

---

[402] Shulchan Aruch, Choshen Mishpat 427:8, Sefaria Community Translation. Also see Mishneh Torah, Murderer and the Preservation of Life 11:4.
[403] A *baraita* is similar to a *mishnah*, authored by the Talmudic sages.
[404] BT Avodah Zarah 15b. Also see Mishneh Torah, Murderer and the Preservation of Life 12:14. On the other hand, see Shulchan Aruch, Yoreh De'ah 151:6.

unwittingly went out with one of these weapons to the public domain, they are liable to bring a sin-offering.[405] Rabbi Eliezer says: These weapons are ornaments for them; just as a person is permitted to go out into the public domain with other ornaments, they are permitted to go out with weapons. And the Rabbis say: They are nothing other than reprehensible and, in the future, they will be eliminated, as it is written:[406] "And they shall beat their swords into plowshares and their spears into pruning hooks; nation will not raise sword against nation, neither will they learn war anymore."[407]

In an Israeli context, Chief Rabbi Shlomo Goren wrote about how a weapon is a sacred religious object:

> Regarding Shabbat observance, a firearm is no different than a Kiddush cup, and a holster is no different than a decorative spread used to cover the challah loaves. . . . . a firearm is something that is needed for Shabbat observance, because it is intended for security, enabling a Jew to celebrate the Shabbat in peace. Even though shooting a gun is a form of igniting fire, something normally prohibited on Shabbat, in situations where life is imperiled, shooting a gun is a mitzvah. . . . .[408]

This is a rather extreme approach that treats a weapon as a religious item. Rabbi Yehoshua Neuwirth comes to a similar conclusion, but with a less glorifying approach:

> A firearm is indeed categorized as *muktzeh*[409] since firing (igniting fire) is prohibited on Shabbat. Nonetheless, carrying a firearm on Shabbat is allowed[410] since it has a definite value as a deterrent—discouraging enemies from attacking Jews on Shabbat. Therefore, it is needed for the observance of Shabbat. Furthermore, since carrying a firearm is a deterrent, there is

---

[405] A sin offering is the punishment for inadvertently carrying a weapon in a public domain on Shabbat.
[406] Isaiah 2:4.
[407] BT Shabbat 63a.
[408] *Mashiv Milchama*. It is important to note that Rabbi Goren was referring specifically to soldiers on guard or reserve duty, which requires them to carry a firearm for protection and to fend off enemy gunfire, and even retaliate if absolutely necessary.
[409] *Muktzeh* refers to items which are forbidden to move on Shabbat for various reasons.
[410] Like Rabbi Goren, Rabbi Neuwirth is referring specifically to those on active duty on Shabbat.

no need for immediate danger in order to carry one. When the
enemies of the Jews know that we are ready to defend ourselves,
mobs are less likely to rise up against us.[411]

On the other hand, a story is told about Rabbi Yisrael Meir HaKohen, known as the Chofetz Chayim (1838-1933), that paints a very different picture of the role of a weapon:

> In 1913, Israel Medintz was a young boy attending the Yeshiva of Raden, which had been established by the Chafetz Chayim. One day young Israel and two friends went for a walk in the woods near the yeshiva. They carried sticks in their hands. They had found the sticks during their walk. Then the Chafetz Chayim himself passed the boys. He greeted them in a friendly manner and stopped to talk to them. "*Kinder,*" he said, "never walk with a stick in your hand. You might be provoked by someone and, before thinking, use the stick to hit or beat someone. A Jew should never carry a stick. Without a stick in the hand, physical violence will not be so easy."[412]

Part of that debate is informed by cultural context and circumstances. The Chafetz Chayim comes from the shtetl-Jew mentality whereas Rav Goren is writing in a time of emboldened Jewish activism and protecting the land of Israel.

In struggling to resolve this cross-generational debate, we learn a powerful message from the processes used to build the *Beit Hamikdash* (the Holy Temple in Jerusalem):

> "Do not build them hewn:"[413] In it [the altar] you may not build them hewn, but you may build them hewn in the sanctuary and in the holy of holies... How, then, am I to understand [the verse] "And hammers, chisels, or any iron tools were not heard in the Temple when it was being built"?[414] In the Temple they were not heard, but outside [where they were hewn] they were heard.

---

[411] *Shmirat Shabbat K'Hilchatah.*
[412] Lawrence J. Epstein, *A Treasury of Jewish Anecdotes* (Northvale, New Jersey: J. Aronson, 1989) 104. This anecdote was supplied by Bernard Medintz.
[413] Exodus 20:22.
[414] I Kings 6:7.

"For if you lift your sword upon it:" R. Shimon b. Elazar was wont to say[415] "Of whole *(sheleimot)* stones shall you build the altar of the Lord"—stones which represent peace (shalom). Now does this not follow a fortiori: If the stones of the altar, which do not see or hear or speak—because they repose peace between Israel and their Father in heaven, the Holy One be Blessed says: "Do not lift iron upon them," then one who reposes peace between a man and his wife, between one city and another, between one nation and another, between one government and another, between one family and another—how much more so will they not meet with adversity![416]

This is relevant to our synagogues today too. The *Shulchan Aruch* (Code of Jewish Law) rules that weapons should not be brought into the synagogue: "Some forbid entering with a long knife or with its blade uncovered."[417] The Tur explains:

"A long knife." Since prayer lengthens one's days, and a knife shortens. And we rule that, here, it implies that with regard to a knife that is not long, there is no concern that the knife will shorten one's days....[418]

For survival, Rabbi Shlomo Zalman Auerbach permits carrying weapons on Shabbat in order to intimidate potential perpetrators:

And nevertheless, it's reasonable to say that it is permitted to carry a rifle or pistol (on Shabbat) in order to intimidate onlookers, for it's reasonable to say that at a time that is not wartime, most of a rifle's function is to intimidate/deter, and because of this intimidation, it's considered necessary.... since it is designated to intimidate... And even the bullets that are in it, since they are intimidating as well, they are considered to be part of the gun.[419]

But aside from questions of legal formalism and of religious principle and law, we can, and perhaps must, ask utilitarian, or consequentialist questions. Do guns

---

[415] Deuteronomy 27:6.
[416] Mekhilta d'Rabbi Yishmael 20:22:2.
[417] Shulchan Aruch, Orach Chayim 151:6, Sefaria Community Translation.
[418] Turei Zahav on Shulchan Aruch, Orach Chayim 151:2.
[419] Shulchan Shlomo, Orach Chayim 108:16.

work? Do they make us safer? After all, it is a mitzvah from the Torah to guard our health and wellbeing: *"V'nishmartem me'od l'nafshoteichem"*—"For your own sake, therefore, be most careful—since you saw no shape when the Lord your God spoke to you at Horeb out of the fire."[420] Interestingly enough, this is the only time that the Torah uses the word *me'od* (very) in a prescriptive, halachic matter. That gives us a sense of how important guarding our health is. So, does gun ownership work? Are we, and our families, safer today with guns in our homes? Does this biblical imperative support gun ownership?

In America today, although some professed gun control opponents would countenance a certain amount of regulation, some want no restrictions on gun purchases.[421] On the other side, many people who champion gun control nonetheless avoid advocating for the abolishing of all guns. Rather, many people call for what they call "sensible gun laws" to reduce gun violence. This includes measures like background checks, safety locks, and bans on semi-automatic weapons. Gun rights would still be intact, as per the Second Amendment, but measures to reduce mass shootings would be put in place. And yet, in 2022 the United States saw 647 mass shootings and 20,200 gun deaths in total.[422]

But based on a more comprehensive definition of mass shootings, as of 2017 there had been, in America, 2,128 mass shootings since 2013, about one per day.[423] In addition, much gun violence occurs outside the scope of mass shootings, as we can see from data that shows nearly 40,000 deaths being linked to gun-related injuries in one year—2017—alone.[424]

Guns have had a brutal legacy in America, even prior to an era that seems filled with consistent mass shootings. Consider how guns were used to maintain the institution of slavery and how the Ku Klux Klan and other national terrorist groups used guns to create a culture of terror. On the other hand, a gun rights advocate would point out that guns have maintained the constitutional commitment to liberty and protection of the individual from the tyranny of the government. And the police use of guns, they might argue, has not been about racial injustice but about societal order.

---

[420] Deuteronomy 4:15. Also see Deuteronomy 4:9: "But take utmost care and watch yourselves scrupulously, so that you do not forget the things that you saw with your own eyes and so that they do not fade from your mind as long as you live. And make them known to your children and to your children's children."

[421] The research discussed here—https://www.pewresearch.org/social-trends/2017/06/22/views-on-gun-policy/—suggests that it's hard to say that there's a gun control "side" and a gun rights "side," with one being extreme and one being moderate.

[422] Gun Violence Archive, last accessed 2023, https://www.gunviolencearchive.org.

[423] Graham Kates: "Report: U.S. averages nearly one mass shooting per day so far in 2017" (*CBS News*, October 3, 2017).

[424] John Gramlich: "What the data says about gun deaths in the U.S." (Pew Research Center, 2022).

The Talmudic rabbis, on both sides, can be seen as eschewing extremism. Yes, a Torah case could be made in either direction with nuance, but only a poor case could be made for the glorification of guns or for the neglect of societies and communities and the failure to protect the vulnerable from unchecked mass gun violence.

A brief review of American history can help us contextualize where we currently stand in connection with gun rights and unjustified violence connected to guns. The Second Amendment was added to the United States Constitution on December 15, 1791, when it, along with the rest of the first ten amendments to the Constitution ("The Bill of Rights") was ratified. It reads: "A well-regulated Militia, being necessary to the security of a free State, the right of the people to keep and bear Arms, shall not be infringed." But fast forward about 150 years (June 26, 1934), and we receive our first piece of federal gun control legislation with FDR's "New Deal for Crime." Then, in 1938, we see the passage of The Federal Firearms Act (FFA) requiring a federal firearms license, which was repealed and replaced in 1968 by the Gun Control Act (GCA), which in many ways broadened the scope of federal gun control, and which was enacted on the heels of the assassinations of JFK, RFK, and MLK. However, pushback came once the pro-gun rights lobby gained power. In 1986, Congress passed the Firearm Owners Protection Act to limit restrictions on gun owners and loosen regulations. But a response came in 1993 with the Brady Handgun Violence Protection Act[425] signed by President Bill Clinton. An assault weapons ban (contained in the "Violent Crime Control and Law Enforcement Act") signed by Clinton in 1994 lasted until 2004. Many attempts to renew this ban have since failed. It is a priority for President Biden now. In 2005, President George W. Bush signed the Protection of Lawful Commerce in Arms Act to protect gun manufacturers. Perhaps the biggest blow to the gun control movement came in 2008 with the Supreme Court's decision, in *District of Columbia v. Heller*, which held that a handgun ban and the trigger-lock requirement violate the Second Amendment, at least in certain contexts.

The debate about the use and sale of guns plays out, of course, well beyond the American context. In Israel, for example, rabbinic authorities have taken different positions regarding the halachic appropriateness of an international arms industry. Some argue that because of the danger inherent in military weaponry, Israel should avoid engaging in the international arms trade, absent a need for such sales to enable arms to be used in ethical war-making (so-called, of course, by those who do not see the term as oxymoronic) or to protect Jews. Others have

---

[425] Named after James Brady, the White House press secretary who was permanently disabled after being shot during an attempt to assassinate President Ronald Reagan.

attempted to justify the export of Israeli military goods as a way of supporting the defense of the State of Israel.[426]

Rather than celebrate machismo, military might, physical strength, and the ability to defeat opposition physically, we might follow a humbler path offered by the military theorist Lao Tzu:

> Good weapons are instruments of fear; all creatures hate them.
> Therefore followers of the Tao never used them.
> The wise man prefers the left.
> The man of war prefers the right.
>
> Weapons are instruments of fear; they are not a wise man's tools.
> He uses them only when he has no choice.
> Peace and quiet are dear to his heart.
> And victory no cause for rejoicing.
> If you rejoice in victory, then you delight in killing;
> If you delight in killing, you cannot fulfill yourself.
>
> On happy occasions precedence is given to the left,
> On sad occasions to the right.
>
> In the army the general stands on the left,
>
> The commander-in-chief on the right.
> This means that war is conducted like a funeral.
> When many people are being killed,
> They should be mourned in heartfelt sorrow.
> That is why a victory must be observed like a funeral.[427]

In the most charitable interpretation, our debate is one rooted in fear. The one who protects weapons is fearful for their own survival. This is understandable. The one who regulates weapons is fearful for another's survival. This is understandable as well. Perhaps the only way to reach some consensus on this debate is not through the perfection of legislation but by transforming our culture, so that ultimately, we live in a society that fosters maximal interpersonal trust. The Jewish people, with our millennia of trauma (along with so many more positive

---

[426] Shlomo M. Brody, "The Halacha of Selling Arms," *Jewish Ideas Daily*, February 5, 2013, http://www.jewishideasdaily.com/5893/features/the-halakhah-of-selling-arms/.

[427] Lao Tzu, *Tao Te Jing*. Translation by Gia-fu Feng and Jane English. (New York: Vintage Books, 2011), #31.

historical truths) informing us, should understandably have sympathy for arguments of self-determination and self-defense. Yet, our people should also have a deep appreciation for removing barriers to health, life preservation, and justice. We must throw off cynicism about the human condition (a characteristic that is often perceived on the far-right) and naivete (a trait frequently ascribed to the far-left). We are neither in a total state of violent chaos nor are we approaching a non-violent utopia in which we can easily anticipate that tomorrow the wolf will lie with the lamb.[428] We can yearn for the messianic era where we will beat our swords into plowshares and our spears into pruning hooks,[429] but we have a long way still to go. May we continue to debate to find the appropriate balance in each society, in each era, but to maximize safety by whatever means, even as we respectfully debate.

While we debate, we must act prudently to reduce gun violence through sensible measures such as restricting machine guns and semi-automatic weapons, requiring background checks, and safety precautions like trigger locks. While more innocent people (family friends, neighbors, strangers) are killed by gun owners in the home than perpetrators killed, we must question the efficacy of the current loose approach to regulating gun use. Just as there are limits on the freedom of speech (most famously that one can't yell "fire" in a theater when there is no fire), so too we must have a healthier notion of liberties that don't lead to extremes such as anti-vaccination, anti-masking, anti-gun control. Lastly, we should identify this not only as a political and religious problem but also as a gender problem. The majority of mass shootings are perpetrated by men.

May we fulfill the prophecy to build a safe, non-violent world where all can thrive.

---

[428] Isaiah 11:6.
[429] Isaiah 2:4.

DEBATE 24.

Capital Punishment vs. Abolishing the Death Penalty

The text of the Torah, read literally, mandates the death penalty as a punishment for specific transgressions. And yet, opposition to the overuse of capital punishment is embedded deep in the Jewish religious psyche and indeed in halachic tradition. The Talmudic rabbis taught that a court that puts others to death too often is a murderous court. How often?

> A sanhedrin that executes once in seven years, is called murderous.
> Rabbi Eliezer b. Azariah Says: once in seventy years.
> Rabbi Tarfon and Rabbi Akiva say: "Had we been members of a sanhedrin, no person would ever be put to death."[430]

But there is a counterargument, of course:

> Rabban Shimon ben Gamaliel remarked: "They would also multiply murderers in Israel."[431]

The Rabbis teach that, based on the value of human life, there are major repercussions for being guilty of taking a life:

> How were the witnesses instilled with fear [not to testify falsely]? Be aware that capital cases are not like monetary cases. In civil cases, one can make monetary restitution and thereby effect his atonement, but in capital cases, he is held responsible for his blood [of the one accused] and the blood of his [potential] descendants until the end of time, for so we find in the case of Kayin, who killed his brother, that it is written [translated literally]: "The bloods of your brother is screaming out to Me."[432] It does not say: "The blood of your brother," rather, "The bloods of your brother," meaning, his blood and the blood of his [potential] descendants.... Therefore man was created alone to teach you that whoever destroys a single life, is considered by Scripture as though he destroyed an entire world; and whoever

---

[430] Mishnah Makkot 1:10, trans. Dr. Joshua Kulp.
[431] Ibid.
[432] Genesis 4:10.

> preserves a single life, is considered by Scripture as though he had preserved an entire world. . . .[433]

And yet, if the rabbis did away with the death penalty as a practical matter, why is it in the Torah in the first place? The rabbis explain (concerning a wayward son):

> Rather, there has never been a stubborn and rebellious son and there will never be one in the future. And why, then, was the passage relating to a stubborn and rebellious son written in the Torah? So that you may expound upon new understandings of the Torah and receive reward for your learning. Rabbi Yonatan says: This is not so, as I saw one. I was once in a place where a stubborn and rebellious son was condemned to death, and I even sat on his grave after he was executed.[434]

Perhaps in our case too we can infer a reason for the inclusion of death penalty references beyond an interest in application of the literal signification of the text. Those references can teach us about the gravitas of crimes worthy of the death penalty. As such, the rabbis can now reinterpret the punishment but always do so knowing that God wants total justice, even though humans aren't necessarily capable of implementing it or even, necessarily, in understanding what it is.

> Does the Divine Law not say, "Eye for eye?" Why not take this literally to mean [putting out] the eye [of the offender]?— Don't think this, since it has been taught: You might think that where he put out his eye, the offender's eye should be put out, or where he cut off his arm, the offender's arm should be cut off, or again where he broke his leg, the offender's leg should be broken. [Not so; for] it is laid down, "He that smites any man. . . "And he that smites a beast . . ." just as in the case of smiting a beast compensation is to be paid, so also in the case of smiting a man compensation is to be paid.[435]

Another explanation is that the death penalty can be imposed by the heavenly court, as it were, even while the earthly judgement must be more lenient:

---

[433] Mishna Sanhedrin 4:5.
[434] BT Sanhedrin 71a.
[435] BT Bava Kama 83b.

> It has been taught: Rabbi Simeon ben Shetah said: May I never see comfort if I did not see a man pursuing his fellow into a ruin, and when I ran after him and saw him, sword in hand with blood dripping from it, and the murdered man writhing, I exclaimed to him: "Wicked man, who slew this man? It is either you or I! But what can I do, since thy blood [i.e., life] does not rest in my hands, for it is written in the Torah, 'At the mouth of two witnesses etc., shall he that is to die be put to death?' May he who knows one's thoughts exact vengeance from him who slew his fellow!" It is related that before they moved from the place a serpent came and bit him [the murderer] so that he died.... From the day the Temple was destroyed, although the Sanhedrin was abolished, the four modes of execution were not abolished:[436] He who is worthy of stoning either falls from the roof, or is trampled to death by a wild beast; he who merits burning either falls into the fire or is bitten by a serpent; he who is worthy of decapitation is either delivered to the [gentile] Government or brigands attack him; he who is worthy of strangulation is either drowned in a river or dies of suffocation....[437]

To be sure, the rabbis did try to find a way around ever directly executing, although it's historically unclear if or how this was actually done:

> He who was flogged and then flogged again [for two transgressions, and then sinned again,] is placed by the court in a cell and fed with barley bread, until his stomach bursts. One who commits murder without witnesses is placed in a cell and [forcibly] fed with bread of adversity and water of affliction.[438]

How can capital punishment be enacted post-Sanhedrin in any event? The Rosh[439] wonders this:

> You surprise me by asking about a capital case. In all of the countries that I have heard of they do not judge capital cases, except here in Spain. When I arrived here, I was most astonished

---

[436] Here the Talmud is advancing the notion referred to above, that if a person is guilty of a crime punishable by death, he will in any case die by similar means.
[437] BT Sanhedrin 37b.
[438] Mishna Sanhedrin 9:5, trans. Dr. Joshua Kulp.
[439] Rabbenu Asher ben Yechiel (1321 CE, Spain).

how they could judge such cases without a Sanhedrin; I was told that this is by permission of the king, and also that the beit din's (Jewish court's) judgment saves lives, since much more blood would be spilled were they [Jews accused of crimes] to be judged by non-Jews. So, I allowed them to continue their custom; but I have never agreed with them about taking life.[440]

Rabbi Moshe Feinstein, author of the multivolume responsa *Igrot Moshe*, wrote a fascinating open letter to Governor Hugh Carey in 1981, in which he dealt with the question about the role of the death penalty in the context of a halachic justice system, such as what the selections from the Talmud and the Rosh discussed above address, and its role in the context of a secular American-style legal system:[441]

> ... The Torah reserves capital punishment for those sins which are very serious such as murder, kidnapping, sexually prohibited relations and idolatry. The perpetrator in these cases is unrestrained and is capable of doing whatever disgusting and cruel acts in the world that are in his heart that he thinks are for his benefit. However, the death penalty is not administered out of hatred to evildoers or fear for the welfare of society, because [the Talmudic Tractate] Bava Metzia (83b) tells us that G-d will punish transgressors.... So on the one hand the purpose of capital punishment is to let people know the severity of these prohibitions so that they will not transgress them. On the other hand, the laws of capital punishment emphasize the importance of each soul and other concerns.[442]

Rav Moshe taught here that while the State of New York certainly has the right, from the perspective of the moral element of the Torah's approach to criminal justice, to execute criminals, the practical outcome of the death penalty will too frequently be unjust.

Even where a death penalty could be upheld, we see that God wants dignity for the executed:

> All that have been stoned must be hanged, says Rabbi Eliezer. But the sages say: None is hanged save the blasphemer and the idolater... How did they hang a man? They put a beam into the

---
[440] Responsa 17:8.
[441] Hugh Carey was the governor of New York from 1975 to 1982.
[442] R. Moshe Feinstein, *Igrot Moshe*, Choshen Mishpat 2:68.

> ground and a piece of wood jutted from it. The two hands of the body were brought together and, in this fashion, [the body] was hanged. Rabbi Yossi says: The beam was made to lean against a wall and one hanged the corpse thereon as the butchers do. And they let it down at once: if it remained there overnight it would transgress a negative command, for it is written, "[Y]ou must not let his corpse remain on the stake overnight, but must bury him the same day. For an impaled body is an affront to God."[443] as if to say: Why was this one hanged? Because he blessed [a euphemism] the Name and the Name of Heaven was found profaned.
>
> Furthermore, every one that allowed his dead to remain overnight transgressed a negative command; but if he had allowed it to remain unburied by reason of honor due to it, to bring for it a coffin and burial clothes, he does not thereby commit a transgression.[444]

And also, imagine if an innocent person was executed. How religiously and morally terrifying; it must be the highest priority to avoid this from taking place, certainly over the wicked being mistakenly saved.

So, as we have seen, the rabbis, while certainly not categorically opposed to capital punishment, saw the death penalty as so extreme a measure that they all but removed it from their system of justice. In contrast, our American system today lacks the highest safeguards to protect the lives of the innocent and, in certain cases, uses capital punishment all too readily.

We do not naïvely believe that everyone on death row is completely innocent of any crime. Yet, too often, people are convicted for crimes they did not commit.

We all agree that a responsible government must have a strong justice system that maintains order and security and that includes appropriate punitive measures. More harmful to our justice system than not catching the guilty, however, is punishing the innocent. Owing to their socio-economic situation or lack of access to legal resources, wrongly convicted people often have no real opportunity to respond to an overwhelming legal system that makes the establishment of innocence difficult. The consequences of this system are not only fundamentally unjust to individuals but also produce racially and otherwise disparate outcomes and therefore skew all sorts of social markers on inappropriate bases. Additionally, it is the taxpayers who are required to pay exorbitant amounts to maintain death rows.

---

[443] Deuteronomy 21:23.
[444] Mishnah Sanhedrin 6:4-5; BT Sanhedrin 46b.

It is time to see the death penalty for what it is: not as justice gone awry, but as a symptom of injustice as status quo. "Deliver them that are drawn unto death."[445] Among the reasons for wrongful convictions, six stand out:

1. **Eyewitness misidentification.** Some of the reasons why eyewitnesses identify the wrong person are not fixable, such as the fact that people are much more inaccurate when they attempt cross-racial identification, but there are many things that police can do when conducting lineups that would decrease false identifications.
2. **False confession.** In one example, four of the five teenagers who became known as the Central Park Five confessed in 1989 to raping and killing a woman in Central Park, but were proven innocent in 2002 through DNA testing—years after being convicted and serving prison time.
3. **Ineffective lawyering.** Defense lawyers mess up, either because they are unskilled and untrained to handle death penalty cases, or because they are so overburdened that it is impossible to do a thorough job on each case.
4. **Police and prosecutorial misconduct.** Sometimes crime labs claim that they have test results when no tests were actually performed, and prosecutors have been known to withhold exculpatory evidence. Unfortunately, enforcement of the rules, which is meant to protect the rights of the accused, is not always effective.
5. **Junk science.** Prosecutors (and, to be sure, lawyers representing private parties as well) rely on scientific methods that do not stand up to rigorous scientific testing. And sometimes, even when appropriate methods are used to develop evidence in capital cases and other criminal matters, those methods are not used properly.
6. **Unreliable testimony.** Witnesses can be unreliable for all sorts of reasons, including the innocent, but real, inability we all have to perceive everything around us with complete accuracy. Even a witness' certainty about a particular perception does not mean that the witness is not mistaken. But beyond innocent, but all too frequent, mistakes in testimony, witnesses' testimony is sometimes skewed by self-interest, such as when a prisoner decides to testify against another prisoner in the hope (and sometimes on the basis of a promise) of favorable treatment from the authorities.

---

[445] Proverbs 24:11, JPS 1917. To be sure, the verse in its context is not actually referring to saving a person on death row, but it is nevertheless apropos here.

How many prisoners are truly innocent? Experts have offered varying percentages in the last decades: Samuel R. Gross and Barbara O'Brien estimated "at least 2.3 percent;"[446] Jon B. Gould and Richard A. Leo put it at 3 to 5 percent;[447] James S. Liebman and his team placed their estimate at 7 percent;[448] and John Roman and his team place their estimate at 5 percent, except for sexual assault, for which the wrongful conviction rate may be as high as 15 percent.[449]

Jewish thinking strongly upholds the principle that the innocent should be spared undue punishment. When God reveals to Abraham his plan to destroy Sodom and Gomorrah (Genesis 18:17-33), Abraham challenges God: "Will you also destroy the righteous with the wicked? If there are fifty righteous people in the city, will you still destroy and not forgive?" When God offers to spare the cities if there are fifty righteous people, Abraham continues to raise the stakes by lowering the number of the righteous, until God decides that if there are even ten righteous people, God will spare the cities. Abraham doesn't press further, but one might presume that an entire city can't be destroyed if even one individual were innocent. Reading the text this way, we can imagine from the time of Abraham, it has been established that punishment should be reserved for the guilty, and against all odds to the contrary, the innocent should be spared.

Today, there are those who are dedicated to ensuring that the innocent do not languish in jail. The National Registry of Exonerations, a joint project of the University of Michigan Law School and the Center on Wrongful Convictions at Northwestern University School of Law, has now recorded 2,858 exonerations since 1989.[450] The Registry highlights the need to scrutinize convictions—especially in the states with the most exonerations, with the two leading states being Illinois and Texas—to ensure that they were honestly obtained and that the defendants had sufficient and competent defense.

The Innocence Project, founded by Barry C. Scheck and Peter J. Neufeld of Yeshiva University's Benjamin N. Cardozo School of Law in 1992, is a group that uses DNA testing and other state-of-the-art technology to establish the innocence of falsely-imprisoned inmates. The staff of lawyers and Cardozo clinic students,

---

[446] Samuel R. Gross and Barbara O'Brien, "Frequency and Predictors of False Conviction: Why We Know So Little, and New Data on Capital Cases," *SSRN*, June 26, 2007, https://papers.ssrn.com/sol3/papers.cfm?abstract_id=996629.

[447] Jon B. Gould and Richard A. Leo, "One Hundred Years Later: Wrongful Convictions After a Century of Research," *SSRN*, last revised February 22, 2011, https://papers.ssrn.com/sol3/papers.cfm?abstract_id=1616359.

[448] Fathom Archive, Capital Punishment in the United States: A Forum on Death-Penalty Issues, https://fathom.lib.uchicago.edu/2/10701044/—"We found that in 82 percent of those cases (state post-conviction cases) where we have the data, the result after you cured the error was very different indeed: a sentence less than death. In 7 percent of those cases, the defendant was acquitted."

[449] John Roman et al., "Post-Conviction DNA Testing and Wrongful Conviction," Urban Institute, June 18, 2012, https://www.urban.org/research/publication/post-conviction-dna-testing-and-wrongful-conviction

[450] The National Registry of Exonerations, http://www.law.umich.edu/special/exoneration/Pages/about.aspx.

along with allies in many states, has thus far exonerated 301 prisoners, who had served an average of nearly 14 years (and 18 of whom had been on death row) using DNA evidence.[451] There are more than fifty Innocence Projects in the United States, under the umbrella of the Innocence Network. They need our support.

One particular case illustrates the great value of the Innocence Project for American society. In 1974, James Bain was convicted of raping a nine-year-old boy in Florida. The primary evidence at the time revolved around the blood type of the semen on the victim's underwear. The jury believed the prosecution's claim that Bain's blood type (AB) was the same as that found on the scene, when in actuality the blood sample was blood type B. Once DNA evidence became available, Bain tried five times to get the Circuit Court to examine his case, but was rejected. Finally, after the Innocence Project became involved, DNA evidence was reexamined, confirming that Bain was not the rapist. James Bain was exonerated and released in December 2009, after serving 35 years for a crime he did not commit.[452]

While we need a justice system, we also need a *system of justice*. Members of our society certainly deserve to be kept safe, which sometimes means that the perpetrators of crimes should be punished and sometimes means that other methods of rehabilitation, some of which might also be viewed as harsh, are warranted. But we must equally ensure that the rights of the innocent are protected. If a prisoner is found to be innocent, then that prisoner should be set free and given fair compensation. Former district attorney, Governor of California, and Supreme Court Chief Justice Earl Warren was well aware of the often-coercive methods by which law enforcement obtained confessions and convictions, and how scrutiny needed to be applied to ensure that only the guilty are convicted and incarcerated. As he said: "Life and liberty can be as much endangered from illegal methods used to convict those thought to be criminals as from the actual criminals themselves."[453]

We must support the work of those who labor to ensure that our criminal justice system is truly just and equitable. This is nothing short of the championing of justice over inequity, and as a community, we must support their work. Jewish community leaders should call for an end to the problematic practice of imposing the death penalty, and also for the development of a fair, equitable paradigm of restorative justice.

---

[451] The Innocence Project, https://innocenceproject.org/exonerations-data/.
[452] Innocence Project, "Longest Serving Exoneree Looks Toward the Future," October 17, 2012, https://innocenceproject.org/news/longest-serving-exoneree-looks-toward-the-future/.
[453] Warren, Earl, and Supreme Court Of The United States. U.S. Reports: Blackburn v. Alabama, 361 U.S. 199. 1959. Periodical. https://www.loc.gov/item/usrep361199/.

Debate 25.

Care for the Vulnerable vs. Education: What does every community need?

Think about the last time you moved. Why did you move? For a job? For a nicer home? To downsize your home? To get into a specific school district? The Talmudic rabbis also thought about moving, and they had specific requirements, or suggestions, when one is looking. Consider this passage in the Talmud:

And it is taught in a *baraita*:[454] A Torah scholar is not permitted to reside in any city that does not have these ten things: A court that has the authority to flog[455] and punish transgressors; and a charity fund for which monies are collected by two people and distributed by three, as required by *halachah*. This leads to a requirement for another three people in the city. And a synagogue; and a bathhouse; and a public bathroom; a doctor; and a bloodletter; and a *velavlar* (scribe) to write sacred scrolls and necessary documents; and a ritual slaughterer; and a teacher of young children.[456]

The Rambam (Maimonides) has his own list:

> In any city where these ten conveniences are not found, a Torah scholar is not permitted to live: a physician, a surgeon, a bathhouse, a comfort-station, running water, as a river or spring, a house of worship, a school teacher, a recorder, a collector of charity, and a tribunal with police powers.[457]

One of the interesting commonalities here is that there should be teachers. After all, shouldn't education be central to our lives as adults, not to mention for our children and grandchildren?

The *Aruch HaShulchan*[458] writes about when a newcomer to the community should be forced to pay their due if they don't do so voluntarily.

---

[454] A *baraita* is similar to a *mishnah*. When the vast number of *mishnayot* (plural of *mishnah*) were redacted, there were many, due to any number of variables, that were not incorporated into the final work. *Baraitot* (plural of *baraita*) are essentially those not included. Their significance is manifested by often being quoted in the *gemara*.
[455] While *makkot* (flogging, or lashes), is viewed today as cruel, it was once relatively common practice. The Torah prescribes flogging for specific situations, and limits the number of lashes to forty. The sages went further, limiting both its application and lowering the number to thirty-nine (so that an error in the count will not lead to exceeding the forty). The flogging was supervised by the *beit din* (court), and was not to exceed more than the recipient could withstand.
[456] BT Sanhedrin 17b.
[457] Mishneh Torah, Dei'ot 4:23.
[458] *Aruch HaShulchan*, authored by Rabbi Yechiel Michel Epstein (1829-1908) is considered a seminal *halachic* work.

> All who dwell in the city are obligated to give to all city *tzedakah* funds, and as such the sages said (Baba Batra 8a) that "whoever dwells in the city for thirty days can be forced to give tzedakah to the public fund along with the rest of the community. If a person dwelled there for three months, they can force that person to give to the food collective. If a person lived there for six months, they can force that person to give to the clothing fund so that they can clothe the poor of the city with it. If a person dwelled there for nine months, they can force that person to give tzedakah to the burial fund so they can bury the poor and cover all burial needs with it.[459]

Should we prioritize an ethic of care when compelling funds? After all, what can be more important than caring for the vulnerable? Or should we prioritize education when compelling funds? After all, what can be more important than education?

The Talmud records how important education was for the rabbis:

> Yehoshua ben Gamla came and instituted an ordinance that teachers of children should be established in each and every province and in each and every town, and they would bring the children in to learn at the age of six and at the age of seven.[460]

On this point, the Meiri[461] teaches:

> It is a positive commandment for a father to teach his son Torah, as it says "You shall teach him." This also applies to his grandson, as it says "You shall make it known to your sons and your grandsons." In any event, every scholar must teach everyone who wants to learn. However, he does not have to pay the teachers himself, except for his sons' and grandsons' [teachers].... until they decreed that teachers of children be appointed in every district and city and to bring the children [to start school] at age 6 or 7 according to the strengths and health of the child. It is explained (in Tractate Sabbath 119b) that we excommunicate every city that doesn't appoint teachers of children. If they still

---

[459] Yechiel Michel Epstein, *Aruch HaShulchan*, The Laws of Tzedakah, 256:15.
[460] BT Baba Batra 21a.
[461] Rabbi Menachem Meiri (1249-1310) was a French talmudist. His commentary to the Talmud, *Beit Habechirah*, is popular in traditional yeshivah learning circles.

don't do so, we destroy [the city]. For the world is sustained only by that which comes out of the mouths of children.... They wouldn't interrupt the study of children in schools even for the construction of the Temple.[462]

Rabbi Eliezer Waldenberg[463] taught that it is not clear that charity for the vulnerable is so different from sustaining intellectual and spiritual pursuits. He wrote:

> The Maharam [a medieval Jewish commentator] allowed the purchase of books for study and lending with charity money. We can apply this to lending books to those who need them for study, for they are poor. And this is like providing spiritual sustenance, which is no worse than supplying physical sustenance to one who lacks it.[464]

On the one hand, humans are animals and we need to honor our biological needs to survive. On the other hand, humans are fundamentally meaning-makers, and as Victor Frankel taught so proudly, we need meaning to survive.

Rabbi Jonathan Sacks wrote about the passing of the golden age for Spanish Jewry. In 1391, the "Spanish equivalent of Kristallnacht" occurred. From that day of destruction of Jewish businesses and the murder of Jews until their full expulsion in 1492, Jews lived under harsh persecution. They lacked basic rights and were constantly pushed to convert to Christianity. Some pretended to convert (Conversos) while others tried to survive while resisting. He explains:

> At the height of this crisis, a gathering of Jews was convened at Valladolid in 1432. It ordained a series of taxes on meat, wine, weddings and circumcisions, to raise funds for public education. They also declared the following:
> "We also ordain that every community of 15 householders [or more] shall be obliged to maintain a qualified elementary teacher to instruct their children in Scripture. They shall provide him with sufficient income for a living in accordance with the number of his dependents. The parents shall be obliged to send their children to that teacher, and each shall pay him in accordance with his means. If this revenue from the parents

---

[462] *Beit Habechirah*, Commentary on Baba Batra 21a.
[463] Rabbi Eliezer Waldenberg (1915-2006) was a highly regarded rabbi and judge in Jerusalem. He was a trailblazer in the field of medicine in *halachah*.
[464] Responsa *Tzitz Eliezer*, Part 9:1, Chapter 2.

should prove inadequate, the community shall be obliged to supplement it with an amount necessary for his livelihood in accordance with the time and the place."

Until modern times, there was no parallel to this Jewish insistence on education as the fundamental right and duty of every person, every child. Nor was this an innovation. It goes back to the dawn of Jewish time. God says of Abraham, "For I have chosen him, so that he will instruct his children and his household after him to keep the way of the Lord by doing what is right and just." Abraham was chosen to be a father and a teacher. In two of the key passages of Jewish faith—the first and second paragraphs of the *Shema*—Moshe places education at the heart of Jewish life: "Teach [these things] to your children, talking about them when you sit at home and when you walk along the road, when you lie down and when you get up."[465]

Consider how essential education has been in the United States. A fundamental Supreme Court ruling in 1954 reads:

> "Education is perhaps the most important function of state and local governments. Compulsory school attendance laws and the great expenditures for education both demonstrate our recognition of the importance of education to our democratic society. It is required in the performance of our most basic public responsibilities, even service in the armed forces. It is the very foundation of good citizenship. Today it is a principal instrument in awakening the child to cultural values, in preparing him for later professional training, and in helping him to adjust normally to his environment. In these days, it is doubtful that any child may reasonably be expected to succeed in life if he is denied the opportunity of an education."[466]

Education is so important that it is a basic right to which all should have access. For some, this is obvious:

---

[465] Rabbi Lord Jonathan Sacks, "Teach Your Children Well," *The Jewish Week*, 2009.
[466] Brown v. Board of Education of Topeka, the landmark 1954 U.S. Supreme Court ruling on racial segregation in schools (The School Funding Gap).

> Describing education and education equality as the "civil rights issue of our time," President Obama called Wednesday for a renewed effort to eliminate the achievement gap between African-American students and others. "Too many of our kids are dropping out of schools," Mr. Obama told a mostly black audience in the ballroom of the Sheraton New York Hotel in Manhattan. "That's not a white, black or brown problem. That's everybody's problem."[467]

Today, if faced with the opportunity, as a philanthropist, to save lives directly or save lives through education, which would we chose? Would we choose humanitarian relief, since it is urgent and direct? Or would we choose education, since we can only pull people out of perpetual poverty and solve social problems with education? And how can we sustain the values that even ensure humanitarian relief is a conversation without education? Just as the Talmud emphasizes both, we too, thankfully, need not choose. Individually and collectively, we can, and must, invest in both.

---

[467] Helene Cooper, "Obama Takes Aim at Inequality in Education." (*The New York Times*, (April 6, 2011).

Jewish Daily Life & Community

Debate 26.

Obedience vs. Meaning:
What is the Purpose of the *Mitzvot*?

Why are Jews commanded to perform *mitzvot*? Several reasons have been offered over the millennia. Some have suggested that the goal is about fidelity. The *mitzvot* are here to strengthen our connection to God through obedience. Even the *mitzvot* that make no sense to us are gifts as a vehicle to connect and serve. The word mitzvah, itself, some argue, actually emerges from a meaning of connection, or relationship. The opposing view is that the *mitzvot* are rational and make sense to us. By extension, they serve a purpose in our personal lives, in our communities, and in the world.

What exactly is referred to by the term *mitzvot*? In general, it refers to the 613 biblical *mitzvot*, or commandments.[468] As the Talmud explains:

> Rabbi Simlai taught: There were 613 mitzvot stated to Moses in the Torah, consisting of 365 prohibitions corresponding to the number of days in the solar year, and 248 positive mitzvot corresponding to the number of a person's limbs. Rav Hamnuna said: What is the verse that alludes to this? It is written: "Moses commanded to us the Torah, an inheritance of the congregation of Jacob" (Deuteronomy 33:4). The word Torah, in terms of its numerical value [gematria], is 611, the number of mitzvot that were received and taught by Moses our teacher. In addition, there are two mitzvot: "I am the Lord your God" and: "You shall have no other gods" (Exodus 20:2, 3), the first two of the Ten Commandments, that we heard from the mouth of the Almighty, for a total of 613.[469]

---

[468] The root of the word *mitzvah* (and the plural *mitzvot*) means command. The term *mitzvot* is also used colloquially in a looser sense to refer to a good deed, even if not commanded by the Torah.
[469] BT Makkot 23b-24a.

On the other hand, some explain that the number 613,[470] while significant, is at the same time somewhat arbitrary, and that there are actually far more commandments.[471] Ibn Ezra writes:

> By way of investigation, the truth of the matter is that there is no end to the number of *mitzvot*, as the verse states, "For every goal I have seen an end, but Your commandment is exceedingly broad" [Psalms 119:96].[472]

The rabbis argue that more important than doing a random good act is performing a *mitzvah*:

> Greater is one who is commanded to do a mitzvah and performs it than one who is not commanded and performs it.[473]

Furthermore, the Torah explicitly states that the *mitzvot* were given for our own good:

> [T]he Lord commanded us to observe all these laws, to revere the Lord our God, for our lasting good and for our survival, as is now the case.[474]

But what exactly does that mean? That the *mitzvot* are to be understood and be of value in this world? Or that they are not understood but benefit us with reward in the next world through our obedience? It isn't clear.

One approach suggests that the benefit is that through the *mitzvot*, we can learn to emulate the Divine and be more God-like.

---

[470] The Hebrew term used for the 613 *mitzvot* is the acronym of its *gematria*, *taryag*, comprised of the letters tav/reish/yud/gimel. On the verse *"Im Lavan Garti"* ("I lived with Laban"), Rashi, quoting a *midrash*, famously adds to Jacob's words: *"v'taryag mitzvot shamarti"* ("and I observed the *taryag mitzvot*"). The word *garti* contains the same letters as *taryag*. Rashi's point is that Jacob, in his declaring to his brother Esau that he had been living with Laban for the past 22 years, is also alluding to the fact that while there he remained faithful to the 613 *mitzvot*.
[471] Many lists of the 613 *mitzvot* have been written over the millennia. Maimonides and Nachmanides, for example, each wrote their own list, and there is much disagreement between them. Maimonides, to cite but one difference, does not list immigrating to Israel (*aliyah*) as a *mitzvah*, whereas Nachmanides does. Each list, however, contains precisely 613 *mitzvot*. The obvious conclusion is that there are indeed more than 613 *mitzvot*, while at the same time there is fidelity and import to that specific number.
[472] Rabbi Abraham Ibn Ezra, Yesod Mora, Shaar 2.
[473] BT Avodah Zara 3a.
[474] Deuteronomy 6:24.

> Follow none but the Lord your God, and revere none but [God]; observe [God's] commandments alone, and heed only [God's] orders; worship none but [God], and hold fast to [God].[475]

So here the goal is character development. Rambam (Maimonides) makes this point clear:

> And all these matters [the *mitzvot*] are to [help us to] overcome our negative inclinations and to correct our traits; and most laws of the Torah are instruction from afar from the Great Adviser [to help us] to correct our character traits and straighten our ways.[476]

As the Midrash says: "The commandments were given only in order to refine humanity."[477]

Rambam, the great rabbinic champion of rationalism, argues that we should strive to uncover the *ta'amei hamitzvot* (the reasoning behind the *mitzvot*).

> Even though all the laws of the Torah are [Divine] decrees . . . it is still fitting that a person contemplate them and give reasons for them as much as they can; and the early Sages said that King Solomon understood most of the reasons of all the laws of the Torah.[478]

The *mitzvot* are divided into two sub-groups: *chukim* (seemingly non-rational) and *mishpatim* (rational). For Rambam, even the *chukim* have an explanation that can be uncovered. Similarly, Rav Saadya Gaon (892-942) argues that revelation and reason can, and must, be in sync with one another. He reasons that if they are not, we have not worked hard enough in either our intellectual work of reason or in our interpretative work of revelation. Ramban (Nachmanides), on the other hand, challenges this project, suggesting that the true goal of the *mitzvot* is all about returning to God.

---

[475] Deuteronomy 13:5, JPS 1985 modified for gender neutrality. Also see BT Sotah 14a.
[476] Rambam, end of Hilchot Temurah. Also see the Ramban's commentary on Deuteronomy 22:6.
[477] Midrash Rabbah, Bereishit 44:1. Also see Midrash Tanchuma, Parshat Shemini 7.
[478] Mishneh Torah, Hilchot Temurah 4:13

> Our Sages taught that "One should be careful with a mitzvah that people treat lightly just as they are careful with a mitzvah that people treat seriously," as all *mitzvot* are precious and coveted. This is because every time a person fulfills any mitzvah, they acknowledge God. And the purpose of all the *mitzvot* is for us to believe in God and to thank God for creating us.[479]

A middle ground, perhaps, could be found in 13th-century Rabbi Aharon of Barcelona's idea that even if we haven't worked out the reasons for the *mitzvot*, behaviorally conditioning ourselves to them will indeed improve us:

> A person is influenced by their actions, and their heart and thoughts follow the acts they do whether they are good or bad. Even one who is a completely wicked person who constantly thinks of doing bad deeds, if they are inspired for the better and put time into fulfilling Torah and *mitzvot*, even if it is not for the sake of Heaven, will turn to the good and overcome their evil Inclination through the power of these actions, since a person's heart follows their actions. Similarly, even if one is a completely righteous person who desires Torah and mitzvot but always involves themself in bad deeds . . . after a certain amount of time they will become a wicked person, for we know, and it is true, that every person is affected by their actions.[480]

On the one hand, it seems humbler to say: "What do we know? Only God knows!" and reject the notion that the *mitzvot* have any discernible goal that we can understand. On the other hand, it seems humbler to say that the *mitzvot* have goals, such as to humble us, and thus we become God-like. After all, once we say that we don't know anything, then we have no real reason to choose Torah over other religious systems. We need intellectual and moral discernment to affirm that this is a moral path worth pursuing. At the same time, one threat in the need for reason is that one may abandon the good path at any moment one feels reason fails to make the proper case. Religious life and moral life, even when separate, and certainly when taken together, require more spiritual roots and grounding than just reason of the moment. Further, the timeless *mitzvot* we've inherited deserve more reverence than to be merely discarded the moment our zeitgeist produces new forms of reason.

---

[479] Ramban's commentary on Exodus 13:16.
[480] Sefer HaChinuch, Mitzvah 16.

Do we ever reach the point in a marriage where we don't need logical reasons to remain married? That love itself is enough to sustain all the various things we do for one another? Perhaps some do. Perhaps others need a good reason for any task they do for their partner. The same is true for Torah and *mitzvot*. At some point, some individuals might be in God-love, and that alone will motivate them to simply immerse in Torah spiritually. Others might not be as God-focused and need good moral reasons for every *mitzvah* they engage in. Once again, each of us are, and must be, quite different. The Torah, through various approaches to the purpose of, and reasons for, the *mitzvot*, can include us all.

The question *What is the purpose of humanity?* is deeply intertwined with our question *What is the purpose of the mitzvot?* Once we understand our life purpose, we can ask what Divine tools have been gifted to us to prepare us to fulfill that deeper purpose. Then we might ask ourselves what it means if we have achieved our purpose and achieved the goal of the mitzvah performed. When I light a menorah, attend a Pesach seder, sing at Kol Nidrei, what am I ultimately trying to achieve beyond just simple performance or attendance? *"Naaseh v'Nishmah;"* we will do and then we will learn. May we commit to righteousness and also commit to learning and growing from the performance of those deeds.

Debate 27.

Reform Judaism vs. Orthodox Judaism

Today, the many different versions, genres, and flavors of Jewish thought and Jewish practice—sometimes called denominations, even though that word doesn't fully capture the uniqueness of one from the other—blend into each other to such an extent that they exist more as a set of blurred lines on a continuum than as distant and distinct points making up some sort of polarity. In the late 18th century, though, as the modern age was beginning, two particular ways of expressing one's Judaism developed that could indeed be viewed as distinct denominations and that could be imagined as polar opposites in both creed and deed: The Reform and Orthodox movements.

Of course, there are other Jewish denominations worth talking about but these two are the earliest and had the most tension in their emergence, so we will begin here. Of course, the main founders of Conservative Judaism were Zecharia Frankel (1801-1875) who founded the Jewish Theological Seminary of Breslau in 1854; and Solomon Schechter (1849 -1915) in the US., who founded the United Synagogue of Conservative Judaism in 1913. Interestingly enough, Frankel broke from the Reform community when it came to praying in German vs. in Hebrew, an issue around liturgy that the Conservative movement continues to grapple with today. The Reconstructionist Rabbinical College was founded in 1967. Renewal doesn't emerge until the late 1960 and early 1970s. Reform and Orthodox Judaism start much earlier. The first Reform Temple opened in Seesn, Germany on July 17, 1810. Dating the founding of Orthodox Judaism is a matter of debate based on when that denominational label was used versus when that style of Judaism was organized (which is obviously much earlier).

Originating in the 1800s in Germany during the Haskalah (enlightenment), Reform Judaism emerged as a liberal response both to some Jews who were rapidly leaving Judaism, even converting to Christianity, and to others who seemed to be stuck in a past that would not even recognize the present world which they inhabited. They wanted to apply scientific study to Judaism (Wissenschaft). A big part of the enterprise was not about rethinking religion as much as gaining societal acceptance with a respect for Judaism. For example, Jerusalem was taken out of the prayer books to demonstrate that Germany was the true home for German Jews. They created much shorter prayer services, took off their kippot, and gave sermons in German instead of Yiddish. They got rid of anything that might lead an outsider to claim that Judaism is strange, like keeping kosher.

One prevailing view was to focus on morality, not ritual. Rabbi Abraham Geiger, one of Reform's pioneers, suggested that his contemporaries should readily change Jewish observance to adapt to the new modern ethos. He argued that this was historically consistent with the Jewish past and that observance always changed to meet the new needs of the moment.[481] In regard to one issue that has become a focal point with reference to which many modern Jewish groups have defined themselves—gender—already in 1837, Rabbi Geiger argued as follows (even as he failed to actualize this point in any complete fashion):

> Let there be from now on no distinction between duties for men and women... no assumption of the spiritual inferiority of women, as though she were incapable of grasping the deep things in religion; no institution of the public service, either in form or content which shuts the doors of the temple in the face of women.

Of course, the first woman Reform rabbi in America, Rabbi Sally Priesand, still was not ordained until June 3, 1972, and the first American Orthodox female rabbi was ordained less than 40 years later; the original egalitarian ethos was in that sense limited, and as such Rabbi Geiger's statement has somewhat limited value as a reference point. Nonetheless, his articulation and assertion of his position set Reform decidedly apart from traditional Judaism. As a concomitant radical departure in the theological sphere, Reform Jewish thinkers generally argued that the Torah is not from God but rather was written by people,[482] that Jewish law is not binding, and that Jews must move away from, and maybe even denounce, all historical practices that are outdated, alienating, offensive, seemingly superstitious, or unhelpful.[483] For the bulk of Reform thinkers, God eventually became not an all-powerful being that we can have a relationship with; rather, God was thought of as a part of the human spirit, not necessarily separate from it. Reform Judaism also came to reject the messianic idea. This shift in thinking showed up liturgically, so that, for example, in regard to resurrection, the reference in prayer to God as "*mechayeh meitim*," the one who brings the dead to life, was changed to refer to the "*mechayeh hakol*," the one who enlivens everything. Similarly, early Reform

---

[481] While Geiger was correct historically, up until that point any changes were considered to be within the confines of *halachah* (Jewish law) and not in opposition to it. Geiger was willing to go beyond that with regard to proposed changes to Jewish communal observance.

[482] Although all agree that the Torah itself was written by Moses, it had been a tenet of Judaism until that point that the Torah was ordained by God. There are divergent opinions on whether the specific, exact words as found in the Torah scroll were dictated to Moses by God or whether God presented to Moses what to write and allowed room for Moses to choose his own words with the approval of God.

[483] Of course, all of these categories and others are subject to personal bias, which led to great debate among Reform thinkers as to what changes were considered acceptable and which are "beyond the pale."

was also anti-Zionist, arguing that finding religious meaning in the Diaspora was the priority and would allow Jews to focus on being "a light unto the nations."[484]

By the second half of the 19th century, the majority of Jews in Germany identified with Liberal Judaism and this new model was what would be exported to America for the building of liberal Jewish America.

One of the early leaders of the Reform movement, Rabbi Isaac Mayer Wise, was very influential in developing Reform Judaism in America in the middle and late 19th century. He wrote the first siddur edited for American Jews (1857), founded the Union of American Hebrew Congregations (1873), founded the Hebrew Union College in Cincinnati (1875),[485] and founded the CCAR, Central Conference of American Rabbis (1889). The approach to *halachah* taken by Rabbi Wise was exemplified by his involvement in an event that came to be known as the Treyfa Banquet. The dinner, held in 1883 to honor the first graduates of Hebrew Union College as well as delegates to a convention of the UAHC, was a lavish affair at which the guests dined on shellfish and had a dessert of ice cream after their meat meal. While Rabbi Wise does not seem to have been responsible for the meal itself, he pushed back hard against Jewish leaders who criticized the non-kosher party, and published an editorial in his newspaper, *The American Israelite*, taking those critics to task for being upset over the laws of kashrut, something considered by that newspaper to be relatively unimportant. The Pittsburgh Platform, a document adopted in 1885 by a group of Reform rabbis, emphasized even further the degree to which Reform Judaism eschewed any focus on ritual in Judaism, and strongly favored treating Judaism as a religion primarily of morality and not so much of ritual. It looked at that time like Reform Judaism was going to be the dominant form of Judaism in America. In 1880, over 90% of synagogues in America were Reform.

A few decades later (1930s), Reform Judaism returned to a more traditional approach, seeking to differentiate itself from its perceived similarity to American Christianity. Reform Judaism also later embraced Zionism.

But over the years, the Reform movement retained a non-traditional perspective on *halachah* or, more commonly, rejected it completely. One of the most prominent 20th-century theologians of the Reform movement was Rabbi Eugene Borowitz.[486] He argued that *halachah*, for the modern Jew, was a "resource," but not binding law.

---

[484] It is important to keep in mind that at the time the landscape of Israel was very different from today. Israel had not yet achieved statehood and Jews were, for the most part, not immigrating to Israel as we are blessed to witness today. Many who declare themselves Zionists today may not have shared this view one hundred years ago.
[485] Today there are three additional campuses (Jerusalem, New York City, and Los Angeles).
[486] Rabbi Borowitz was Professor of Education and Jewish Religious Thought at the New York School of Hebrew Union College-Jewish Institute of Religion, where he taught from 1962 until his death in 2016. He was the only

> I do not see how even in principle, Jewish law can be imposed on such a Jewish self. Rather, with autonomy essential to selfhood, I avidly espouse a pluralism of thought and action stemming from Jewish commitment.[487]

Here he is not only speaking of the idea that *halachah* is not of Divine origin but also that religious law itself can never be binding for the modern person.

Notwithstanding the views of leaders such as Wise and Borowitz, Reform Judaism has hardly lacked religious imperatives. Thus, while Reform has prioritized the ethical over the ritual, Reform thinking grounded ethics in religious doctrine. So, although some non-Reform rabbis were involved in the civil rights movement of the 1960s,[488] Jewish participation in that movement came mostly from the ranks of Reform rabbis and Reform Jews. Protesting injustice was not a secular political act as much as a Jewish act. For Reform Judaism, egalitarianism is taken for granted, since equality is a fundamental principle. Similarly, intermarriage is widely embraced today by Reform Judaism, since there should be no barriers to love. And the Reform movement defines its faith in terms of "the Covenant between God and Israel as expressed over the generations in the teachings of an ever-evolving Torah and tradition."[489]

Over the course of time, Reform suffered losses in its numbers due to assimilation out of Reform Judaism (just as members of other sectors of Jewish society have assimilated into the broader American—indeed, world—populace), even as the late 20th and early 21st centuries have seen a strengthening of more traditional brands of Judaism. Nonetheless, more American Jews check the "Reform" box when given the choice than that of any other grouping. Reform Judaism today, primarily an American phenomenon, is the largest stream of Judaism in America and Canada. However, in Israel, Europe, South America, South Africa, and other places in the world, Reform Judaism is not nearly as prominent.

While Reform Judaism tends to appear somewhat monolithic, by contrast there is really no one Orthodox Judaism. Reform Judaism has one umbrella organization (URJ),[490] one rabbinic association (CCAR), one social action agency

---

Jew to have served as President of the American Theological Society, and he was seen by many as the "dean" of American Jewish philosophers. He also served as the editor of *Sh'ma*, which was called a journal of Jewish responsibility, a magazine of Jewish social concern that he founded in 1970 and edited for 23 years.

[487] "The Autonomous Jewish Self," *Modern Judaism* 1984.

[488] Rabbi Ahron Soloveichik was a vocal proponent of civil rights, as was Rabbi Eliezer Silver, the voice of the Orthodox rabbinate in Cincinnati. Orthodox activists such as Rabbi Saul Berman, then a yeshiva student, and later Rabbi Tzvi Blanchard and Rabbi Abraham Joshua Heschel, protested as well.

[489] "What is Reform Judaism?" Union for Reform Judaism. https://urj.org/what-we-believe/what-is-reform-judaism.

[490] Earlier known as The Union of American Hebrew Congregations (UAHC).

(RAC), and one global organization (the World Union for Progressive Judaism). Orthodox Judaism, on the other hand, is fractured among various Hasidic groups, different non-Hasidic ultra-Orthodox factions, Sephardic and Ashkenazi communities, and so-called Centrist Orthodoxy, Modern Orthodoxy, and Open Orthodoxy. There are countless different Orthodox umbrella organizations and rabbinic associations, and there is often enormous division between these camps. While Reform is centralized and decisions of ethics committees are binding from within that hierarchy, for Orthodoxy, different factions reject the authority of others (i.e., the leadership of different Hasidic groups such as Chabad and Satmar, halachic decisors affiliated with Yeshiva University and Yeshivat Chovevei Torah,[491] and even members of wider subgroups such as Sefardim and Ashkenazim).[492]

The general approach of mainstream Orthodoxy might be articulated as holding that the Torah is the word of God, that *halachah* is binding, that sweeping halachic change is largely antithetical to Jewish authenticity, and that gender differences are not only to be embraced but largely celebrated. Rabbis, in the Orthodox world, were originally and traditionally seen as authority figures whom one sought for a ruling.[493] Like early Reform, early Orthodoxy, too, was not Zionistic. For the Orthodox, this wasn't about the ethical primacy of the Diaspora but rather about a need to wait for the Messiah, and a rejection of the secular pioneers who were too quick and eager to roll up their sleeves and create a secular state not guided and informed by Torah and *halachah*.[494] Orthodox Judaism embraced a strict adherence to the rulings found in traditional rabbinic texts regarding observance of Shabbat, kashrut, niddah, and other Torah and rabbinic laws. In Orthodoxy, it is not only the Torah (the "written law") that is viewed as binding, but also the Talmud (the "oral law"), which leaves, for the most part, virtually no room for flexibility. And in much of Orthodoxy, insularity came to be seen as a value because Orthodox Jews at large did not want to be influenced by an outside culture that could lead to even the slightest bit of assimilation. Many Ultra-Orthodox Jews, like those in Brooklyn and Monsey, still speak only Yiddish, with the goal of preventing interaction with the world at large. (Many who do

---

[491] YU and YCT are mentioned here by way of example only. Many other yeshivot, as well, each view their worldview as the only valid one, to the exclusion of the validity, or true orthodoxy, of others.

[492] The inclusion of Ashkenazim on this list seems appropriate, as so much of pre-World War II European Judaism was both Ashkenazi and Orthodox. Including Sephardim among Orthodox Jews is, however, a more complex proposition, as the divide between Orthodox and non-Orthodox camps is not a feature of the Sephardi world to the same extent as it is among Ashkenazim.

[493] Differences have arisen over time and between groups as to the scope of authority that rabbis hold in areas such as political and personal decision-making, as opposed to strictly within the realm of *halachah* (and its concomitant written responsa).

[494] To be sure, there were some Orthodox rabbis (today they would perhaps be called Ultra-Orthodox), such as Rabbi Yitzchak Yaacov Reines, the founder of the Zionist Mizrachi movement, and Rabbi Naftali Zvi Yehuda Berlin, who were Zionists, but they were outliers in their time.

speak English only do so when necessary for business or other pressing needs).[495] At the same time, many Orthodox Jews have embraced the culture of the broader world, even as they carefully sift through those elements of general culture that enhance a way of life guided by Torah and those that could undermine it.

For Orthodox Jews, serving God with ritual and Torah study are particularly central. A visitor to an Orthodox service or event might hear less talk about ethics and more about observance of the law than they would when among other denominations; although most Orthodox Jews who consider the point likely take it for granted that the law is ethical and that to be an Orthodox Jew means to be an ethical one. Many Orthodox Jews assume a belief in the rebuilding of the Temple and the coming of the Messiah along with the resurrection of the dead, although much disagreement exists even within Orthodox Judaism about the meaning of the terms "Messiah" and "resurrection," and what it might mean for the Temple to be rebuilt and for the sacrificial service to be restored.

For many Ultra-Orthodox Jews, the modern State of Israel provides needed benefits and is certainly meaningful, even though some Haredim[496] shun not just the idea of a modern Jewish state but even choose not to live in Israel for religious reasons. For many religious Zionists, however, the return to the land is the birth of the messianic era, and the government, although secular, is also a crucial part of the redemption. This vision of Zionism was articulated in early formulations by Rabbi Abraham Isaac Kook and developed further by his son Rabbi Zvi Yehuda Kook and his followers, with the belief that the State of Israel in its current formation will ultimately become a totally halachic state.[497] Still, many Orthodox Jews and leaders feel that the end goal of a purely halachic state is not a necessary aspiration, so long as all Jews can call Israel their home and those who wish to live a halachic lifestyle are free to do so.

The term "Orthodox" is often used as a proxy in umbrella fashion to include the various forms of traditional Judaism that existed before the modern era and that made up almost all pre-Enlightenment rabbinic Judaism. The term "Orthodox" isn't actually mentioned (or at least not recorded), however, until it was used in a 1795 Berlin publication called the Berlinische Monatsschrift. The term was used to describe those who were in opposition to the Enlightenment. While the Reform used "Orthodox" as an insult to show how barbaric the traditionalists

---

[495] This phenomenon is found in certain communities in Israel as well, where its constituents avoid speaking Hebrew except when necessary.

[496] Haredim is the Israeli term for Ultra-Orthodox Jews. The term Haredim literally means "those who adhere," and is based on the verse (Isaiah 66:5) which refers to Torah abiding Jews as "*hachareidim el devaro*," ("who adhere to His words").

[497] Rabbi Dr. Alex Kaye argues in his book, *The Invention of Jewish Theocracy* (New York: Oxford University Press, 2020), that the idea of a modern halachic state is a very late innovation and not authentic to earlier Jewish tradition.

were, the people described by this term at the time didn't like the fact that this foreign title emerged from Christian-German discourse. They preferred titles such as "Torah-true" (*gesetztreu* in German).

At some point after the advent of Orthodox Judaism, an Orthodox subculture that ultimately came to be known as Modern Orthodoxy came into existence. One feature of the Modern Orthodox approach is its perception of secular knowledge as a positive force to be incorporated into Jewish thought, rather than, at most, something to be studied for utilitarian purposes. Some will ascribe the birth of Modern Orthodoxy to Moses Mendelssohn (18th-century Germany), although others credit Mendelssohn with birth of the Reform movement. The Modern Orthodox were attracted to Mendelssohn's idea of being a Jew at home and a person in the streets[498] whereas the Reform would be attracted to the articulation from Judah Leib Gordon. Others will point to Rabbi Shimshon Raphael Hirsch (19th-century Germany), who championed the idea of "*Torah Im Derech Eretz*," "Torah alongside the way of the world." He was the founder of Neo-Orthodoxy what would today be called Modern Orthodoxy. This camp wasn't like the other Orthodox camps. For example, he said you can shave your beard. Also, instead of fighting with Reform Judaism, he said it was best to just leave each other alone. Still others will point to Rabbi Joseph B. Soloveitchik (20th-century New York). He was affiliated with Yeshiva University, whose motto is "Torah U'Madda," which literally means "Torah and science," although in this context it is intended to imply and refer to "Torah and general knowledge."

While Orthodox Jews can be found throughout America, the majority live in the eastern Tri-State area.[499] The largest Orthodox yeshiva outside of Israel is found in Lakewood, New Jersey. You will find Orthodox synagogues (especially Chabad houses) in virtually every modern country in the world.

The relationship between the Orthodox and Reform camps has developed in a variety of contexts. In the 19th century, the Reform rabbinate pushed back on Orthodoxy when the Reform movement moved to erode traditional halachic practice. But the matter went both ways. Rabbis such as the German educator Rabbi Yaakov Ettlinger organized anti-Reform manifestos.

Israeli Reform and Orthodox Jews tend to live in very different communities and do not interact much, although conflicts do occasionally emerge.[500] And

---

[498] Orthodox maskilim (enlightenment thinkers) like Reines, Pines, Lifshitz, and Yaavetz were far more moderate in their engagement than were Reform thinkers. An 1878 poem by Judah Leib Gordon, "Kotzo shel yo" is where "Be a Jew at home and a man in the streets" originates.

[499] The Tri-State area refers specifically to New York, New Jersey, and Connecticut, but for the purposes of our discussion it is used loosely and also includes Massachusetts and Pennsylvania. Other areas, such as Chicago and its suburbs and Los Angeles, have large Orthodox populations as well.

[500] The overwhelming majority of Israeli Jews who identify neither as Haredi nor Orthodox view themselves as Hiloni (literally meaning "secular," here referring to a lack of religious observance). Still, virtually all Israelis,

while the Chief Rabbinate imposes its rules upon the entirety of the State of Israel (notably regarding many status issues and lifecycle processes), there is only a miniscule Reform movement in the state. If one read the news of "Women of the Wall," one might think that Reform and Orthodox Jews are clashing constantly. The reality is, though, that many leaders of that effort to allow women access to prayer opportunities at the Western Wall are either affiliated with branches of Judaism other than Reform or have no specific affiliation. Indeed, many members and sympathizers of Women of the Wall often go out of their way to wear tefillin, something many men involved in Reform Judaism do not regularly do.

In America, one significant difference between Judaism as practiced today in Orthodox communities on one hand and Reform communities on the other has to do with Jewish identity. The accepted norm within Orthodoxy is that one is only considered a Jew based on either matrilineal descent or a halachic conversion, while the Reform movement accepts both patrilineal descent as well as a less rigorous form of conversion which does not require of the convert a commitment to halachic observance. Conversions through the Reform movement have become a right for someone who wants it, and the process will be clear and short in order for the convert to be welcomed. Converting for marriage is also acceptable to some members of the Reform movement. These divergences have made the potential for unified peoplehood very difficult. For some Jews, there is simply no way to redefine a Jewish status through patrilineal descent. Others do not see themselves as having the option of working with other groups that don't accept these new terms of Jewish status as acceptable. Many in each group see the other group's approach as offensive. A related challenge also emerges with regard to weddings. Although this was not always the case, today intermarriage is largely not considered to be an impediment in the Reform world.[501] A related and ironic debate has to do with whether a Reform wedding is halakhically valid. Reform rabbis do not require a *get* at divorce.[502] On the one hand, if a Reform wedding is not valid and the couple civilly divorces without a halachic get, if either member of the couple were to remarry, they could perhaps not have to face the prospect of having children from the new union to be considered *mamzerim* (illegitimate offspring).[503] On the other hand, considering the original wedding to be invalid could be viewed as offensive to the Reform rabbi who performed it. A somewhat

---

even Hilonim, observe deep-rooted traditions such as lighting Chanukah candles, conducting a seder on Pesach, and fasting and attending synagogue services on Yom Kippur.

[501] Earlier, in 1909, the CCAR said that intermarriage is "contrary to the traditions of the Jewish religion." This was reinforced again in 1947 and yet again in 1973.

[502] A *get* is a Jewish divorce.

[503] In light of such a ruling by Rabbi Moses Feinstein (20th century, New York), arguably the most highly respected halachic authority of his time, many young men and women who otherwise would be precluded from marrying a Jew, i.e., would have been considered *mamzerim*, are permitted to do so.

related issue that seems to represent an Orthodox-Reform divide has to do with same sex marriage. Reform Judaism appears to accept that institution in ways that Orthodoxy has rejected.

Fast forward over a century and it is not difficult to find warm engagement between Reform rabbis and Orthodox rabbis. In an unprecedented exchange in 1978 between the Lubavitcher Rebbe and Rabbi Joseph B. Glaser, the Executive Vice President of the CCAR, they shared their different views on the Constitution and the role of religion in the public square. Rabbi Glaser argued for a strict separation of religion and state. The Lubavitcher Rebbe argued that religion (Torah) should be present everywhere possible. In regard to the Lubavitch practice to have Hanukah menorah lightings on government property, Rabbi Glaser urged the Lubavitcher Rebbe to "direct a cessation of... lightings or other religious observances on public property." He argued that this was:

> a violation of the constitutional principle of separation of church and state as is the erection of Christmas trees and creches depicting the birth of Jesus. It weakens our hand when we protest this intrusion of Christian doctrine into the public life of American citizens.[504]

One step toward humility is for each member of a denomination to name the shortcomings of the denomination. As Rabbi Yitz Greenberg once remarked: "It doesn't matter what denomination you are as long as you're ashamed of it." Are Reform Jews really doing enough to keep authentic Judaism intact and to slow down trends toward mass assimilation? Are Orthodox Jews really doing enough to proactively adapt and evolve and not distort timeless values by freezing the law with new layers of stringency? The problems are clear; the solutions are not.

So, can we still be one people?

The concept of Jews as a single, unified people seems, at least in hindsight, to have emerged with fiery conviction and ubiquity with the Diaspora that began two thousand years ago, and to have been rearticulated as a reality accepted by so many in the immediate aftermath of the Holocaust. Jews were considered to be a singular nation in the Diaspora; it did not matter that we were separated by thousands of miles, oceans, languages, and cultures; in the eyes of so many, we were one people. This was also what made the State of Israel in the land of Israel so important: the promise of a country where Jews could gather, live, and become a unified people with the same language, culture, religious practices, and identity.

---

[504] Prof. Jonathan Sarna, "Menachem Mendel Schneerson, Letter to the Jewish Community of Teaneck," *The New Jewish Canon* (Boston: Academic Studies Press, 2020), 323.

However, this idea of oneness seems to be just that: an idea, or more precisely, an unrealized aspiration for unity in a time of constitutional turmoil.

Rabbi Jonathan Sacks, in his preface to *One People?*, writes:

> Jewish Unity: The phrase is deceptively simple. It is easier to invoke than to understand, and is beset by irony. The idea that Jews are "one people" has emerged as a, perhaps the, dominant motif of post-Holocaust Jewish reflection. It is a constant presence in the public rhetoric of contemporary Jewry. It evokes passion and conviction, but seldom clarity. Set against the reality it seeks to describe, it is an aspiration, not an achievement; a myth rather than a reality. Not since the first and second centuries CE have Jews been less united. Rarely has it been harder to state what constitutes them as "one people." That, in itself, should not surprise us, because demands for unity surface only at times of great internal conflict.[505]

Today we may be inclined to perceive ourselves as part of one people due to a shared language, a shared history, a shared tradition, a shared land, shared values, and other commonalities. But it is not our shared membership in a people that unites us. Indeed, will the trends toward embracing a post-ethnic Judaism continue? It is the very values we cherish that unite us, with the goal of being an *am kadosh* (a holy people). We do not merely share some inexplicable tribal-bonding affiliation. When we prioritize our mere existence—our survival over our values—we depreciate that very existence, we make our survival less significant. I encourage our unity to be based on Jewish tradition, common values of justice, ethical responsibility, truth, and peace, and not only on a singular conception of national peoplehood. The shifting nature of both Orthodox and Reform movements over their relatively short history stands witness to the fact that what endures as Jewish identity is a shared tie to an ancient wisdom whose values and mores have evolved over the generations, whose Judaism is not some form of static nationalism. We must not only *survive* as a people but also must—and can—*thrive* as a people. To do that, we must redirect our respective orientations beyond ourselves toward the other, living with the other in the realm of common ideas and ideals, in order to find our collective way back into, and realizing, the dream of true Jewish unity.

---

[505] Jonathan Sacks, *One People?: Tradition, Modernity and Jewish Unity* (Littman Library of Jewish Civilization, 1993), Introduction.

Debate 28.

A Life of Study vs. A Life of Action: Which is Greater?

Is religion fundamentally about a life of study or a life of action? Is Judaism primarily about the inner psyche or the external world? Are we to focus on improving the self or the lives of others? The Talmudic rabbis debated the relationship between learning and action. Here is a well-known passage:

> Rabbi Tarfon and the Elders were reclining in the loft of the house of Nit'za in Lod, when this question was asked of them: Is study greater or is action greater? Rabbi Tarfon answered and said: Action is greater. Rabbi Akiva answered and said: Study is greater. Everyone answered and said: Study is greater, but not as an independent value; rather, it is greater as study leads to action.[506]

"Action" for the rabbis could have meant observance of *mitzvot*, and not action in the general sense we mean today as moderns when we think about activism. I wonder whether Rabbi Akiva, even though he championed study over action, thought about action as "activism" in the sense that he was, along with many of his contemporaries, all about engaging in civil disobedience to the rules of the Romans who prohibited some study and some action. But we can think about the category which we call *mitzvot* as going beyond those rules that we find in the Torah or the Shulchan Aruch, as being a category aligned with its colloquial usage by so many today to include all good done to help others.

In the end, the rabbis taught that the primary purpose of learning is not merely seeking truth (which many saw as secondary), but rather to serve as a catalyst for improved action. "Rava was wont to say: The objective of Torah wisdom is to achieve repentance and good deeds."[507]

Rabbi Aharon Lichtenstein, the highly regarded Rosh Yeshiva of Yeshivat Har Etzion, grappled with the sad and disturbing phenomenon that spending one's entire day engrossed in learning can sometimes paralyze one from moral action:

> A couple of years after we moved to *Yerushalyim*, I was once walking with my family in the *Beit Yisrael* neighborhood, where R. Isser Zalman Meltzer used to live. For the most part,

---

[506] BT Kiddushin 40b.
[507] BT Berakhot 17a.

it consists of narrow alleys. We came to a corner, and found a merchant stuck there with his car. The question came up as to how to help him; it was a clear case of *perika u-te'ina* (helping one load or unload his burden). There were some youngsters there from the neighborhood, who judging by their looks were probably ten or eleven years old. They saw that this merchant was not wearing a *kippa*. So they began a whole *pilpul*,[508] based on the *gemara* in [Tractate] *Pesachim* (113b), about whether they should help him or not. They said, "If he walks about bareheaded, presumably he doesn't separate *terumot u-ma'asrot*,[509] so he is suspect of eating and selling untithed produce..."

I wrote R. Soloveitchik a letter at that time, and told him of the incident. I ended with the comment, "Children of that age from our camp would not have known the gemara, but they would have helped him." My feeling then was: Why, Ribbono shel Olam, must this be our choice? Can't we find children who would have helped him and still known the gemara? Do we have to choose? I hope not; I believe not.[510] If forced to choose, however, I would have no doubts where my loyalties lie: I prefer that they know less gemara but help him.[511]

One can be immersed in study but forget kindness. The Netziv[512] writes:

> And we explained that they [the Rabbis of the Second Temple] were righteous and devout and toiled in the study of Torah. Yet they were not upright in the ways of the world. Therefore, because of the baseless hatred in their hearts toward one another, they were suspicious of one whom they saw act not according to their opinion of the fear of God, that he was a Sadducee or heretic. And because of this, they came to bloodshed through division and to all of the evils in the world until the Temple was destroyed. On this there was justification of the [Divine] judgment. Because The Holy One Blessed Be He is upright and

---

[508] *Pilpul* refers to Talmudic debate and analysis.
[509] *Terumot* and *ma'asrot* are a reference to tithing.
[510] Of course, what is really at issue here is not the boys' learning and knowledge of this excerpt from the *gemara*, but rather not having also learned from their teachers how and when to apply it to everyday living.
[511] Rabbi Aharon Lichtenstein, *By His Light* (Jersey City, New Jersey: Ktav, 203), 249.
[512] Netziv is an acronym for R' Naftali Tzvi Yehuda Berlin, the famed *rosh yeshiva* of the Volozhin yeshiva in what is today Belarus.

does not tolerate righteous people like this, rather ones who also conduct themselves in an upright manner in the ways of the world and not in a manner which is warped, even though it is for the sake of Heaven, because this causes destruction of creation [and] obliterates the settling of the Land.[513]

Once we have concluded that action is indeed primary, we might ask whether we should prioritize acts of *chesed* (kindness) or acts of *tzedakah* (justice). The rabbis explore this:

> The Sages taught that acts of kindness are superior to charity in three respects: Charity can be performed only with one's money, while acts of kindness can be performed both with his person and with his money. Charity is given to the poor, while acts of kindness are performed both for the poor and for the rich. Charity is given to the living, while acts of kindness are performed both for the living and for the dead.[514]

And yet, as Jews, we know how central learning is. We learn substantive Jewish law. We learn the stories of the early Israelites and their descendants. And we learn to be able to hold and live with the complexities of our lives.[515]

To engage in action on a high level, one needs to be able to have both intellectual and spiritual complexity. This is one of the many areas where learning may not necessarily lead to action but rather may enhance action. We are so influenced by the Sages' notion of "learning," but for the Prophets, who flourished prior to the Sages, "learning" meant something else. Consider Isaiah:

> Learn to do good. Devote yourselves to justice; Aid the wronged. Uphold the rights of the orphan; Defend the cause of the widow.[516]

For Ramban (Nachmanides), one of the reasons for higher learning is that the Torah itself cannot give us all the answers. We must continue to learn, to interpret, and to assess the proper path.

---

[513] *Ha'Emek Davar*, Introduction to Genesis.
[514] BT Sukkah 49b. In fact, burying and tending to the needs of the deceased are considered the truest form of *chesed*, and are referred to as *chesed shel emet* (true *chesed*), as the recipient cannot repay the bestower.
[515] Rav Kook, for example, in his *Shemonah Kevatzim*, 6:212, teaches that an advanced self is able to hold contradictions.
[516] Isaiah 1:17.

> Initially, God said that you should observe the laws and statutes which God had commanded you. Now God says that, with respect to what God has not commanded, you should likewise take heed to do the good and the right in God's eyes, for God loves the good and the right. And this is a great matter. For it is impossible to mention in the Torah all of a person's actions toward their neighbors and acquaintances, all of their commercial activity, and all social and political institutions.[517]

The rabbis taught:

> Rabbi Elazar quoted this verse: "God has told you, O mortals, what is good, and what the Lord requires of you: Only to do *mishpat* (justice), to love *chesed* (kindness), and to walk humbly with your God" (Micah 6:8). What does this verse imply? "To do justice" means to act in accordance with the principles of justice. "To love goodness" means to let your actions be guided by principles of loving-kindness. "To walk humbly with your God" means to assist needy families at their funerals and weddings [by giving humbly, in private] . . .[518]

Here, we must continue to learn that which we have not yet received. The Torah is broad and expansive. Rav Kook, among others, taught that to be a student of Torah means that we increase peace in the world. Torah learning is about debate but it is this debate that enables a deeper clarity of truth and more robust moral action:

> There are those who mistakenly think that world peace will be built through agreement in positions and opinions. Therefore, when they see Torah scholars investigating and delving into the wisdom of the Torah, and through their investigation more and more possibilities are brought up, they think that this is a source of controversy and the opposite of peace. But such is not the case, for it is impossible for true peace to come to the world except through the abundance of peace. The abundance of peace means that all sides and opinions will become evident,

---

[517] Ramban on Leviticus 19:2:1.
[518] BT Sukkah 59b.

and it will become clear how there is room for all of them, each according to its own standing, place, and substance.[519]

And so, we must learn. We must act. But when we learn, we must engage in a type of learning that will lead to more action and better action. Sages must increase peace in the world.

To be sure, for the kabbalists, the realm of *asiyah* (the kabbalistic term for action) is not just about moral action but about deeply spiritually transformative action. *Asiyah* is the type of creative processing that, on a mystical level, is most accessible to the human actor when considered in contradistinction to the other types of coming into being: *yetzirah* (formation), *bri'ah* (creation), and *atzilut* (emanation). In this regard, Rav Kook taught: "All actions, all *mitzvot*, all customs, are no more than manifold instruments, each containing within itself a few sparks of the supreme light."[520]

We can wonder how emotions are translated into action. Susan Sontag addresses this question:

> Compassion is an unstable emotion. It needs to be translated into action, or it withers. The question is what to do with the feelings that have been aroused, the knowledge that has been communicated. People don't become inured to what they are shown—if that's the right way to describe what happens—because of the quantity of images dumped on them. It is passivity that dulls feeling.[521]

Rabbi Dessler, the eminent early 19th-century *mashgi'ach ruchani* (spiritual counselor) at the esteemed Ponovezh Yeshiva, taught:

> A human being who has overcome his *yeitzer* (inclination) once, feels clearly in their heart that they are distancing themself from fantasy, and resolving to grasp truth vigorously. But one who has never overcome their inclination, cannot discern this, for their experience teaches them that whenever they desired an evil thing, the desire enslaved them with no escape; therefore, they cannot understand the idea of free choice, because in

---

[519] Avraham Yitzchak HaCohen Kook, *Olat Ra'aya*, Volume one, 330.
[520] *Ikvei Hatzon*, 25.
[521] Susan Sontag, *Regarding the Pain of Others* (New York: Picador, 2003), 101.

examining the sources of their actions they see only external causes and effects.[522]

The point is not that we are convinced that a particular action is free, but that we know ourselves to be capable of freedom to engage in action. This insight has enormous educational implications.

Rav Kook teaches here:

> As a person rises in knowledge and understanding, in the study of Torah and in the cultivation of good attributes, in their intellectual and moral propensities, they march forward toward the future... By perfecting their ways and actions, personal and social, there is open to them a great light that directs them to endless progress.[523]

Through learning, a person progresses. As they progress, they become enlightened. Their newly perceived light inspires them back to further learning and action. And so, we must work to ensure that the increased action we're undertaking actually enhances our interaction with the outside world and our efforts at making it a better place, while strengthening our inner life as well.

Rabbi Yehudah Amital, the founder of Yeshivat Har Etzion and co-Rosh Yeshiva, wrote:

> The acceptance of human frailty does not dictate sufficing with low levels of spiritual achievement; rather, it means that one should not deceive oneself about one's level and should make sure that actions (especially *humrot*, stringencies) are consonant with inner levels of spirituality.[524]

Similarly, Rabbi Joseph B. Soloveitchik taught:

> Judaism has always believed that wherever actions are fair and relations are just, whenever man is able to discipline himself and develop dignified behavioral patterns, the latter are always accompanied by corresponding worthy emotions. Feelings not manifesting themselves in deeds are volatile, and transient

---

[522] Rabbi Eliyahu Dessler, *Treatise on Choice*, vol. 1, 112.
[523] Abraham Isaac Kook, Bokser (Mahwah, New Jersey: Paulist Press, 1978), 232.
[524] Rabbi Yehudah Amital, *Jewish Values in a Changing World* (Jersey City, New Jersey: Ktav Publishing House, 2005), 94.

deeds not linked with inner experience are soulless and ritualistic. Both the subjective as well as the objective component are indispensable for the self-realization of the religious personality.[525]

As Jews, we learn, we act, and we reflect, and then we use our ability to reflect to learn some more and to act on the basis of our learning as a way of making our learning more meaningful. We know the danger of skipping any step in that process. To learn, to grow, and to hold ourselves accountable, we must never stop translating our learning into action and our action back to learning.

"Learning leads to action" should not be read empirically to mean that learning will inevitably lead to action, but read rather as prescriptive and aspirational, meaning that our learning should and must lead to action. Study is more important only when it is the type of study that leads to action.

Many traditional communities might find it easy to keep acting in their traditional ways, failing to incorporate the inner meaning of the texts and traditions that they learn, but it is the learning that enables them to grow and to evolve, preserving some actions and evolving in others.

One of the most moving images in the Bible is Moses floating down the Nile. His mother, Yocheved, fearing the wrath of the Egyptian taskmasters, sends her three-month-old child down the river, praying for his salvation. Miraculously, Moses is spotted by the daughter of Pharaoh, who risks her life to save him. Bitya, as she is known, merits eternal life for her courage and kindness.

When we examine the verse carefully, we will notice an important detail. The Torah describes the scene as Bitya witnesses the baby in the floating basket. "She opened it and saw the baby. He was crying, and she felt sorry for him. 'This is one of the Hebrew babies,' she said."

The Midrash comments that the tears of Moses are what aroused the compassion of Bitya. The crying aroused her mercy and she moved outside her comfort zone to save him. In that instant, she set into motion the redemption of the Jewish people. Moses becomes the savior, prophet and master teacher of Torah, but the catalyst for that transformation was her attention to the crying baby.

We must never forget the baby who is crying. This message is crystallized in a well-known story about the Baal HaTanya, Rabbi Schneur Zalman of Liadi, the first Lubavitch Rebbe, and his son, Rav Dov Ber.

When Rabbi Dov Ber was a young man, he lived in the same house as his father. One night, while Rav Dov Ber was deeply engrossed in his studies, his youngest

---

[525] Rabbi Joseph B. Soloveitchik, "Marriage," in *Family Redeemed* (Jersey City, New Jersey: Ktav Publishing House, 2000), 40.

child fell out of his cradle. Rabbi Dov Ber heard nothing. But Rabbi Schneur Zalman, who was also immersed in study in his room on the second floor, heard the infant's cries. The Rebbe came downstairs, lifted the infant from the floor, soothed his tears, placed him back in the cradle, and rocked him to sleep. Rabbi Dov Ber remained oblivious throughout it all.

Later, Rabbi Schneur Zalman admonished his son: "No matter how lofty your involvements, you must never fail to hear the cry of a child."

Rabbi Yehuda Amital repeated this story often. He explained that this was one of the founding principles of his Yeshiva: learn Torah but still hear the baby cry. In this vein, he explained that when he saw the plans of the study hall and it did not have windows, he immediately requested that the study hall have big windows installed. A house of study must be connected to the outside world to hear the cries of the world outside.

Sometimes, indeed, we must act first. Consider the Israelites responding "*Naaseh v'nishmah*" at the edge of Mount Sinai. "We will do and we will learn." They were prepared to accept and act before understanding. The pathway to Jewish enlightenment is not through isolated meditation but through mitzvot, the realm of action. This is one of the greatest insights Judaism has offered to the world.

We must always aspire to lead lives of faith but never at the expense of ignoring the cries in our communities. When we express compassion, when we hear and act to alleviate the cry of the "baby," our deeds may be the catalyst for a world of redemption, goodness and peace.

Our learning must enable us to hear and to respond, always to recognize the potential impact of our actions.

DEBATE 29.

Tamar Ross vs. Judith Plaskow: Paradigm-Shifting Feminism vs. Traditional Feminism

This debate is being framed through the lens of Jewish feminism. We are not looking at anti-feminism which would be the mainstream position for almost the entirety of Jewish history prior to the past few decades. This position suggests that we must preserve the patriarchy and the matriarchy and that to keep balance, men should lead in society and women should hold families together. For those proponents in the past and today, to disrupt that order is to challenge the foundation of everything good. This was, of course, not only the Jewish approach for millennia but the pervasive human approach for millennia.[526] On the opposite end, we also won't be looking at anti-Jewish radical feminism which suggests that since all men controlled religion for millennia, that all of religion is fundamentally corrupt and to be discarded. Instead, we will look at a spectrum of ideas emerging from Jewish feminists who value Judaism, albeit in very different ways, yet who also are willing to address the major problems that emerge with new feminist paradigms. In Israel, these feminists were grappling with women's role in society at large since the whole state is the Jewish playing field. In America, these feminists were mostly looking at ritual life since the Jewish institutional world is the Jewish playing field.

We also won't explore the realm of theology as much as the role of ritual and *halachah*. In some ways, Jewish feminists have it easier than Christian feminists since God, for Jews, never existed in male flesh as Christians believe God did with Jesus. On the other hand, Hebrew is a gendered language and while virtually everyone will agree that God is not a man or woman, the tradition inevitably used male and female language to describe God (most commonly male).

Of course, among the great leaders in Jewish tradition we will find countless women, including some of the most famous Biblical figures, such as the four Matriarchs,[527] as well as Miriam, Devorah, Esther, and Ruth. We'll also find Beruriah in the Talmud, Golda Meir as Prime Minister of Israel, and Ruth Bader Ginsburg as an icon of a Jewish commitment to justice. We can learn from Anne Frank, Hannah Senesh, the political activist Emma Goldman, and the biblical scholar

---

[526] To be sure, one can be anti-feminist and still believe there should not be violence against women, that women who must work should be treated equally, and that women should have full rights, etc. They may separate what is a legal right from what is a moral good, in their view. There are different roles but they are to be equally valued. On the other hand, they may just fully be sexist and reject the idea that women have equal value and dignity.

[527] Of course, an argument might be made that six Matriarchs should be counted, as the twelve tribes can be traced back to six women (with the addition of the maidservants Bilhah and Zilpah, whom Rachel and Leah gave to Jacob in order to bear children), but that raises an entirely separate point, unrelated to this essay.

Nechama Leibowitz. There are countless Jewish women today and throughout Jewish history we should know about; it behooves us to familiarize ourselves with their stories and teachings. Nonetheless, a gap remains. As in every society, the voices of Jewish men have dominated the history.

In as early a source as the Biblical text, women were already described as resisting their exclusion. Let's revisit the story of the daughters of Zelophehad:

> The daughters of Zelophehad, of Manassite family—son of Hepher son of Gilead son of Machir son of Manasseh son of Joseph—came forward. The names of the daughters were Mahlah, Noah, Hoglah, Milcah, and Tirzah. They stood before Moses, Eleazar the priest, the chieftains, and the whole assembly, at the entrance of the Tent of Meeting, and they said, "Our father died in the wilderness. He was not one of the faction, Korah's faction, which banded together against the Lord, but died for his own sin; and he has left no sons. Let not our father's name be lost to his clan just because he had no son! Give us a holding among our father's kinsmen!" Moses brought their case before the Lord. And the Lord said to Moses, "The plea of Zelophehad's daughters is just: you should give them a hereditary holding among their father's kinsmen; transfer their father's share to them. "Further, speak to the Israelite people as follows: 'If a man dies without leaving a son, you shall transfer his property to his daughter. If he has no daughter, you shall assign his property to his brothers. If he has no brothers, you shall assign his property to his father's brothers. If his father had no brothers, you shall assign his property to his nearest relative in his own clan, and he shall inherit it.' This shall be the law of procedure for the Israelites, in accordance with the Lord's command to Moses."[528]

One fascinating *midrash* interpreting this Biblical passage blames the injustice on men claiming that God, of course, loves women and men equally:

> "And the daughters of Zelophehad came forward"—When the daughters of Zelophehad heard that the land of Israel was being divided among the tribes with portions given to the males but not the females, they gathered together to seek counsel. They said, "The mercies of God are not like the mercies of people.

---
[528] Numbers 27: 1-11.

> People have more concern for males than females. But the One who said and brought forth the world is not like this. Rather, God's concern is for both males and females. God's concern is for all, as it is said, "God gives sustenance to all flesh" and "who gives beasts their food" and "God is good to all and God's mercy is upon all God's works."[529]

Too often, the term "feminist" gets co-opted to mean something that it is not. In the minds of its opponents, "feminist" and "feminism" are catch-all terms reserved only for individuals who loudly (and bluntly) seek to destroy centuries of gender norms without respect to the past. This isn't the case historically and it surely isn't the case in the present time. Furthermore, the need for feminism isn't only social, but spiritual as well.

One of the great tragedies of human history, and perhaps of the human condition, is that the needs of men and boys have been consistently prioritized over those of women and girls. Wherever one looks, gender inequality is endemic to every segment of societal and communal life. From politics, business, the arts, and academia to religious institutions and major league sports, women are undervalued for their contributions, their effort, and their natural talent. Discrimination against female workers is rampant in the labor force, despite women making up nearly half the working population.[530] And though there is some evidence that the pay gap is narrowing, the reality that women are often paid less than their male counterparts persists.[531]

But even beyond the confines of the workplace, there are still lasting issues with how women are portrayed and depicted in modern culture. Despite normative societal factors, female bodies are used as platforms for merchandise, political demagoguery, and empty glamor. Millions of women are left vulnerable because their needs are not seen to be on par with those of men.

But through it all, to be a socially conscious feminist means that one recognizes sexism and calls it out fervently. It means seeing sexism in the workplace and combating it forcefully. No one should be treated as inferior based on gender (or supposed gender roles). To be a feminist means that one sees the plight of women and stands in solidarity with them, whether or not the observer is a woman. In the *midrash* about Zelophehad's daughters, the Talmudic rabbis explain that while people may have the capacity to be sexist, God completely and utterly rejects such

---

[529] Sifrei Bamidbar 133.
[530] Keri A. Potts, "Same Gap, Different Year: IWPR says wage gap persists." Institute for Women's Policy Research, September 16, 2020, https://iwpr.org/same-gap-different-year-iwpr-says-wage-gap-persists/.
[531] Carolina Aragão, "Gender pay gap in U.S. hasn't changed much in two decades," Pew Research Center, 2023, http://www.pewresearch.org/fact-tank/2017/04/03/gender-pay-gap-facts/.

views. God understands that the different-gendered beings of Creation have real differences, yet S/He desires equal rights for both, since they are created with equal dignity. We are instructed to follow God's compassionate ways. In so doing, we are not only calling out injustice and rooting it out for the benefit of future generations, but also fulfilling the holy *mitzvah* of *v'halachta bidrachav* (imitatio Dei). While in prior eras, our understanding of revelation was still evolving alongside historical progress, embracing a discriminatory ideology in our time is to reject the God of Israel.

In every tradition and in every civilization, women historically have been marginalized. With the advent of the Enlightenment, new challenges and opportunities emerged for women. Many men and women resisted, and still resist, breaking from traditional gender roles. Others call for women's rights and even women's liberation. The Jewish world is no different. Secular Jews, by and large, often take equality for granted. Ultra-Orthodox Jews, by and large, take for granted difference and separation. But what about everyone in between? How have Jews affiliated with the Reform, Conservative, and Modern Orthodox movements, and those movements themselves, among other Jews and other streams of contemporary Judaism, engaged with Jewish identity and Jewish texts vis-à-vis the rise of feminism?

Dr. Judith Plaskow[532] critiqued Cynthia Ozick[533] for trying to help Jewish tradition remain intact while also arguing for women's inclusion. Plaskow argues that women can't have their cake and eat it too by retaining the "old Judaism" while at the same time experiencing the "new Judaism."

> The fact [that] Ozick... is reluctant to explore the theological underpinnings of women's status, places her in the mainstream of Jewish feminism. The Jewish women's movement of the past decade has been and remains a civil-rights movement rather than a movement for "women's liberation."[534] ... It has focused on getting women a piece of the Jewish pie: it has not wanted to bake a new one!
>
> ... Of the issues that present themselves for our attention, halakhah has been at the center of feminist agitation for religious change, and it is to halakhah that Ozick turns in the hope of altering [the] women's situation... Underlying specific halakhot, and outlasting their amelioration or rejection is an assumption

---

[532] Dr. Plaskow is recognized by many as the first Jewish feminist theologian. She served on the faculty of Manhattan College for 32 years.
[533] Cynthia Ozick is an American short story author.
[534] Judith Hole and Ellen Levine, *Rebirth of Feminism* (New York: Quadrangle Books, 1971), ix-x.

of women's Otherness far more basic than the laws in which it finds expression. If women are not part of the congregation, if we stand passively under the huppah, if, even, in the Reform movement, we have become rabbis only in the last ten years, that is because men—and not women with them—define Jewish humanity. Men are the actors in religious and communal life because they are normative Jews. Women are "other than" the norm: we are less than fully human.[535]

In Dr. Plaskow's book *Standing Again at Sinai: Judaism from a Feminist Perspective*, she explores just how empty Jewish tradition can be for women, given, in her view, how it was crafted entirely by men. Taking a similar approach, Professor Rachel Adler emerged from the Orthodox world but left and spent her career teaching theology in the Reform world. She writes about how deep the challenges are for Jewish feminists:[536]

> Being a Jewish woman is very much like being Alice at the Hatter's tea party. We did not participate in making the rules, nor were we there at the beginning of the party.... When our external reality is absurdity and madness, it is difficult for us to retain internal coherence. We begin to ask, "Who are we, really?" We are being invited by Jewish men to re-covenant, to forge a covenant which will address the inequalities of women's position in Judaism, but we ask ourselves, "Have we ever had a covenant in the first place? Are women Jews?"
>
> The problem of "methodolatry"[537] cannot be dismissed as an "Orthodox problem." It is a meta-halakhic problem, touching all Jews who believe the tradition possesses some relevance to modern Jewish life. Any wedding, for example, at which the groom says, "Behold, you are sanctified to me with this ring according to the laws of Moses and Israel," and any divorce issued unilaterally by the husband... is utilizing the categories of acquisition and manumission in which divorce in which men

---

[535] Judith Plaskow, "The Right Question is Theological," in *On Being a Jewish Feminist* (Schocken Books, 1983), 223-27, 230-32.
[536] Rachel Adler, "I've Had Nothing Yet So I Can't Take More," *Moment* 8, no. 8 (September 1983), 22, 24, 26.
[537] Methodolatry is defined by the Collins Dictionary as the "worship of a method that employs it uncritically regardless of ever-changing particulars."

and women are equals could be constructed only by uprooting those entire categories of the tradition.[538]

Of course, Jewish feminism is not limited to the Reform and Conservative world. The Orthodox feminist, perhaps the founder of Orthodox feminism as we know it, Blu Greenberg, wrote in the early 1980s:

> I do not wish to imply that Jewish women were oppressed. This is far from the truth. Given the historically universal stratification of the sexes, plus the model of the Jewish woman as enabler and the exclusive male (rabbinic) option of interpreting the law, there could have been widespread abuse of the powerless. But this did not happen. In fact, the reverse is true; throughout rabbinic history one observes a remarkably benign and caring attitude towards women.
>
> Nevertheless, there is a need today to redefine the status of women in certain areas of Jewish law. First, a benign and caring stance is not discernible in every last instance of rabbinic legislation. Second, paternalism is not what women are seeking nowadays, not even the women of the traditional Jewish community. Increasingly, such women are beginning to ask questions about equality, about a more mature sharing of responsibility, about divesting the power of halakhic interpretation and legislation outfits [from] singular maleness.
>
> The techniques of reinterpretation are built right in the system. It was the proper use of these techniques that enabled rabbinic Judaism to be continuous with the past, even as it redefined and redirected the present and future. The techniques also allowed for diversity, for allowances based on local usage, for a certain kind of pluralism....
>
> ... [W]here there was a rabbinic will, there was a halakhic way.[539]

---

[538] Adler ultimately addressed this issue directly, and in her 1999 book *Endangering Judaism* she offered a novel, egalitarian form of the Jewish marriage contract, a *brit ahuvim* (lovers' covenant), for use by heterosexual and gay couples in lieu of the classical Jewish wedding contract, the *ketubah*. In this work, Adler explicitly rejected *kinyan* (acquisition) on the part of the husband toward his bride in the Jewish wedding ceremony as inherently patriarchal and unjust.

[539] Blu Greenberg, *On Women and Judaism: A View from Tradition* (Philadelphia Jewish Publication Society, 1981), 39-42, 43-44, 46.

Blu Greenberg doesn't think traditional Judaism missed the mark. Yes, there were errors, but overall, Judaism is wise and compassionate. Nonetheless, there are major opportunities for greater inclusion while honoring the beauty of the tradition passed down.

Similarly, Professor Tamar Ross[540] wishes to keep rabbinic Judaism intact but also "Expand the Palace of Torah," as she put it, to be more inclusive:

> If feminist morality is more than a passing fad, it is likely that the interpretive tradition will discover that some of the values expressed by the feminists are indeed those of the Torah and should be pursued accordingly. The fluidity of meaning that allows for this does not require that we understand that the Sinaitic revelation was incomplete. Other feminist values may be considered as opposing the values of the Torah and as such be rejected. Still other matters may remain in the realm of the permissible but not obligatory. Such a solution could be no less effective than claims to divine intervention in history in avoiding the theological pitfall of faulting the existing biblical text. Sufficient to this task should be an underlying assumption that the multiple meanings inherent in a divine message become apparent only through a protracted process of rabbinic interpretation.[541]

Building off a teaching of Rav Kook, in a Hegelian fashion, Professor Ross argues that we can both keep our past that was beautiful and right for its time while embracing a new model that is more right for our time in continuity with that past. Torah becomes greater as it progresses.

Professors Ross (an Orthodox Jewish feminist) and Plaskow (a liberal Jewish feminist) engaged in a robust, but friendly, debate about the path forward. Professor Ross wrote:

> As is to be expected of a religious university in Israel, Bar Ilan boasts an unusually high proportion of Orthodox women teaching and studying in the program. Despite their obvious awareness of radical feminist theory with regard to sex and gender, and their preoccupation with issues of women's equality, none

---

[540] Tamar Ross teaches Jewish philosophy at Bar Ilan University and is a specialist of religious feminist philosophy.
[541] Tamar Ross, *Expanding the Palace of Torah: Orthodoxy and Feminism* (Hanover, NH: Brandeis University Press, 2004), 221-23.

of them appears to be a purist in this matter. Although they welcome unprecedented opportunities for women to study religious texts, engage in active careers outside the home, and militate for equal rights in home and marriage, many of them cover their hair, wear skirts rather than pants, attend synagogues with separate men's and women's sections, and recite traditional prayers suffused with male-centered God imagery. They also tend to have families with more than the average number of children, although they might typically assume a greater degree than is usual in Israeli society of sharing with their spouses in child-rearing and in the assumption of responsibility for other domestic tasks. In other words, though they circumvent sharply stereotypical gender distinctions, such women continue—at least on the symbolic and ritual level—to observe many of the practices that perpetuate the more enduring sexual differentiations against which radical feminism rails, and which it claims are responsible for continued inequality between the sexes.[542]

She continues:

> For the Orthodox feminist, the Jewish element in her feminism is not merely a description of the nature of the burden of tradition that she must contend with in order to achieve equality. Due to the more complex nature of her commitments and loyalties, she will not be inclined to view the traditional conception of gender as a totally negative affair. Many aspects of her womanhood are cherished elements of her self-identity and communal attachments, or serve as signifiers of other values that she has internalized. For her, the sanctification of differences between men and women in Jewish tradition is corroborated by her sense that such differences bear true benefits despite the risks. What might these benefits be?.... Finally, there may be strong theological arguments for the preservation of gender distinctions. Feminist theologians have alleged that such distinctions lead to a transcendent God-image that does not address women's spiritual inclinations, which more naturally veer to viewing the universe as a web of interconnected relations and

---

[542] "The View from Here: Gender Theory and Gendered Realities - An Exchange between Tamar Ross and Judith Plaskow," *Nashim* 13 (Spring, 2007), 220.

the individual ego as a more permeable self. However, some of the so-called male depictions of God may be valuable to women. The vision of God as outside us may be crucial to the experience of prayer as a dialogic activity. The notion of divine providence may be as necessary to the development of human morality and social responsibility as policing is to the preservation of law and order. And the notion of a God who stands over and above the created universe may be valuable in imagining a God who is more than the projection of our subjective desires. . . . This pragmatic stance, which concentrates more on negotiation, compromise and piecemeal victories than on radical deconstruction of sexual differences, has been disparaged by critics of Orthodox feminism as "bargaining with patriarchy" and viewed as an inadequate response to the demands of a rigorous feminist sensibility. It has also been regarded as a travesty of religion, complying with immoral notions of justice. I believe that such objections are misplaced and fail to appreciate the virtues of a more nuanced feminist response to binary gender distinctions, one that is connected to the real world and what people think and feel on the ground. I believe they also involve a misconception of the nature of religious tradition, forcing it into a position that clips its wings.[543]

For Reform Judaism, the Bible itself is flawed—not simply because it is human-authored and not God-written and thus necessarily fallible—but because of the more obvious reason of its patriarchal ethos. Rabbi Dr. Gunther Plaut wrote:

> While the Torah records a number of laws in which men and women are treated equally, it is on the whole male-oriented. The male has rights the female does not enjoy. She is to be wife and mother, invested with inherent dignity, to be sure, but by law and social order relegated to a second-class status.[544]

Already much earlier, in 1837, Rabbi Abraham Geiger, one of the pioneers in Reform Judaism, argued:

---

[543] Ibid., 221, 222, 227.
[544] Gunther Plaut, *The Torah; A Modern Commentary* (New York: Union for American Hebrew Congregations, 1981), 1218.

> Let there be from now on no distinction between duties for men and women... no assumption of the spiritual inferiority of women, as though she were incapable of grasping the deep things in religion; no institution of the public service, either in form or content which shuts the doors of the temple in the face of women.[545]

In the past half century, North American Jewish feminists—across the various denominations—have made leaps and bounds in ensuring the inclusion of women in ritual life as well as in the elevation of women to positions of respect and communal leadership. More recently, Jewish feminism has grown to address more systemic issues such as advocacy for comprehensive forms of sex education and by trying to address the plight of *agunot* (women who are unable to obtain a *get*—a religious writ of divorce—from their husband). There is certainly much work still to be done in all of these areas, in each of the denominations. And yet, the ritual concerns—all of which are essential—are too often the concerns of the more privileged.

As Jews living in an increasingly globalized world, we must widen the umbrella of our concerns to include, and indeed to prioritize, the cries of women and girls in bondage around the world. Grave injustices plague our sisters, both at home and abroad. We cannot ignore their plight and other justice issues; we dare not only focus on the more parochial ritual issues.[546]

What sociologists call "the feminization of poverty" reflects the reality that, throughout the world, two out of three impoverished adults are women. More than half of the world's food is produced by women, often while maintaining the home, yet these women earn only a fraction of what men earn. These injustices, among many others, necessitate a response from our community. American Jews, regardless of their gender, must be at the forefront of campaigns concerning HIV, micro-lending to women, education for girls, and women's health. In doing so, we realize the teaching of Proverbs 31: 25-26 that "Strength and dignity are her clothing... She opens her mouth with wisdom."

Unfortunately, we do not have to look overseas to find oppression and systemic discrimination against women. One pressing issue here in the U.S. is paycheck fairness. Currently, on average, women between the ages of 45 and 64 who work full-time earn only 72% of the salary of men of the same age, working in the same position, would earn. This inequality often compromises women's abilities to

---

[545] Rabbi Barry L. Schwartz, *Judaism's Great Debates* (Philadelphia: Jewish Publication Society, 2012), 27.
[546] Ruth Messinger, the former President of American Jewish World Service, is an important role model for American Jewish feminists who are interested in ritual inclusion but more focused on global equality issues.

meet their own needs, to provide for their children's future, and to plan for their retirement.

In a similar sense, the equitable labor problem is found in the Jewish community as well. Approximately 75% of the Jewish communal workforce in America consists of women, yet the number of women participating on Jewish nonprofit boards and at the pinnacle of Jewish leadership is astonishingly low, at only 25%. Women constitute roughly 70% of the staffs of Jewish Federations, yet as of 2008, not one of the top 20 Federation leaders has been a woman. Additionally, maternity leave at Jewish organizations is deficient. A recent survey exposed that only about 35% of Jewish organizations offer paid time off to mothers after giving birth.

We can return to the earliest texts of our tradition to help us comprehend the biblical origin of radical injustice toward women and their plight, but we can also look at those same texts to provide us with models of how we must act in our present world when faced with injustice. Eve, the first woman, was cursed with the pain of childbearing after the sin of eating the forbidden fruit. Adam, the first man, was given his own curse: "By the sweat of your brow shall you eat bread." How can we stand by while women of the world, daughters of Eve, are burdened with the curses of both Adam and Eve? It is by and large the women around the world who bear the major brunt of agricultural labor, who continue to die in childbirth, and who continue to be infected with AIDS by promiscuous men.

We should look to the biblical leader and heroine Esther for inspiration. Esther risked her life on behalf of the broader community, in response to Mordechai's rallying cry, "And who knows if you have reached this royal position to address a crisis such as this?" American Jews have attained unprecedented influence, just like Esther in the court of King Achashverosh, and we must channel our influence toward addressing these issues. Who knows if we have reached this privileged position for a crisis such as this? As Esther well understood, all of our achievements will be lost in the abyss of history if we fail to help our brothers and sisters around the world in need.

We, Jewish feminists and otherwise, must unite to address the needs beyond our own gates. We must join the Biblical prophetess Miriam in her universal song of freedom. Furthermore, the above-quoted *midrash* reminds us that, in our own day, we dare not neglect the drowning nations as we celebrate our own victories. The song for equality must be heard across the seas. Only then can we fully rejoice at the liberated crossing of our own proverbial Red Sea.

DEBATE 30.

Auschwitz vs. Sinai:
Which is the More Central Jewish Narrative Today?

Today, Jews have two primary frameworks for developing their Jewish identity: disempowered victim and empowered responsible agent. Of course, one can hold both narratives, but for most, we find that one identity is more dominant. For some Jews today, the Holocaust is the most central memory (actual or vicarious) fostering their identity. For other Jews, Sinai is the most central narrative, often articulated as a kind of "memory," within which to develop identity. One chooses to use their energy to call upon others to "remember," or one uses their energy to engage in and promote religion. And the two are not necessarily mutually exclusive. We therefore need not debate who is right; rather we merely need to understand the complexity.

To be sure, identifying the Holocaust as the central Jewish historical event can lead one to be either a particularist or a universalist. One could invoke "Never Again" solely as a slogan for security within the Jewish community alone. Alternatively, one could also invoke the slogan as a call to combat genocide in Africa. Recall Elie Wiesel's words from his 1986 Nobel Prize acceptance speech, in which he explicitly connected his memories to his activism. "I remember," Wiesel said, "it happened yesterday or eternities ago.... That is why I swore never to be silent whenever and wherever human beings endure suffering and humiliation."

The 20th-century philosopher Emil Fackenheim connected the decimation of the Jewish people in the 1930s and 1940s to a religious narrative. He argued that after Auschwitz, there is now a 614th biblical commandment: working to maintain the continuity of the Jewish people.[547]

Rabbi Yehuda Amital also argued for a new religious mandate based on our collective memory of mid-20th-century reality as experienced directly by European Jewry and less directly by other residents of the Jewish world: "In Auschwitz, they did not check people's tzitzit before sending them to the gas chambers; should we check tzitzit before regarding someone as a brother?" For Rav Amital, fundamental to the Jewish ethos is the adamant resistance against judging another's religious worldview and practice.

Rabbi Dr. Yitz Greenberg went one step further, arguing that the shift suggested by contemplation of the Holocaust is not only in our behavioral tolerance but even deeper: in our understanding of religious truth itself.

---

[547] Emil L. Fackenheim, *The Jewish Return to History* (Schocken Books, 1978), 19-24.

> We are told that the path back to Eden is barred by the blade of an ever-turning fiery sword. Is it too poetic after Auschwitz to see in this image a hint of being thrust into a world, illuminated by the flames of the Shoah, in which all existence and all claims must be viewed with clear-eyed, sober realism, exposed in all their limits?
>
> In the flawed, finite, wounded world that we inhabit, error and limit are incorporated in the essence of the truth. Recognition of this concept is the key to respecting other people; constructive channeling of this insight can prevent the destructive floods that flowed forth from past absolutisms. The only way to wholeness is to heal the world and to work to take the poison out of absolutism without eroding all values and truth in the process.[548]

While some have invoked the Shoah to deepen our faith in the miraculous within what would otherwise present itself as a dark and gloomy world, others, even religious teachers, have invoked the Shoah to challenge our faith. Rabbi Joseph Telushkin writes:

> In a similar vein, I once heard the late theologian Rabbi Eliezer Berkovits suggest that on Yom Ha-Shoah (Holocaust Memorial Day), Jews should gather in synagogues and say... nothing. While most Jews feel it appropriate on Yom Ha-Shoah to recite the Kaddish prayer in honor of the six million, Berkovits reasoned that since the Kaddish is a prayer that praises God, it is more appropriate to offer no prayer at all, such silence constituting a form of protest against God for not using His power to stop the Holocaust.[549]

Consider, on the other hand, a deepening of faith based on the notion that God promised early on that there would be curses and there would be blessings. Rabbi Shlomo Riskin often tells a particular story to show this approach.

---

[548] Rabbi Dr. Yitz Greenberg, "Theology after the Shoah: The Transformation of the Core Paradigm," *Modern Judaism* 26:3, October 2006.
[549] Joseph Telushkin, *You Shall Be Holy* (New York: Harmony/Rodale, 2006), 400. To be sure, Kaddish is of course also recited by mourners, which seems at first glance to run counter to Berkovits' reasoning. On the other hand, one could make a claim for the Shoah being an exception to this otherwise logical connection.

Rav Riskin was praying at the Klausenberger Rebbe's shul. This Rebbe had lost his wife and eleven children in the Holocaust. He was one of the last to leave Europe as he told people that a captain does not leave a sinking ship before the passengers.

He eventually got out, and on the Shabbos morning that Rabbi Riskin came to pray, something unusual happened: When the Torah reader came to the passage of *tochechah* "rebuke," or curses that would befall the Jewish people due to our straying from the Torah, and tried to read those verses quickly and quietly—as is the custom—the Rebbe said only one word: "hecher" (louder).

The Torah reader was confused that the Rebbe would go against tradition and decided to proceed quickly and quietly, assuming he had heard wrong, but then the Rebbe turned around to the congregation with his eyes blazing and banged on the lectern, "Ich hobgezogt hecher." (I said louder!) he shouted. "Let the Master of the Universe hear! We have nothing to be afraid of. We have already received all of the curses—and more. Let the Almighty hear, and let Him understand that the time has come to send the blessings!"

Rabbi Riskin was trembling, other congregants quietly sobbed. The Torah reader then read the verses loudly and slowly. At the end of the services, the Rebbe turned back to the congregation with deep love in his eyes, "Mein tayere shvestern un birder, my beloved sisters and brothers, the blessings will come, but not from America. God has promised the blessings after the curses, but they will only come from the land of Israel. Let us pack our bags for the last time." Soon after that Shabbos, the Rebbe led his congregation to Israel, where they settled in Netanya.[550]

But viewing the tragedy of the Holocaust as the defining narrative of Jewish identity is far from the only way to think about what it means to identify as a Jew in the 21st century. We can also think about what it means to be a Jew by imagining ourselves experiencing divine instruction as to how to live life as a Jew, as described in the narrative of the Sinaitic revelation. And we might ask what the relationship is between a revelation-consciousness and a tragedy-consciousness.

---

[550] Rabbi Shlomo Riskin, "Shabbat Shalom: Parshat Ki Tavo" (excerpt), August 19, 2013, Ohr Torah Stone, https://ots.org.il/parshat-ki-tavo-5773-rabbi-riskin-text/.

We can contemplate the linguistic and phonetic similarity between the name Sinai (the place of revelation) and the word *sinah* (hate). At Sinai, we were charged to be a voice of conscience in the world. But such a role, lofty as it is, can indeed inspire hate from others. How popular is it to be the source of moral critique regarding the evils of our day? How loved were the biblical prophets, who also served as social critics, in their time?

Rabbi Jonathan Sacks wrote about the primacy of the Sinaitic experience for all of the communal and moral significance emerging from that moment.

> At Sinai they acquired *heirut*, their "constitution of liberty" as a nation. It was then that they discovered that *God reveals Himself in the form of laws*. For only the rule of law creates the possibility of a society on which my freedom respects yours. Law—a law that treats everyone equally, rich and poor, native born and stranger—is the institutional embodiment of collective as opposed to individual freedom. At Sinai, the Israelites were transformed from a community of fate into a community of faith, from an *am* to an *edah*, meaning a body politic under the sovereignty of God, whose written constitution was Torah. At that moment a fundamental truth was established: that a free society must be a moral society, for without the rule of law, constrained by the overarching imperatives of the right and the good, freedom will eventually degenerate into tyranny, and liberty, painfully won, will be lost.[551]

Given its historical—or at least imagined—placement as the formative moment of Jewish peoplehood, and perhaps the Jewish religion, one might suggest that all future events could be understood within the framework of Sinai or that any new defining event is included retroactively in the Sinai experience. A famous Talmudic passage[552] illustrates how Moshe was terrified upon prophesying that Rabbi Akiva would teach Jewish law that he himself didn't understand. Moshe was comforted; however, when he heard Rabbi Akiva state that what he was teaching was also revealed to Moshe at Sinai: A revelatory process was put into place, producing new results to new generations that previous generations could never have fathomed, and this enduring connection was solace to the initial recipient of the Torah.

---

[551] Rabbi Jonathan Sacks, *A Letter in the Scroll* (New York: Free Press, 2004), 119-120.
[552] BT Menachot 29b.

Rav Kook explains that embracing Sinai as central does not leave it as a mere historical experience.

> The blessing recited before studying Torah concludes with the words "Who gives the Torah," in the present tense, though the Torah was given on Mount Sinai three thousand years ago. In reality, God is constantly giving the Torah anew. In every age, the Torah flows constantly within the interior of the soul.[553]

Sinai involves ongoing revelation and so new meaning-making continues to emerge from the revelation experience for any Jew immersed within a spiritual consciousness. From a rationalist, or perhaps existentialist perspective, Rabbi Soloveitchik shows how embracing tradition in our time can emerge from an intellectual place. For the Rav, the same way we can use our minds to study science, we can use our minds to study *halachah*.

> He[554] does not search out transcendental, ecstatic paroxysms or frenzied experiences that whisper intonations of another world into his ears. He does not require any miracles or wonder in order to understand the Torah. He approaches the world of *halacha* with his mind and intellect just as cognitive man approaches the natural realm. And since he relies upon his intellect, he places his faith in it and does not suppress any of his psychic faculties in order to merge into some supernal existence. His own personal understanding can resolve the most difficult and complex problems. He pays no heed to any murmurings of [emotional] intuition or other types of mysterious presentiments.[555]

We know today from Pew studies that along with the development of an increasingly secular American Jewish people, the narrative of Auschwitz has taken precedence over the narrative of Sinai. In some respects, at least, this is not surprising. Auschwitz is a provable event and recent in history. Sinai is not provable and, to the extent it can be viewed as historical, occurred over 3,000 years ago. Also, the story of Auschwitz intersects with American Jewish political identity, whereas religious identities are, in some ways, less and less relevant in the public discourse.

---

[553] Orot, vol. 1, 61.
[554] Rabbi Soloveitchik is referring here to the one he calls "halakhic man," meaning a person devoted to, and observant of, *halachah* (Jewish law).
[555] Rabbi Joseph B. Soloveitchik, *Halakhic Man* (Philadelphia: Jewish Publication Society of America, 1991), 79.

Consider a clash between the two narratives in the context of the contemporary State of Israel. In considering the rules of immigration, the State of Israel decided that the Holocaust would be more central than Sinai in the "Who is a Jew?" debate. To be a Jew for the purposes of the "Law of Return" (the law that allows a Jew to become a citizen of Israel with no waiting period), a strict Sinai view is not embraced; rather, the Holocaust view is. Anyone whom Hitler considered a Jew is a Jew for immigration purposes: that is, anyone with one Jewish grandparent may become entitled to immediate citizenship. For other purposes, however, the secular state gives the Chief Rabbinate, which is currently controlled by Ultra-Orthodox leadership, the decision as to who is a Jew.[556]

Further, a typical secular argument for Israel is that it's a place of refuge from horrific events like the Holocaust. A typical religious argument for Israel, on the other hand, is about Israel as an actualization of a prophetic dream and an opportunity to fulfill the mandates of the Torah. Are Jews primarily victims today based upon our history or primarily empowered agents for change?

It is completely understandable, for personal and collective reasons, why one would make the Holocaust the most central part of one's identity. It is also completely understandable why one would include the Holocaust as only one among many Jewish historical experiences within the broader Sinai narrative. It also makes sense why one might embrace both but keep them separate: i.e., suggesting that we have no religious tools from Sinai to make any meaning of such a tragic event as the Holocaust.

Each Jew is charged with the imperative to find the Jewish path that works for them. We are obliged to find the path that allows each of us to grow and to contribute to society in the most productive fashion.

---

[556] Although the Law of Return grants *aliyah* rights as an immigrant, someone wishing to proceed under this law must generally provide, among other documentation, a letter from a rabbi testifying to their Jewish identity, either through birth or conversion, although for these purposes a conversion need not meet the standards that the Rabbinate would apply in determining Jewish identity in non-immigration situations. (Other rules are in place for one not wishing to be considered a technical *oleh*).

On the Self

DEBATE 31.

Love:
Emotion vs. Deed,
Emotion-based Love vs. Deed-based Love

The Torah is deeply concerned with many types of love. Here is an example of one kind, that of love of one's spouse (or is this an example of the love of a son for his late mother?):

> Isaac then brought her into the tent of his mother Sarah, and he took Rebekah as his wife. Isaac loved her, and thus found comfort after his mother's death.[557]

We also learn that one should "Love your fellow as yourself."[558] Rabbi Akiva goes so far as to say: "This is the fundamental principle of the Torah."[559] For the Talmudic rabbis, although the Torah speaks elsewhere of the importance of loving the stranger,[560] this particular *mitzvah* often has to do with our fellow Jews:

> One should love each and every Jew with a "soul love." That means: One should have compassion on each Jew and on their possessions just like one has compassion on themself and their [own] possessions, for it says, "and you shall love your fellow as you love yourself." The specific laws of this *mitzvah* are included in the general principle of the *mitzvah*, that a person should deal with their fellow just like they would deal with themself; to guard their possessions and protect them from any damage; and if speaking about them, they should speak of their praises; and take compassion for their honor; and not to elevate your honor on account of their humiliation....[561]

There is another way that this principle is taught, not based on whom and what you love but based on what you hate:

> There was another incident involving one non-Jew who came before Shammai and said to him: Convert me on condition

---
[557] Genesis 24:67.
[558] Leviticus 19:18.
[559] Sifra, Kedoshim 4:12; Mishnah, Nedarim 9:3.
[560] Deuteronomy 10:19.
[561] Sefer HaChinukh 243:1-3.

that you teach me the entire Torah while I am standing on one foot.⁵⁶² Shammai pushed him away with the builder's cubit in his hand. (This was a common measuring stick and Shammai was a builder by trade.) The same gentile came before Hillel. He converted him and said to him: "That which is hateful to you do not do to another; that is the entire Torah, and the rest is its interpretation. Go study."⁵⁶³

The rabbis are interested in other kinds of love as well. They taught:

> All love that is dependent on a specific cause will disappear once that factor is no longer present, but the love that is not dependent on a specific cause will never disappear.⁵⁶⁴

Rav Samson Raphael Hirsch teaches that love cannot be superficial:

> Wherever love is rooted in the spiritual and moral worth of the beloved individual, there the love will be as abiding as the values on which it was founded. But a love based on physical attraction will not outlast those fleeting charms.⁵⁶⁵

When we love, we should not be concerned with our own pleasure, but rather focus on the well-being of the recipient of our love. A *Mussar* story makes this point well:

> Rabbi Leib Chasman, spiritual supervisor of [the] Chevron Yeshivah, once saw a student eating fish with great relish. "Tell me, young man," he asked him, "do you love fish?" The student answered in the affirmative. "If you love fish," replied Rabbi Chasman, "then you should have cared for the one on your plate. You should have fed it and tried to make it happy. Instead, you are devouring it." As the student groped for a proper response, the rabbi explained: "Obviously, you don't love fish. You love yourself!"⁵⁶⁶

---

⁵⁶² While some take the words "while standing on one foot" literally, it may simply be akin to the common expression "in the blink of an eye."
⁵⁶³ Babylonian Talmud Shabbat 31a.
⁵⁶⁴ Pirkei Avot 5:16.
⁵⁶⁵ Rabbi Samson Raphael Hirsch, *Chapters of the Fathers* (New York: Feldheim Publishers, 2014), 89.
⁵⁶⁶ Rabbi Aharon Feldman, *The River, the Kettle, and the Bird* (New York: Feldheim Publishers, 1987), 26–27.

Also emerging from the *Mussar* camp, Rav Eliyahu Dessler, spiritual advisor of the Ponevezh Yeshiva, taught that giving, not receiving, is what fosters love:

> The love between man and woman is a fascinating phenomenon... The source of this love is the fact that they complement one another. For God has created men and women incomplete on their own, as the Sages say, "Any man who is not married is not a complete human being." Thus, on his own, man is incomplete and cannot function properly. The completion they bring each other creates love, since, as we have seen previously, giving to another fosters love. The love that exists between them makes them want to give happiness and satisfaction to each other... I always say to couples at their wedding, as follows: "Take care to always wish to bring joy and pleasure to each other as you do now. And be aware that the moment that you begin making demands on each other, happiness will escape you."[567]

Rav Dessler teaches that the root of *ahava* (love) is *hav* (to give). The one who gives more has the potential to love more.

The prolific 20th-century author and teacher Rabbi Aryeh Kaplan similarly explained that we don't love another just for what they do for us but for who they are (even as he expresses this view anachronistically in language that assumes that in a relationship between a man and a woman, the man is the one who loves and the woman serves as the object of this love):

> The most perfect love in the world is between parent and child. When a mother holds an infant in her arms her heart overflows with a most unique love. She has this love not because she expects anything from the child but merely because the child exists.[568] Love between parent and child exists because parent and child feel like one. The bond between a man and woman is a reflection of this.

---

[567] *Michtav Me'Eliyahu*, Vol. 1, 38.
[568] One of course could add that a mother loves her child because she carried him/her during pregnancy and gave birth to that child.

The Torah teaches that man and woman were originally created as a single, androgynous unit.[569] God then separated the two, making man and woman into independent persons. Thus, man and woman began as a single entity, and togetherness is a natural tendency to be one. Adam recognized this as soon as Eve was separated from him. He said, "Now this is a bone from my bones and flesh from my flesh."

Adam was saying that when a man marries, he takes the natural love that he has for his parents and directs it toward his wife.[570]

Rav Hirsch further teaches:

> "V'ahavta l'rei'acha kamocha" ("You shall love your neighbor as yourself") ... is not the person themself, but everything that pertains to this person, all the conditions of their life, the weal and the woe which makes up their position in the world. To this, their weal and their woe, we are to give our love as if it were our own; we are to rejoice in their good fortune, and grieve over their misfortune as if it were our own. We are to assist in everything that furthers their well-being and happiness as if we were working for ourselves.... For the demand of this love is something which lies quite outside the sphere of the personality of our neighbor.... Nobody may look on the progress of another as a hindrance to their own progress, or look on the downfall of another as the means for their own rising, and nobody may rejoice in their own progress if it is at the expense of their neighbor.... Their own self-love too is only a consciousness of his duty. They see in themself only a creation of God, entrusted to himself to attain the bodily, mental, and earthly existence, and for which God had given them directions in God's Torah.[571]

There are three primary love relationships in the Torah: 1. Love of one's fellow Jew; 2. Love of God; 3. Love of the stranger. These three, as we've seen in all we explored above, are interconnected. Consider the relationship between love for one's spouse and love for God:

---

[569] Genesis 1:27. This notion is based on a strict reading of the verse, which states that "God formed man in His image... male and female He created them." Genesis 2 provides us with a very different picture of the creation of man, with the more well-known narrative that God first created man and only afterwards created woman as a separate entity from one of his ribs. (The biblical word *tzeila*, meaning rib, also means side. The verse can therefore be understood to imply that God formed woman from one of man's sides). Indeed, these two different narratives give birth to Rabbi J. B. Soloveitchik's thesis of what he calls Adam 1 and Adam 2.
[570] Rabbi Aryeh Kaplan, *Made in Heaven* (Moznaim Publishing Corporation, 1983), 11.
[571] Rav Hirsch, Leviticus 19:18.

> At the time that the Israelites would go up [to the Temple in Jerusalem for their festivals, the *kohanim*] would roll back the curtain [of the Holy of Holies] and show them the Cherubim, who were clinging to each other. And they would say to them: "Look, your love before God is like the love of a man and a woman."[572]

We see here that different kinds of love are separate but also interconnected in many ways. C.S. Lewis argues that there are 4 types of love: Affection (storge), Friendship (philia), Romantic (eros), and Charity (agape). The Rambam (Maimonides) offers a different threefold model of love:

> There are three types of love: Love due to what one stands to benefit from the other; love of pleasure; and love of virtue... Love of virtue is when two people desire the same valuable thing, the essentially good, and each one wishes to collaborate with the other in obtaining that ideal for both of them.[573]

For the Rambam, following Aristotelian thought, one level of loving another is being a virtue partner with them. After all, the Talmud teaches that without a life partner, one is missing so much:

> Rabbi Tanchum said that Rabbi Chanilai said: Any man who does not have a wife is left without joy, without blessing, without goodness... In the West, Eretz Yisrael, they say: One who lives without a wife is left without Torah, and without a wall of protection... Rava bar Ulla said: One who does not have a wife is left without peace.[574]

This idea of covenantal commitment is one that Rabbi Joseph B. Soloveitchik develops as well:

> The Bible equated the great historical covenant binding the charismatic community to God with the limited private covenant that unites two individuals in matrimony. On the one hand, the great covenant has been compared by the prophets, time

---

[572] BT Yoma 54a.
[573] Rambam's commentary on Pirkei Avot 1:6.
[574] BT Yevamot 62b.

and again, to the betrothal of Israel to God; on the other hand, the ordinary betrothal of woman to man has been raised to the level of covenantal commitment. Marriage as such is called *berit*, a covenant.[575]

Rabbi Soloveitchik reflects upon this phenomenon as a metaphysical ethical summons:

> Within the frame of reference of marriage, love becomes not an instinctual reaction of an excited heart to the shocking sudden encounter with beauty, but an intentional experience in reply to a metaphysical ethical summons, a response to the great challenge, replete with ethical motifs. Love, emerging from an existential moral awareness, is sustained not by the flame of passion, but by the strength of a Divine norm whose repetitious fulfillment re-awakens its vigor and force... The ethical yearning to create and share existence with someone as yet unknown redeems *hedone* by infusing it with axiological normative meaning and thus gives it a new aspect—that of faith.[576]

We have demonstrated that, despite the stereotype that Judaism isn't a religion of love—which even Jews have often embraced in an effort to distinguish themselves from Christians—Judaism is indeed a religion deeply concerned with love. We have seen that there are many different kinds of love for different people and for God.

But how do we fulfill that love? Some might argue that love is merely a passionate emotion, but many Jewish thinkers argue against this approach, prioritizing love acted upon over love simply felt. Rabbi Soloveitchik wrote elsewhere:

> The Bible spoke of the commandment to love one's neighbor (Leviticus 19:18). However, in Talmudic literature, emphasis was placed not only upon sentiment, but upon action, which is motivated by sentiment. The Hoshen Mishpat, the Jewish code of civil law, analyzes not human emotions but actual human relations. The problem of Hoshen Mishpat is not what one feels toward the other, but how he acts toward him.[577]

---
[575] Rav Soloveitchik, *Family Redeemed* (Jersey City, New Jersey: Ktav Publishing, 2000), 41-42.
[576] Ibid.
[577] Ibid., 40.

Following the approach that love is not just an emotion but is actualized through deed, Rabbi Jonathan Sacks wrote:

> What is *hessed*? It is usually translated as "kindness" but it also means "love"—not love as emotion or passion, but love expressed as deed. Theologians define *hessed* as covenant love. Covenant is the bond by which two parties pledge themselves to one another, each respecting the freedom and the integrity of the other.... *Hessed* (love) is an act of engagement. Justice is best administered without emotion. *Hessed* exists only in virtue of emotion, empathy, and sympathy, feeling-with and feeling-for. We act with kindness because we know what it feels like to be in need of kindness. We comfort the mourners because we know what it is to mourn. *Hessed* requires not detached rationality but emotional intelligence.... Societies are only human and humanizing when they are a community of communities built on face-to-face encounters—covenantal relationships. Emmanuel Levinas was right to see the concept of a "face" as fundamental to our humanity. Society is faceless; hessed is a relationship of face to face. The Pentateuch repeatedly emphasizes that we cannot see God face to face. It follows that we can only see God in the face of another.[578]

So, it is not enough to help another and at the same time not feel any emotional connection to them. It is also certainly not enough to feel fervent passionate love for another but not to take responsibility for their care. The deed is primary, but the emotion is connected to the deed. This is why Judaism does not advocate boundless love. Love made real through deed is dependent on the resources that make deeds possible, resources such as time and energy which are, by their very nature, limited. But love that is bound by the need to prioritize among the deeds that actualize that love can nonetheless be, and perhaps must be, as deep and as meaningful as any other love.

We can strive for a world of *ahavat chinam* (baseless love) but we can also realize that as humans we are not capable of the Divine love: infinite unconditional love. As humans, our capacity to love is more limited, conditional, and finite. Nonetheless, we can strive to be more like God, loving others fully, through emotion and deed.

---

[578] Rabbi Jonathan Sacks, *To Heal a Fractured World* (New York: Schocken, 2007), 45-55.

DEBATE 32.

Body vs. Soul

Are humans to be defined primarily by our bodies and our physical features, or by our soul (our deeper, spiritual essence)? Are my responsibilities to another more about a concern for the other's body or their soul?

Right from the creation story, we learn that humans are most certainly a combination of both body and soul:

> The Lord God formed man from the dust of the earth. He blew into his nostrils the breath of life, and man became a living being.[579]

Rashi explains that this verse teaches that humanity emerges from both "the upper and lower spheres—the body from the lower spheres and the soul from the upper spheres."[580]

But which will dominate: The desires of the body or the aspirations of the soul? The great Torah commentator, Kli Yakar, explains:

> For the "living soul" is the eternal, intellectual spirit. If you examine Who breathed [the soul into man], you will find that it refers to a Divine soul from above. But the verse tells us that even though God breathed an intellectual, living soul into man, nevertheless in the beginning of his existence, man was simply another living spirit, like all other creatures, for man is born as a wild animal and his perfection depends on the diligence of his efforts and the correctness of his choices when he matures with age.
>
> However, at the beginning of a person's existence, even though a living soul was already placed within him, the soul is not yet actualized, but is merely potential within him, and if he does not gird himself with diligence to wage God's war, he will remain on the level of an animal. But an ox or a sheep or goat is born with its full level of perfection on the day of its creation, and it does not perfect itself further.
>
> The Torah revealed this to us so that a person should not make the mistake of thinking that since he was born complete,

---
[579] Genesis 2:7.
[580] Rashi's commentary on Genesis 2:7.

> he will achieve his perfection without effort. It is not so! Rather, everything depends on a person's actions; he always has the ability to exchange intellect for nature or nature for intellect. This is why the Torah does not say about the creation of man, "God saw that it was good," because when man was created, it was not yet apparent in what way he was good.[581]

One might have thought that since human beings have a soul, they are therefore pure and their actions are naturally good. But this is not the case, Kli Yakar explains. The soul demonstrates potential but the body has its own desires. Humans have the choice to live by body or by soul, or by a combination of the two.

For some, this is not just a simple duality but a constant war. Rabbi Moshe Chaim Luzzatto[582] teaches:

> The two are then in a constant state of battle. If the soul prevails, it not only elevates itself, but elevates the body as well, and the individual thereby attains his destined perfection. If he allows the physical to prevail, on the other hand, then besides lowering his body, he also debases his soul. Such an individual makes himself unworthy of perfection, and thus divorces himself from God. He still has the ability, however, to subjugate the physical to his soul and intellect, and thereby achieve perfection.[583]

For others, the body and soul are not at war but rather supporting one another. The Talmud relates:

> Antoninos, the Roman emperor, said to Rabbi Yehuda HaNasi: The body and the soul are able to exempt themselves from judgment for their sins. How so? The body says: The soul sinned, as from the day of my death when it departed from me, I am cast like a silent stone in the grave, and do not sin. And the soul says: The body sinned, as from the day that I departed from it, I am flying in the air like a bird, incapable of sin. Rabbi Yehuda HaNasi said to him: I will tell you a parable. To what is this matter comparable? It is comparable to a king of flesh and blood who had a fine orchard, and in it there were fine first fruits of a fig tree,

---

[581] Kli Yakar's commentary on Genesis 2:7.
[582] Rabbi Moshe Chaim Luzzatto is also known by his acronym, Ramchal.
[583] *Derech Hashem* 1:3:2, translated by Rabbi Aryeh Kaplan (New York: Feldheim Publishers, 1997), 45, 47.

> and he stationed two guards in the orchard, one lame, who was unable to walk, and one blind. Neither was capable of reaching the fruit on the trees in the orchard without the assistance of the other. The lame person said to the blind person: I see fine first fruits of a fig tree in the orchard; come and place me upon your shoulders. I will guide you to the tree, and we will bring the figs to eat them. The lame person rode upon the shoulders of the blind person and they brought the figs and ate them.
>
> Sometime later the owner of the orchard came to the orchard. He said to the guards: The fine first fruits of a fig tree that were in the orchard, where are they? The lame person said: Do I have any legs with which I would be able to walk and take the figs? The blind person said: Do I have any eyes with which I would be able to see the way to the figs? What did the owner of the orchard do? He placed the lame person upon the shoulders of the blind person just as they did when they stole the figs, and he judged them as one.[584]

The great 20th-century *Mussar* teacher Rabbi Shlomo Wolbe explains the above passage as follows:

> The powers of the soul and the powers of the body are both "guards" of the beautiful orchard, which is man and his world. The only difference between them is that the powers of the body are blind, while the powers of the soul have sight. The drive to live impels us to take care of our health, and in dangerous situations it activates all of our abilities to preserve our lives. The desire to reproduce impels us to establish a home and have children. Jealousy impels us to try to earn a respectable living. Love of children impels us to take care of our offspring and raise them. All of our capacities, then, are excellent "guards" for a person. But they do not know why they are guarding us—they are blind.
>
> The soul is the guard who has eyesight. It sees the goal and can give our lives direction—what to strive for, whom to serve, what to achieve. That is the soul's purpose in guarding the "orchard of life," to ensure that we do not use our inborn abilities in vain. Rather, we will know how to direct them toward our true

---

[584] BT Sanhedrin 91a and 91b.

goal. But the soul is lame. It does not have the ability to carry out its drives and desire on its own accord. For that purpose, it needs the body.[585]

One might mistakenly conclude that since the soul is so much loftier, that we are not concerned with the body. Yet, even Rambam (Maimonides), who in typical Aristotelean fashion is far more interested in the mind than the body, teaches:

> A person should ensure that his body is complete and strong so that his soul will be adequately fit to know God, because it is impossible to understand and fathom wisdom when a person is hungry, sick, or if one of his limbs is in pain ... Rather, his body should be complete and strong to serve God. And even when he is sleeping, a person should have the intention that he is allowing his mind and body to rest in order that he should not become sick, which would prevent him from serving God. Thus, his sleep becomes part of his Service of God.[586]

Indeed, caring for the body is part of our service of God. A key element of the spiritual experience of *simchat Yom Tov* (joy on the holiday) and *oneg Shabbat* (delight of shabbat) is to eat delicious food. When we feed the body, we are "feeding" the *neshamah yeteirah* (the extra soul that emerges on shabbat). One might think that denying the body its physical pleasures makes one a more spiritual person. The Talmud disagrees. Living an ascetic life can in fact be transgressing:

> R. Eleazar HaKappar B'rebbi said: Why does the Torah state, "And make atonement for him [the nazzarite], for he sinned against the soul?"[587] Against what "soul" did the nazzarite sin? It can only be because he denied himself wine. If, then, this man who did no more than deny himself wine is termed a sinner, how much more so is this true of one who is ascetic in all things![588]

---

[585] *Alei Shur* Vol. I, 143.
[586] *Mishneh Torah*, Hilchot Dei'ot 3:3. Indeed, Rambam goes even further and spells out a specific diet that he believed one should adhere to. To this day, there are individuals who follow Rambam's diet.
[587] Numbers 6:8
[588] BT Nazir 19a; BT Nedarim 10a.

Now to be sure, there is an authentic Jewish traditional approach toward asceticism that we cannot deny;[589] however, as we have seen, it can be argued that the dominant thrust of Jewish tradition is about the elevation and sanctification of, rather than the deprivation of, the body.

On the other hand, we would certainly be skeptical of ideologies that make the pleasure of the body an end in itself. Rav Wolbe teaches:

> Bodily sensation is the foundation of all of Western culture. That is what brought about the development of science, art, sculpture, and sports in ancient Greece. (An indication of this is the "gymnasium," a place where sports were conducted by unclad athletes, and from which their schools developed.) The way of Torah begins with a person learning to view his body as a tool for the service of God, not [solely] for enjoyment. The holy books refer to the body as an "encasement for holiness."[590]

We care about the body not as a hedonistic end in itself but rather as a vehicle toward the spiritual good. The Torah does not prohibit everything that is wrong and inappropriate. In fact, Ramban (Nachmanides) famously taught that one could be a *naval birshut haTorah* (a glutton with the permission of the Torah)[591] specifically pointing to overindulgence (in food and in sexual relations).

The human body does not entirely resemble God, since God has no body, according to virtually every Jewish thinker. The soul, on the other hand, is indeed quite similar to God. The Talmud explains:

> Just as the Holy One, Blessed be He, fills the entire world, so too the soul fills the entire body.
> Just as the Holy One, Blessed be He, sees but is not seen, so too does the soul see, but is not seen.
> Just as the Holy One, Blessed be He, sustains the entire world, so too the soul sustains the entire body.

---

[589] There is of course one day of the year, Yom Kippur, in which we do indeed focus solely on the soul and refrain from the five basic physical, pleasurable activities (eating and drinking, bathing, anointing, wearing leather shoes, and sexual relations) in order to heighten our spiritual awareness. Doing so merely one day a year, and being sure to not overdo it, is viewed as healthy by the Torah, and helps to center us.

[590] *Alei Shur* Vol. I, 59.

[591] Ramban's commentary on Leviticus 19:1. Fascinatingly, Ramban asserts this notion of *naval birshut haTorah* as his understanding of the *mitzvah* of *kedoshim tihyu* (the command that we must be holy). He explains the *mitzvah* this way: "*Kadeish atzmecha b'mutar lecha*" ("sanctify yourself with that which is permitted to you").

> Just as the Holy One, Blessed be He, is pure, so too is the soul pure.
> Just as the Holy One, Blessed be He, resides in a chamber within a chamber, in His inner sanctum, so too the soul resides in a chamber within a chamber, in the innermost recesses of the body.
> Therefore, that which has these five characteristics, the soul, should come and praise He Who has these five characteristics.[592]

Just as God is hidden to the eye, so too, the soul is hidden from the mind. The Zohar teaches that the deepest truth about the universe is that which we cannot see with the eyes on our faces but only through the eyes of the soul. And so, for some, the goal in life is to use the body primarily as a vehicle to actualize the soul. Consider this teaching of Rabbi Moshe Chaim Luzzatto:

> ... if the purpose of the creation of man had been for his station in this world, it would not have been necessary for such a distinguished and sublime soul to be placed in him. The soul is greater than the angels themselves, and certainly it does not derive any enjoyment from any of the pleasures of this world. This is what our Sages taught us in Midrash Kohelet (Kohelet Rabbah 6): "'And the soul will also not be filled'—This is analogous to an ordinary citizen who marries the Royal Princess. Even if he brings her everything in the world, it means nothing to her, since she is the King's daughter. Similarly with the soul, even if we bring it all the physical delights of the world, they mean nothing to it since it comes from the upper spheres."[593]

How about our relationship to others? Rabbi Moshe Feinstein, one of the greatest *halakhic* authorities of the 20th century, taught that through modeling we can affect the souls of others.

> "Thus, a person should understand that the soul inside him is holy and pure and has the ability to influence and sanctify his body. When he is sanctified, he will also exert an influence on his surroundings, so that anyone who associates with him will

---

[592] BT Berakhot 10a. This comment is made regarding the verse "Let all souls praise God" (Psalms 150:6).
[593] Rabbi Moshe Chaim Luzzatto, *Mesilat Yesharim* Ch. 1.

learn from his deeds and will also become holy and pure, and thus he will bring sanctity to the entire world."[594]

Interestingly enough, in Jewish eschatology, there is concern for both the body and the soul in the afterlife. For the body, this is *techiyat hameitim* (the resurrection of the dead). For the soul, there is the concept of *gilgulim* (reincarnation) and *olam haba* (the world to come—the world of souls).

The human body is most certainly physiologically complex, but there is only one name for the body. The soul, on the other hand, may be deemed even more complex by virtue of the fact that it has five names/dimensions: *nefesh* (soul), *ruach* (spirit), *neshamah* (breath), *yechidah* (singularity or oneness), *and chayah* (lifeforce).[595] The soul operates on so many levels. For the Hasidim, the soul even operates through the body and through the physical world (*avodah b'gashmiut*).

In the end, we see that many Jewish thinkers embrace a duality and a binary. Some even suggest there is a war. But we might also challenge the binary of body vs. soul. Perhaps the two are more interconnected and intertwined than we might imagine or experience? Rabbi Yisrael Salanter famously taught that another's physical needs are my spiritual needs. This is to say that we are indeed focused on our souls, but the way to do that is through care of others' bodies. When we construct a more just society that honors the bodies of others (access to healthcare, food, water, rest, etc.) our souls are elevated. One of the most unique aspects of Jewish thought is that both the body and soul are crucial to our *avodat Hashem* (service of God) and our actualization of our potential. Being completely soulful without the body does not make sense in Jewish thought, in this world. On the other hand, performing deeds without any spiritual intentionality is certainly not a noble pursuit either. We need to learn to resist the temptations of hedonism in society today and of radical spirituality that neglects the body as well. We are to strive for a healthy dose of both.

---

[594] *Derash Moshe*, 303.
[595] *Bereshit Rabbah* 14:9.

Debate 33.

Zealousness vs. Tolerance

Should we be certain and forceful with our ideas? Should we be uncertain and unconvincing? Somewhere in between? This is a crucial religious and moral question. It's also a question relevant to all who believe in anything passionately, beyond the moral and religious, whether theological, political, or intellectual in nature.

The case for *kinah*[596] (zealotry) is easy to make. It is the story of Pinchas:

> The Lord spoke to Moses, saying, "Phinehas, son of Eleazar son of Aaron the priest, has turned back My wrath from the Israelites by displaying among them his passion for Me, so that I did not wipe out the Israelite people in My passion. Say, therefore, 'I grant him My pact of friendship. It shall be for him and his descendants after him a pact of priesthood for all time, because he took impassioned action for his God, thus making expiation for the Israelites.'"[597]

Pinchas acts with zealotry upon witnessing an act of moral depravity, and God seemingly rewards him. The Talmud explains:

> What did Pinchas see that led him to arise and take action? Rav says: He saw the incident taking place before him and he remembered the *halachah* (law). He said to Moses: Brother of the father of my father (as Moses was the brother of his grandfather Aaron), did you not teach me this during your descent from Mount Sinai: One who engages in intercourse with a gentile woman, zealots strike him? Moses said to him: Let the one who reads the letter be the *parvanka* (agent) to fulfill its contents.[598]

There is a fascinating principle, found in several places in the Talmud,[599] of *halachah v'ein morin kein* ("this is the *halachah*, but we do not teach it"). In the case of Pinchas' zeal, this principal may indeed apply. In other words, while his actions were correct, we shouldn't necessarily teach others to act accordingly.

---

[596] *Kinah* means zeal or zealotry. Interestingly, the same term also means jealousy.
[597] Numbers 25:10-13.
[598] BT Sanhedrin 82b.
[599] BT Shabbat 12b.

In fact, the Ben Ish Hai[600] wants to limit the application so that we don't seek to emulate this behavior.

> "Did you not teach me this during your descent from Mount Sinai," that's the version in the Gemara. "Teach me" and not "teach us" in the plural, and it seems that only for this one incident, just for me (Pinchas) you taught this law, as it was certain from On High that I (Pinchas) will fulfill it. . . .[601]

The Netziv[602] also seeks to limit the application by saying that Pinchas' intentions were only for heaven. How many today in their zealotry could claim that?

> "Because he was zealous for his God," he deserves the covenant of peace, not only because he "has turned back My wrath" through his zealousness, and had he not reached God's wrath, he would not have deserved the covenant of peace. Not so, but rather because he was zealous for his God, was his anger and wrath only for the sake of heaven. Therefore, he received the covenant of peace.[603]

Nonetheless, many religious zealots today, as well as other biblical figures, indeed believe that they're acting purely for the sake of heaven and not out of rage or ego, and therefore have the license to act. How else can we understand the zealotry of Dina's brothers who slaughter the people of Shechem?

The case for tolerance, on the other hand, is not hard to make either. We learn in Proverbs: "A calm disposition gives bodily health; Passion is rot to the bones."[604] We are to master the trait of *menuchat hanefesh* (equanimity) rather than be led astray by our desires and passions. Song of Songs has even stronger fighting words for extremism:

> Let me be a seal upon your heart, Like the seal upon your hand. For love is fierce as death, Passion is mighty as Sheol; Its darts are darts of fire, A blazing flame.[605]

---

[600] Generally referred to by the name of his work, Ben Ish Hai, Yosef Hayim ben Yehoyada (1835-1909) was a Baghdadi master *kabbalist* and *halachist*.
[601] Ben Ish Hai, Sanhedrin 82b.
[602] Netziv is an acronym for Rabbi Naftali Tzvi Yehuda Berlin (1816-1893), the dean of the famed Volozhin yeshivah.
[603] Ha'amek Davar, Numbers 25:2.
[604] Proverbs 14:30.
[605] Song of Songs 8:6.

The Ramban (Nachmanides) teaches:

> The only place where we find the language of jealousy/zealousness, is in matters of *avodah zarah* (idolatry). And this is so because Israel is the one God consecrated... and if God's people, God's own servants, turn to other gods, God is jealous just like a man is envious of his woman when she goes with another or his servant, when he takes on another master, and the same language is not so with regard to other nations, to whom God gave the heavenly array.[606]

Let's fast forward from the Torah to the Talmud to see how the rabbis explore this issue. Rabban Yochanan ben Zakkai, one of the most influential rabbis in the Talmud,[607] can be seen as the quintessential model for living with equanimity.[608] We learn about his religious personality:

> The Sages said about Rabban Yochanan ben Zakkai, the teacher of Rabbi Eliezer: In all his days he never engaged in idle conversation; and he never walked four cubits without engaging in Torah study and without donning phylacteries; and no person ever preceded him into the study hall; and he never slept in the study hall, neither substantial sleep nor a brief nap; and he never contemplated matters of Torah in alleyways filthy with human excrement, as doing so is a display of contempt for the Torah; and he never left anyone in the study hall and exited; and no person ever found him sitting and silent, i.e., inactive; rather, he was always sitting and studying; and only he opened the door for his students, disregarding his own eminent standing; and he never said anything that he did not hear from his teacher; and he never said to his students that the time has arrived to arise and leave the study hall except on Passover eves, when they were obligated to sacrifice the Paschal lamb, and Yom Kippur eves, when there is a mitzvah to eat and drink abundantly. And Rabbi Eliezer, his student, accustomed himself to model his conduct after his example.[609]

---

[606] Ramban's Commentary on the Torah, Exodus 20:2.
[607] Pirkei Avot 1:1, 2:8.
[608] For more on how Rabban Yochanan ben Zakkai lived, see BT Sukkah 28a, BT Yoma 39b, BT Berakhot 28b, Jerusalem Talmud (JT) Nedarim 5:6. Also see Mesechet Sofrim 16:8-9.
[609] BT Sukkah 28a.

We can, perhaps, learn people's character best in times of crisis. Indeed, here we learn a lot about Rav Yochanan ben Zakkai:

> Vespasian said to him: If there is a barrel of honey and a snake [*derakon*] is wrapped around it, wouldn't they break the barrel in order to kill the snake? In similar fashion, I am forced to destroy the city of Jerusalem in order to kill the zealots barricaded within it. Rabban Yochanan ben Zakkai was silent and did not answer. In light of this, Rav Yosef later read the following verse about him, and some say that it was Rabbi Akiva who applied the verse to Rabban Yochanan ben Zakkai: "I am the Lord... Who turns wise men backward and makes their knowledge foolish" (Isaiah 44:25). As Rabban Yochanan ben Zakkai should have said the following to Vespasian in response: In such a case, we take tongs, remove the snake, and kill it, and in this way we leave the barrel intact. So too, you should kill the rebels and leave the city as it is.[610]

This was such a scary time. Virtually everything was destroyed. The Temple was burnt down; the Jews were murdered and exiled. Rabban Yochanan ben Zakkai, almost miraculously, now has an audience with the villain and he is in a position to make requests. Instead of fighting or pushing back or making major demands, he requests to keep Judaism alive through study and learning.

Consider the reply of one with zealotry on the other hand, that of the Bar Kochba revolts.

> Rabbi Yochanan said: "Eighty thousand pairs of horn-blowers were sent to siege on Betar, and each of them was in charge of a number of troops, and there was the Ben Kozva[611] (Son of Kozba), and he had two hundred (soldiers of) "chopped fingers."
>
> The Sages sent for him and said to him: How much longer will you continue to mutilate people of Israel? He said to them: And how else should I check them? They sent for him and said: Anyone who does not tear the cedar out of the Lebanon do not write it in your list...

---

[610] BT Gittin 56a.
[611] Ben Kozva, also pronounced Koziba, is synonymous with Bar Kochba.

> What was the power of Ben Kozba? They said: When he went to war, he would catch the bullet-stones in his limbs, and would kick them back and kill some people.
> Rabbi Yochanan said: When Rabbi Akiva saw Ben Kozva, he would say: "A star has shone from Jacob" (Numbers 24:17)—the star of Jacob has shone—this is the Messiah, the king. Rabbi Yochanan ben Torta said: Akiva, weeds will rise in your cheeks, and still the son of David does not come.[612]

Bar Kochba offered a very different path than Rabban Yochanan ben Zakkai did. We can be reminded, as Bar Kochba was deemed by some to be a messianic figure, that in Jewish thought there are two messiahs. There is Moshiach ben Yosef (the one who will violently lead a war toward redemption) and Moshiach ben David (the one will then usher in a new era of peace). These two figures of redemption resemble the paradox of finding redemption through zealotry and yet also through peace.

One might say that the Rabban Yochanan ben Zakkai tradition is followed today by the Haredim (ultra-orthodox population) and the Bar Kochba revolts are still playing out today with the proactive, sometimes militant, Zionists (who are willing to physically fight for freedom).

North American Jews, who are not asked to fight physically for survival, will easily have a very different idea of violence and resistance than those required to serve in the army and to enlist their children. Of course, army service should not be equated with zealotry, and living in the Diaspora should not be equated with being tolerant. It is far more complicated than that.

But the question remains: Should we use violence to protect that which we cherish most? The hawks say yes while the doves say no. The Haredi population, by and large, says no,[613] while the Zionists say yes (at least as it pertains to state-building). There is naturally a correlation between believing strongly in something and being willing to fight for it. A religious person is often more likely to be zealous. A relativist is perhaps less likely.

We can look at another example from the 20th century:

> David Ben Gurion and his moderate Zionist party (the Haganah) urged independence through intense lobbying and other

---
[612] Bar Kochba: Midrash Eicha Rabba 2:4. Translated by Rabbanit Michal Kohane.
[613] While this is true regarding protecting the land and State, many Haredim are of course militant regarding other issues which they hold dear. While one may not condone their behavior or agree with their sentiments, such as blocking traffic and/or throwing stones, those engaging in such behavior, for the most part, truly believe that they are in the right and are "waging the war" to protect Judaism as they see it.

political means. Menachem Begin and his minority militant organization (the Irgun) were more aggressive; they attacked British targets. The most notorious occurred at Jerusalem's King David Hotel, resulting in military and civilian casualties alike.

Although they shared the same goal of independence, the internal dispute over resistance to the British escalated. Eventually Ben Gurion said the Irgun had to be stopped, and he ordered a boat full of Irgun arms to be sunk. Israelis continue to argue about the role of the Irgun and Ben Gurion's decisions, and about the degree to which external threats to Israel's security should be met with negotiation or force. The debate over resistance to evil is alive and well. [614]

Any value held in its extreme is very dangerous, as we have learned from religious zealots such as Baruch Goldstein (who committed the Hebron massacre) and Yigal Amir (who assassinated Yitzchak Rabin). So too, to be a relativist who won't fight for anything leads to being silent and passive when facing evil. So, while the debate of Bar Kochba vs. Rabban Yochanan ben Zakkai, between the Haredim and the Zionists, between Pinchas and the masses, lives on, we must learn when to stand up, how to stand up, how to be passionate about our values, but also to show restraint. In social change work today, it is crucial that we have passion but equally crucial that we place enormous checks upon that passion to be sure we maintain balance and are always level-headed.

---

[614] Rabbi Barry L. Schwartz, *Judaism's Great Debates* (Philadelphia: Jewish Publication Society, 2012), 46.

DEBATE 34.

Calm vs. Tension:
Is Life About Struggle or Peace?

One the one hand, our tradition emphasizes over and over the value of inner *shalom* (peace). On the other hand, our tradition emphasizes again and again the value of struggle. So, which is it? Do we want calm or tension?

Another way to frame this debate is in the context of pleasure versus asceticism. For many schools of philosophy and religion, the goal is asceticism.[615] We are to be in battle with our temptations and engage in a negation of evil desires. It is a form of counter-naturalism arguing that we are naturally flawed. The world is not naturally good, according to this school of thought, and the human body has desires that must be overcome. We should exist with some level of guilt and shame for what we are and how we behave. Nietzsche disagreed with this approach and argued that we should affirm all of our existence, including all that is necessary about us as individuals. We should love fate. He argued that when we are creating our system of meaning that we should not feel trapped by the systems that have been passed down to us. He offers us a paradox: we can fight evil but also affirm it. He is arguing against "being" in favor of "becoming" (against a fixed mindset in support of a "will to power"). He wants to increase our responsibility for making meaning of our lives rather than see us submit to what others tell us we must be. Struggle is a necessary part of life and it is beautiful, and we should reaffirm struggle positively rather than have some negative war against the self and against the necessary.

Struggle may sound attractive until it is real. After all, struggle was largely considered to be the curse placed upon Adam and Eve for eating the fruit.[616] It is difficult to persevere through struggles, for all of us. But what's the alternative? To live in a false reality? Would you strap yourself to a machine and spend your whole life lying on a table living in the illusion of a very pleasurable life if you could? Or would you rather have a less pleasurable but real life, where you go through the experiences firsthand? Of course, if one was extremely sick or in prison for life, you can perhaps imagine them choosing the first option. But the fact that almost

---

[615] Buddhism and Hinduism are ascetic in nature. Islam, while not necessarily ascetic, does indeed preach certain ascetic practices, such as abstention from drinking wine. This approach to wine consumption is diametrically opposed to our Jewish practice of using wine for the recitation of *kiddush* and *havdalah*, and, perhaps most famously, for the four cups at the Passover *seder*. Even more telling is the fact that wine is the only drink that merits its own *berachah*, "*borei peri hagafen*," translated as "Who creates the fruit of the vine." (It is interesting to note that this *berachah* also applies to grape juice, and that nowadays it is considered permissible by many *halachic* authorities to use grape juice as a substitute for wine for all of the above rituals.)
[616] Genesis 3:14-19.

all of us would say yes to option two is proof that we are seeking more than just pleasure in life. Plato famously said: "Better to be a sad Socrates than a happy pig."

Is suffering ultimately good? Hedonism means doing all possible to avoid pain and maximize pleasure. Certainly, life is about more than pleasure, even while it is important. In addition to pleasure, people also pursue meaning, purpose, morality and happiness which includes more than just pleasure. Humans are complex, all of us. We can view Motivational Pluralism[617] in two ways: First, that different people are motivated differently; and secondly, that each individual is motivated by multiple motives. We can embrace both physical pleasure and existential struggle, work and rest, tension and calm.

But struggle should raise the moral bar, not lower it. One of the great plagues within some religious schools of thought today is that if you say, "this is a real struggle" and "we have to live in tension," then virtually anything can become morally justifiable. We, therefore, for example, can't help the *agunah* (a woman chained to a marriage she doesn't want) but we can cry with her. We can't do anything for the gay person at risk but be pained that we must marginalize them further. We can't say anything "political" but rather sit forlorn in isolation, with our ideological purity, in the tension of not fitting in to society.

But the goal of all religious and moral life is not merely to struggle as an end but rather to struggle as a means to gain deeper moral clarity. And not every moral choice is an *akeidah* (where we must faithfully and fearfully bind children upon an altar), some Soloveitchik or Kierkegaardian moment of "the teleological suspension of the ethical."[618] Struggle is deeply valuable in intellectual and spiritual life and necessary for one's integrity, but the ultimate goal must be moral clarity and moral leadership. We must engage in responsible interpretation guided by cherished Jewish values that balance often-competing interests of justice, equity, compassion, legal continuity, human dignity, sanctifying God's Name, etc.

It's true we may find value in moving away from what some of our friends, less committed to tradition, experience as no struggle at all, since all of Judaism and personal ethics can be viewed as virtually synonymous. On the other end of the religious spectrum, too, some of our dear friends don't feel tension, since they can just fully and almost blindly submit to *da'at Torah* (the judgement of their religious authorities) and silence autonomy, critical moral thinking, and even remove the guilt of imperfect decision-making.

---

[617] Motivational Pluralism is the idea, in its most simple form, that people operate based on multiple motives, not a singular one. Many try to argue that humans fundamentally are selfish, or fundamentally only want pleasure, or fundamentally are driven by fear, etc. Motivational Pluralism offers the suggestions that humans are more complex.
[618] Robert Gordis, "The Faith of Abraham: A Note on Kierkegaard's Teleological Suspension of the Ethical." *Judaism*, 25:4 (Fall 1976), 414.

To be sure, I want to acknowledge that there is, of course, great diversity within those religious schools of thought and I respect the integrity of their various approaches. But, indeed for me, there is real virtue to living in a tension between Torah & conscience, law & morality, religious law and natural morality. I believe there is a greater value in making the struggle so real and actualizing the holy opportunities, that we move from existential paralysis to moral responsibility. I wonder if we can still attract folks interested in that approach to this enterprise anymore, or if too much damage has been done? Where you're out if you don't conform in what is becoming a fear-based culture? Where passive crying is constantly chosen over active humble and courageous leadership?

It's a Purim question: Will we just get drunk[619] and rehash the old narrative and old tensions over and over as if we still live in some ideal time of the past, be it 1880 Poland or 1930 Paris, or 1970 Washington Heights, or 1985 Alon Shvut, or will we sober up and frame the new, urgent narrative of today? Will we see the palace that we stand within today where we're called to respond or will we transport ourselves back to an imaginary realm that is so intellectually critical in the minutia that no room is left for any contemporary moral reasoning and leadership?

The Torah understands that humans are fallible, and thus tries to establish guidelines for the utmost purity. The Torah is concerned with our everyday moral behavior due to the dual nature of our service to other people and to God, through Divine mandate and earthly obligation.

The nazirite takes three strict prohibitions upon himself: drinking wine, cutting his hair, and—most essentially—becoming ritually impure.[620] The nazirite, in his singularly stark representation of an uncontaminated faith, presents a paradox: Judaism shuns asceticism, but the nazirite must abide by a highly regimented code that restricts pleasure, thereby taking on an aspect of asceticism. And even more so, such an individual is considered both "holy unto God" for his spiritual commitment, yet is also commanded to bring a sin offering after his season of asceticism. (Some suggest that this action is due to the sin of denying himself the pleasures of this world.)

How do we reconcile the fascinating contradictions of the nazirite? For if the Torah intends for us to reject asceticism, yet gives precious space to describing the obligation of an ascetic, there must be a deeper meaning to the text here.

---

[619] BT Megillah 7b, states that one is required to get drunk, or at least drink to excess, on Purim. This seeming edict is then followed by a story which raises the danger in getting drunk, hence, perhaps, negating this practice. The medieval commentators and codifiers heavily debated this issue, and it is an even stronger, and more urgent, topic of discussion today, given what we now know about the effects of alcohol, and the real danger of driving while intoxicated.

[620] Numbers 6:1-21.

And of course, there is, though it does delve into esoteric territory. The Talmudic rabbis teach that one who embraces a path of asceticism and denies themself the pleasures of this world is sinning:

> R. Eleazar HaKappar B'rebbi said: Why does the Torah state, "And make atonement for him, for he sinned against the soul"?[621] Against what "soul" did the nazirite sin? It can only be because he denied himself wine. If, then, this man who did no more than deny himself wine is termed a sinner, how much more so is this true of one who is ascetic in all things![622]

Ignoring a world that we are meant to enjoy goes against the values inherent in Creation. Why would God create a world if God's creations are not meant to enjoy its splendor? Consequently, the rabbis teach that we are accountable to God if we do not enjoy the pleasures of this world.[623]

Rabbi Shimshon Raphael Hirsch pithily suggests that we will be accountable to God for the permitted pleasures of this world that we do not enjoy and will even be asked at the gates of heaven: "Have you seen my Alps?"

Now, it goes without saying that there is significant moral value in curbing our appetites and not pursing every pleasure we dream of. The biblical passage of the nazirite, in this sense, is a subtle warning against extremism. We must be measured in every aspect of our lives, from what we eat, to how we work, to how we conduct ourselves in sexual matters. And, to be sure, the Torah imposes numerous restrictions upon food consumption, sexual conduct, and the tasks we may perform on Shabbat, among many others. Further, it doesn't hurt to take on a personal stringency based upon a religious and moral commitment.

The story of the nazirite reminds us that we should never reject wholeheartedly what the world has to offer. But at the same time, we shouldn't succumb to every excessive opportunity. The prevailing Jewish orientation toward life is to embrace an ideology that is life-affirming and pleasure-affirming. We are not meant to retreat from the affairs of the world, nor are we to take unrestricted advantage of every delight that exists. Moderation of life's pleasures is critical, though we need not go to the lengths of the nazirite to avoid temptation. We are to balance joy in life with healthy measures of holiness. And in this space, we truly experience wondrous opportunities for awe, reverence, and renewal.

---

[621] Numbers 6:8.
[622] BT Nazir 19a; BT Nedarim 10a.
[623] Jerusalem Talmud (JT) Kiddushin 4:12.

So, we should indeed struggle, but we should also enjoy life. We should embrace pleasure, but also have limits. We should take on challenges, but also embrace inner peace. After all, Shlomo Hamelech (King Solomon) concludes one of his most famous proverbs with the words "Her ways are pleasant ways, And all her paths, peaceful."[624] The Rambam says the Torah was only given in the world to enhance "mercy, kindness, and peace in the world."[625] He was likely referring to outer peace but certainly the value is relevant to our discussion of inner peace as well.

What it means to be a person of empathy is to bring the struggle of others into our own. We are not only to listen and understand but to move into allyship. There is personal struggle but there is also collective struggle where our human unity and solidarity is manifest. It can be a privilege to "choose" struggle rather than have struggle thrust upon us, but it is, indeed, our sacred responsibility as well. Yaakov's name was changed to Yisrael because he struggled with God and humanity. That is the fate and destiny of the Jewish people: we will be at peace with God but we will also be immersed in perpetual struggle.

---

[624] Proverbs 3:17.
[625] Mishneh Torah, Hilchot Shabbat 2:3.

DEBATE 35.

Humor vs. Seriousness

On the one hand, we have a heavy mission that we must take seriously. We can't mess around. On the other hand, life is to be enjoyed and enjoyable, and laughing is not only a means to that end but is also healthy and normal. Does our tradition prioritize humor or seriousness?

In the Talmud, the Rabbis taught that humor is valuable in Torah study, as it warms people's hearts and brings joy into the learning. For example, before starting to lecture or teach, Rabbah, the Talmudic sage, "would say something humorous and the Sages would be cheered. Ultimately, he sat in trepidation and began teaching the *halakha*."[626] Religious education and humor go together nicely. This is because humor, among many other benefits, can connect us, can make learning fun and help sustain the learner's interest, can foster humility, and can help cultivate moral imagination.

One Talmudic passage even teaches that making others laugh gives one an automatic ticket to heaven!

> These two also have a share in the World-to-Come. Rabbi Beroka went over to the men and said to them: What is your occupation? They said to him: We are jesters, and we cheer up the depressed. Alternatively, when we see two people who have a quarrel between them, we strive to make peace."[627]

Humor also presents a challenge to the educator, as it can serve as a distraction and lead to frivolity.[628] The Rabbis were sensitive to this, too. While of course striking the right balance is necessary and a challenge, one episode in the Talmud shares how one rabbi tried to conquer his delight in humor.

> On the day that Rabi laughed, punishment would come upon the world. So he said to Bar Kappara [who was a humorist]: "Do not make me laugh, and I will give you forty measures of wheat." He replied, "But let the Master see that I may take whatever measure I desire." So he took a large basket, pitched it over, placed it on his head, went [to Rabi] and said to him, "Fill me the forty measures of wheat which I may demand from you."

---

[626] BT Shabbat 30b.
[627] BT Taanit 22a.
[628] Jackie Mason was a pulpit rabbi before rising to fame as a comedian. It was his humor and jokes in his sermons that drew people in to the synagogue, and it was at that point that he realized he may have a future in comedy.

Thereupon Rabi burst into laughter, and said to him, "Did I not warn you not to jest?" He replied, "I wish but to take the wheat which I may [justly] demand."[629]

Societies from pagan times to the present have designated certain occasions or days when the usual societal discipline was relaxed or completely done away with (think of ancient spring festivals and present-day Mardi Gras in New Orleans or Carnival in Europe). For us, Purim is a time when we may drink wine,[630] and the usual discipline is often thrown off. The custom of the Purim *shpiel*,[631] the whimsical play put on by *yeshivah* students and community members, is the most prominent example of this practice.

The history of the Purim *shpiel* merits examination. In the 15th century, Ashkenazi families created humorous plays based on parody rhymes of the Book of Esther. Eventually, these grew into public performances, often of a bawdy nature. By the following century, it was customary for Purim *shpiels* to be staged performances in the home, and wealthy families brought in performing companies to stage elaborate productions. By the 18th century, the *shpiel* branched out to include other Biblical episodes, and grew to include musical instruments and longer narratives. At times, the content was deemed offensive, to the extent that, for example, the leaders of the Jewish community in Hamburg banned all Purim shpiels in 1728. Today, the Purim shpiel varies from community to community. It tends to be light-hearted, festive, and replete with silly costumes and playacting.

Fortunately, the humor that is on display in Purim *shpiels* and other religious contexts is not only therapeutic, but it can help us learn as well. In many *yeshivot* and *midrashot*,[632] the Purim *shpiel* includes satirizing faculty members, which when done in good taste, can serve as a catalyst for students and faculty to develop a stronger relationship.

On the other hand, Rabbi Ovadia Yosef[633] expresses his concerns on this subject in a responsum:

---

[629] BT Nedarim 50a.

[630] Drinking wine is associated with Purim because wine plays a significant role in the Purim story as recorded in the *megillah*. While the Talmud records that one should get drunk on Purim, it is equally noted that putting oneself and others in danger is never permissible. For this reason, Rambam (Maimonides) writes that on Purim one should simply drink enough to induce one to take a nap. Others, such as Rama (Rabbi Moshe Isserlis, Ashkenazi commentator of the Shulchan Aruch) suggest that one should merely drink a bit more than one would normally drink.

[631] The word *shpiel*, of Yiddish origin, literally means a play or production.

[632] In modern Israeli Hebrew, *yeshivah* typically refers to a male institution and *midrashah* to a female one. *Yeshivot* and *midrashot* are the plural forms.

[633] Rabbi Ovadia Yosef was the Rishon Letzion, the Sefaradi Chief Rabbi of Israel, 1973-1983.

I have seen in writing that the Gaon, Rabbi Shimon Sofer, died from the anguish he suffered in the wake of the insults hurled at him on Purim. May the good Lord atone for this. God forbid, then, that this custom should continue, and especially not in the holy *yeshivot*, which must serve as an example of love, honor and awe of Torah. It is a *mitzvah* to forcefully object and absolutely abolish this evil custom, the word *minhag* (custom) being a transmutation of the word *Gehinnom*.[634]

Of course, *leitzanut* (frivolity), mockery, *lashon hara* (hurtful speech), and insensitivity are not the goals, nor are they acceptable outcomes, of humor in religious life or in education. I recall Purim *shpiels* that went overboard in roasting educators at a certain *yeshivah*. Clearly, some of those rabbis felt hurt by what students considered to be holiday jokes. Some who witnessed this banned future Purim *shpiels* there.

Studies over the past 15 years have yielded interesting data on the positive role of humor in learning:[635]

- Students in a statistics course retained more knowledge when the lectures included humorous material that related to the course material.
- Students were more likely to log into an introductory psychology course when they had a professor who made self-deprecating jokes and included cartoons and other topical material in lectures.
- A 1999 study demonstrated that students perceived instructors who injected humor in the classroom as being more intelligent and concerned with students than instructors who did not.
- Laughter, which reduces stress hormones such as cortisol, can even be used to lighten the atmosphere in a classroom during a test, and can improve students' performances on those tests.

While concerned educators will rightly point out that humor should not take over in a class setting, because students will consider everything to be a joke and

---

[634] Yechaveh Da'at V, no. 50.
[635] Zak Stambor, "How laughing leads to learning" (American Psychological Association, 2006), https://www.apa.org/monitor/jun06/learning

there will be little learning, these studies show that humor is nevertheless helpful in many situations.

Many jokes enter a gray area. While a joke may appear innocent and playful, it can leave a lasting scar on another. My teacher Rabbi Avi Weiss told me that he committed to not telling jokes in sermons anymore (only self-deprecating ones) after he offended a congregant with what he thought was an innocent, loving, and playful joke. We must be so careful with our behavior and words and tremble with *yirat shamayim* (awe of heaven), yet, at the same time, we should strive to be humble and not take ourselves so seriously that we cannot laugh and play a bit. After all, as we mentioned above, such gentle behavior can bring joy and healing to others. My teacher Dr. Carl Hammerschlag, of blessed memory, used to travel to conflict zones, as a psychiatrist dressed as a clown, with Patch Adams, because he knew that laughter was a crucial part of healing from trauma.

Jerry Seinfeld often offered such a uniquely Jewish form of humor in the TV series *Seinfeld*. They would analyze the micro-dimensions of social phenomena in a Talmudic fashion. To what may be obvious to learned Jews was hilarious to a general American popular culture audience. Many other Jewish comedians tapped into unique Jewish wisdom to help build the scene of American comedy.

Rabbi Avraham Yitzchak Kook taught that joy does not involve evading evil and the challenges of life, for this would not be true joy. It would simply be masking the reality of the world in which we are living. Rather, there must be a constant desire to integrate life and join with a greater spiritual force, and this can arouse true joy.[636] In this vein, humor can be used to bring in new life perspectives and elevate one emotionally, in turn creating the potential for new spiritual heights.

Does God have a sense of humor? If so, perhaps this too is a religious pursuit for us and a Divine character trait to emulate? May we succeed in infusing humor and joy into our lives, and may it be the type of joy that elevates us and those around us to a higher purpose.

---

[636] Rav Kook, *Ein Ayah Berakhot*, no. 61.

The State & Authority

DEBATE 36.

Hobbes vs. Anarchists: A King vs. No King

God is *haMelech* (the King). We do not need an earthly king to govern us. That is the approach that many Jewish thinkers have taken. And while all agree that we need some form of governance,[637] the only question being whether that should entail having a king, other Jewish thinkers have suggested that a monarchy is a perfectly fine, perhaps even ideal, government model.

With the advent of modernity, we witnessed the opportunity to uproot and dismantle the old order. Some were revolutionaries while others were desperately working to preserve order. This is where Hobbes comes in. Thomas Hobbes famously argued that by a "right of nature" one would feel they have no obligations. One would assume they are free to do anything in the name of survival and to live a life of self-interest. He thus contends that we need government power to prevent humanity from eating each other alive. Hobbes rejected the assumption that by our nature we are sociable. The other major civilizations (such as the Greeks and Christian culture) had largely assumed that we were inclined to live with each other. Hobbes thought our nature is isolation and self-interest, and that living collectively is extremely difficult and therefore needs to be tightly governed. We would need contracts to manage order in society, and those contracts must be strictly enforced.

Ethics, for Hobbes, is something else. Ethics leads us beyond our nature and beyond governance into the realm of doing what is good for others—beyond what is good for oneself.

To be sure, the Talmudic rabbis had themselves offered such an idea that government was needed primarily to prevent violence, long before Hobbes:

Rabbi Hanina, the vice-high priest, said: pray for the welfare of the government, for were it not for the fear it inspires, every man would swallow his neighbor alive.[638]

Rabbi Yitz Greenberg directly connects the above teaching with Hobbes:

> This is a Hobbesian view. Since people act out of power and selfishness, they would be in a state of perpetual warfare with each other were [it] not for the restraining power of the government. By this logic, as Hobbes argued, government has the right to be authoritarian and not subject to the changing will of the citizens.[639]

---
[637] Establishing a court, or governing system, is one of the *sheva mitzvot B'nei Noach* (seven Noahide laws).
[638] Pirkei Avot 3:2, trans. Dr. Joshua Kulp.
[639] Yitz Greenberg, *Sage Advice* (New Milford Connecticut: Maggid Books, 2016), 111.

The rabbis were clearly addressing living under a foreign king. When it comes to a king of Israel, the biblical and rabbinic texts speak with ambivalence toward the king.

Looking back to the *Tana"ch*,[640] we see that this conversation emerges during the period of the *shoftim* (judges). The text demonstrates that prior to Israelite monarchies, Israeli society was anarchistic. "In those days there was no king in Israel; every person did that which was right in their own eyes."[641] The prophet Shmuel (Samuel) critiques the Jews for wanting a king. Why should we want to be like all the other nations? We should do what's right out of love of God and a desire to live a virtuous life, not out of fear of a king. Further, we should build a government that actualizes a Torah lifestyle, he argued, not one of political expediency emulated after the surrounding nations. The people were explicit in their asserting that other nations are the example they want to follow. "So that we too may be like all other nations that our king may lead us and go before us and fight our wars."[642] But Shmuel objects both on practical grounds, because a king will abuse his power, and also on theological grounds, because "the Lord your God is your King."[643] There is further reason to object. In many cultures (Philistine, Egyptian, etc.) the king is considered to be a god. In the Torah, however, every king was assigned a prophet to keep the king at bay and remind the king, and society, of the king's imperfections. But it is not hard for a king to come to believe himself a god. We must avoid raising up humans to too high places of glory.

Later rabbis want us to avoid engaging with governments. "Love work, hate acting the superior, and do not attempt to draw near to the ruling authority."[644] Rabbi Kalonymus Kalman Shapira of Piasetzno (the Piasetzno Rebbe) wrote: "In a place where holiness is revealed, there is no rulership and honors."

Similarly, we can ask: Why was the Torah given in the desert, outside the land of Israel? If the pinnacle of the journey for the Jewish people was arriving in the land, then shouldn't revelation have happened then? Rather, one might suggest that the Torah was given in the desert precisely because it is outside of society, outside of government and sovereignty.

The 19th-20th-century Polish kabbalist Rabbi Yehuda Ashlag taught:

> Altruistic Communism will finally annul the brute-force regime completely, for "every man did that which was right in his own eyes." .... Indeed, there is nothing more humiliating

---

[640] *Tana"ch* is an acronym for Torah, Nevi'im, and Ketuvim (Pentateuch, Prophets, and Writings).
[641] Judges 21:25.
[642] Judges 8:20.
[643] I Samuel 12:12.
[644] Pirkei Avot 1:10, trans. Dr. Joshua Kulp.

and degrading for a person than being under the brute-force government.[645]

There were some Orthodox thinkers who were anarchists, such as British Orthodox Rabbi Yankey-Meyer Zalkind, the above-mentioned kabbalist Rabbi Yehuda Ashlag, Chabad rabbi of the early to mid-20th-century Rabbi Abraham Yehudah Khein, Chabad Rabbi Yehudah-Leib Don-Yakhia, Rabbi Aharon Shmuel Tamaret of early 20th-century Poland, and others. Some are drawn toward spiritual ideas that are anti-authoritarian. Some are drawn by political ideas as anti-nationalist or anti-Zionist. Others support libertarian-communism. Still others may simply reject all forms of government they see around them, with all their coercion and corruption.

Rabbi Soloveitchik at times champions a form of anarchism, suggesting that humans are meant to be free and not restrained. He only concedes that there is a need to have law and order to prevent a breakdown of society. Consider this passage:

> Bondage to man excludes Divine friendship. The beloved must tear down all the social and political barriers that fence in the individual and imprison his initiative and liberty. The charismatic person is anarchic, liberty-loving; he frees himself from all the fixed formulas and rhythms of an urbanized civilization and joins a fluid, careless, roving nomad society. An ancient Egyptian document describes the nomads as follows: 'Here is the miserable stranger... He does not dwell in the same spot; his feet are always wandering. From times of Horus he battles, he does not conquer, and is not conquered.'[646] The stranger is indomitable; he may lose a battle, yet had never lost a war. He will never reconcile with political subjection. Roaming, wandering, he will escape persecution and oppression. When the need arises, the nomad stands up and fights for his freedom and many a time proves superior in battle to the settled king. Abraham's heroism on the battlefield is the best illustration."[647]

Of course, far more numerous than religious anarchists have been the Jewish secular anarchists, such as Emma Goldman, Mikhail Bakunin, Leo Tolstoy, and

---

[645] Rabbi Yehuda Ashlag, "Building the Future Society," Kabbalah.info, http://www.kabbalah.info/eng/content/view/frame/3811?/eng/content/view/full/3811&main.
[646] Buber, *Moses*, 25.
[647] Rabbi Joseph Soloveitchik, *The Emergence of Ethical Man* (Jersey City, New Jersey: Ktav Publishing, 2005), 153.

Noam Chomsky. Relatedly, figures such as Martin Buber and Gershon Scholem argued for non-nationalist manifestations of Zionism.

But, in the end, monarchy won out in Jewish history. The Jews embraced countless Jewish kings, and Jewish traditional teachings on messianism argue that the monarchy will return. But where does that leave us now? We have an ancient Jewish history of monarchs and a future eschatological destiny of monarchs, but what about in modern times? Today, Jews live with unparalleled history under Israeli sovereignty, and participate in a sovereign government in the United States. Of course, both the United States and Israeli governments are democracies, but all Jews must abide by the decisions and laws of those governments just the same.[648] One could argue that Jews have never been safer in even one location in all of history, not to mention in two locations simultaneously. Both Israeli and American security require strong governments. So merely on the level of self-protection, it is simple to make a case for strong centralized government. But even beyond that, the state of Israel and the United States do enormous good for the global community (even alongside the inevitable harm that each does). Professor Michael Walzer argues that the monarchy model sows the roots for later democracy.[649] So, do we want an authoritarian king today? No, of course not. But does our traditional embrace of the monarchy set a trajectory toward the arguably most desirable form of government, democracy? Yes!

Rabbi Jonathan Sacks, in *The Dignity of Difference* and other works, argues that there must be more than just government and the market. Liberals want bigger government and more regulations on the market. Conservatives want smaller government and fewer regulations on the market. But Rabbi Sacks argues that there must be a third element: society. Yes, there is a need for government and for a marketplace but we need the realm of ideas, communities, and values to inform how both of those operate.

There's just so much that governments (whether in the form of a monarchy or a democracy) cannot do for us.

> Governments can't legislate happiness or ban depression, but public policy can play a role in ensuring that people have time to relax with friends, and pleasant places to do it.... For many governments, both national and local, preventing crime is a far higher priority than encouraging friendship and cooperation. But, as Professor Richard Layard of the London School

---

[648] Rabbi Ahron Soloveichik argued that breaking the law of the land is a Torah prohibition. For example, one who exceeds the legal speed limit also transgresses a Torah law.
[649] "Is Democracy a Religious Value? Professor Michael Walzer interviewed by Rabbi Shmuly Yanklowitz" (Valley Beit Midrash on YouTube, 2020), https://www.youtube.com/watch?v=illhD6wzbAg.

of Economics has argued in this recent book *Happiness: Lessons from a New Science*, promoting friendship is often easy and cheap, and can have big payoffs in making people happier. So why shouldn't that be a focus of public policy?[650]

So, for those of us living in America today, where does that leave our thinking? Susan Neiman writes in her book *Moral Clarity*:

> Americans, he [Robert Kagan] concluded, are Hobbesians, while Europeans are Kantians; Europeans have withdrawn into a cocoon that is shielded from the harsh circumstances of conflict only because the U.S. remains in the anarchic and unstable center of history, acknowledging how bad things really are and using military power to prevent them from falling apart entirely. Europeans think we have reached the Kantian dream, in which ideas of peaceful negotiation, international courts, and common concern for sharing global wealth make things work. But though we, too, would like to live in a dream world, Americans recognize the hard facts of this one, and are resolute enough to respond to them—thereby taking on the burdens that allow Europeans to dream on.[651]

It is very difficult to stop thinking about Hobbes' ideas and The Social Contract. As the global political drama continues to unfold, he makes the case for how a government-less society would lead to "the war of every man against every man" in which life would simply be unbearable. Without a government that holds control, humans would live in a natural state of constant war. Everyone would be, in Hobbes' words, constantly afraid and living in "continual fear, and danger of violent death; and the life of man solitary, poor, nasty, brutish and short." We witness this reality in the book of Judges: "In those days there was no king in Israel; everyone did that which was right in his own eyes."[652] As unhappy as we can be with the state of nation-states today and the chosen officials, we can still work to muster up the appreciation that most of these regimes are maintaining some order and preventing lawless chaos. We have a sacred obligation to protest the unjust policies of governments, but it is also wise, and our responsibility

---

[650] Peter Singer, *Ethics in the Real World* (Princeton, New Jersey: Princeton University Press, 2017), 201, 203-204.
[651] Susan Neiman, *Moral Clarity* (Princeton, New Jersey: Princeton University Press, 2009), 31-32.
[652] In fact, the entire book of Shoftim (Judges) follows a pattern: First, "everyone did which was right in his own eyes." God then sent an enemy to oppress the Israelites, followed by God sending them a *shofeit* (judge) to urge them to repent and keep them in line. With the death of each *shofeit*, the pattern repeats itself.

and obligation, on some level, to support the order that governments provide to society even when we disagree with the elected officials running them (tyrants, despots, and fascists excluded, of course). It's not easy to strike the right balance between protesting and supporting governments that are misguided. Each of us can learn to play our unique role. Hobbes still provides us something to think about 350 years after his death.

And so, in democracy today, rather than submit to authority, we should argue about the just society safely and fairly. The 20th-century Quaker American author and activist Parker Palmer writes:

> Human beings have a well-demonstrated capacity to hold the tension of differences in ways that lead to creative outcomes and advances. It is not an impossible dream to believe we can apply that capacity to politics. In fact, our capacity for creative tension-building is what made the American experiment possible in the first place. As I argue in this book, America's founders—despite the bigotry that limited their conception of who "We the People" were—had the genius to establish the first form of government in which differences, conflict, and tension were understood not as the enemies of a good social order, but as the engines of a better societal order.[653]

He continues on:

> From the separation of powers and system of checks and balances among the executive, legislative, and judicial branches to the tug-of-war between federal and state governments to our adversarial system of justice, American democracy was intended to generate, not suppress, the energy created by conflict, converting it into social progress as a hydroelectric plant converts the energy of dammed-up water into usable power.[654]

American democracy was developed to be specifically in contrast to a monarchy. By dividing power between executive, legislative, and judicial branches of government, for example, the framers of the U.S. Constitution sought to avoid any absolute claims to power. Democracy can be a way to balance our spiritual pull toward anarchy with our spiritual pull toward monarchy. We seek order and control,

---

[653] Parker J. Palmer, *Healing the Heart of Democracy*, (Jossey-Bass, 2011), introduction, xx.
[654] Ibid., 15.

but we also seek to make God the only one above us. We don't want lawlessness but we don't want tyranny either. Democracy, in its best form, provides order and checks and balances but also ensures there is no authoritarian king. What matters in a democracy, as opposed to a monarchy, is that an election takes place and that there is accountability after the election. I think we may need to consider moving away from thinking of a monarchy as a valid future Jewish model (aside from a newer version, the "figurehead model" that we see in modern countries today such as Thailand and Britain). Our Jewish case for democracy does not need to be a literal one. Rather, we should be consequentialists. The Torah wants a just society, and choosing a political system is in some ways a means to an end (of creating that just society). Of course, the means must be just as well (i.e., honoring the dignity of the citizens). The Torah wants us to be healthy, but that doesn't mean we follow medieval science. So too, we need a "healthy" society, but dare not revert to archaic (possibly even dangerous) models.

We are left with many questions. We see different types of democracies around the world. Which model do we believe leads to the best consequences and ought to be the Jewishly embraced form of modern government? And, outside the role of persuasive educator and religious leader, what should the political power be of a philosopher-king-messiah?

Democracy is not perfect and it is remarkably fragile. Even today, we see countless threats to democracy here in America through gerrymandering, the filibuster, the electoral college, foreign threats (like Russian intervention), social media campaigning, dark money, an insurrection, and more. Each era has its own unique challenges to sustain and build a just government. Too much is at stake for preserving the collective good through schools, medical responders, law enforcement, sanitation, foreign defense, and so much more. We cannot allow the far-right threats to government to win out. We also can't let neo-anarchy prevail on the far left where there is a call to completely dismantle policing, abolish border control, and reject any justifications for war (including self-defense). As religious people, we care about human motives and that people do what is good because it is good, not just because it is the law. Nonetheless, some things are so important that requiring them to be done is more important than relying on volunteerism in an effort to mold character. For example, the poor must be fed and we cannot rely on charity in the interest of cultivating altruism. How to achieve all goals to protect the vulnerable while also allowing enough freedom for citizens to grow in their agency and character is not an easy matter.

These questions and more are worth pondering, as we do our utmost, during our own lifetime and within our form of government, to preserve and better society.

DEBATE 37.

Halachah vs. State:
What is the vehicle for progress?

How might Jews define progress? And once we've defined that, what are our best vehicles for progress? When Jews have been powerless, we could hope and dream that God, or Mashiach, would come to intervene with power. Or perhaps, in some mystical way, our performance of mitzvot were transforming the world.

Today, when Jews have access to more power than ever before in history (with Israeli sovereignty and with American Jewish security) new questions emerge about how we influence the world. For some, we still change the world through our obedience to Jewish tradition. For others, we can now change the world through universal acts of *tikkun olam*. For yet others, the *medinah* (the State of Israel) is the most powerful vehicle not only for Jewish survival but for global influence. It is quite amazing to realize, for example, that so many modern technological innovations and inventions were created in Israel.[655] In addition, more *yeshivot* and *midrashot* (institutions of higher learning) exist today in Israel than in any other time in Jewish history. Secular biblical learning, too, is experiencing a renaissance, with the advent of *batei midrash* (study halls), classes, and lectures all offered by, and for, the non-religious. Written works of several contemporary secular biblical scholars, such as Avigdor Shinan, Yair Zakovitch, and Meir Shalev have even become mainstream and are found in many an Orthodox Jewish home. None of this would be transpiring today if Israel were not an independent state.

As an early religious Zionist, it is not entirely clear that Rav Kook viewed the state itself as the primary vehicle for moral progress.[656] What is clear, though, is that he believed that the Jewish people, collectively with sovereignty, living in the holy land, is the vehicle for moral progress,[657] and that our particular role has a universal impact. So, while *halachah* has an important role to play in our progress as Jews, it is only true in that the collective Jewish people engage it toward a greater end. Putting it another way, the performance of *mitzvot* or the study of Torah in a vacuum, without viewing that very action or study as a vehicle to influence and better the world, is not progress at all. To be sure, theologies of redemption are very complicated in Jewish thought, and most certainly in the thought of Rav

---

[655] Israel has contributed greatly to the fields of economics, technology, agriculture, mathematics, science, optics, and more. Waze, Soda Stream, and Firewall, to name but a few, were all created in Israel. See https://en.wikipedia.org/wiki/List_of_Israeli_inventions_and_discoveries for a rather comprehensive list.
[656] While Rav Kook was the first Ashkenazi chief rabbi of British Mandatory Palestine, he died in 1935, 13 years prior to the creation of the independent state.
[657] It is well known that Rav Kook would visit members of non-religious kibbutzim, encouraging them in their holy work of building the land of Israel.

Kook.[658] But it is clear that the return to the homeland and the renaissance of Jewish life is a major part of the progress toward redemption. The state will enable the great gifts of the Jewish people to offer a bright light to the world.

Rav Kook reflects on the relationship between an earlier monarchy and a new democracy:

> Aside from this, it seems reasonable that at a time when there is no king, these privileges revert to the hands of the nation as a whole, since the prerogatives of monarchy also pertain to the general condition of the nation. In particular, it seems that every Judge who arises in Israel has the status of a king, as regard several royal prerogatives, particularly those pertaining to governance of the nation.[659]

The relationship between nationalism and universalism is a complex one. Professor Tamar Ross explains Rav Kook's approach:

> The raison d'être of the Jewish people is to gather all the special qualities that serve to define the respective national characters of the other nations and weld them together as varying expressions of a common moral urge. R. Kook equates this moral urge with religious faith, or the striving for perfection. The unique task of the Jewish people is to harmonize and readjust the mass of expressions of this cosmic urge, and form them into a cohesive unity, by establishing and enforcing mutual reciprocation, and providing a general spiritual context for a plurality of diverse units. Reflecting the divine unity in this manner, the Jewish people serve as the special instrument of divine revelation. It is in the Jewish people's way of life and creativity that the process of revelation finds its fullest expression.... Its purpose is to provide a model of harmonization on a national scale (the widest scale capable of recognizably bearing the joint experience necessary to found a common life) that will eventually be adopted by humanity at large and obviate the need for nationalism altogether. The world is not yet ready to adopt this cosmopolitan model when it is represented by individuals,

---

[658] While Rav Kook penned many works, much of his writing is very deep and mystical. Many of his views and positions therefore remain unclear to the average reader.
[659] Rav Kook, Teshuvah, *Mishpat Kohen*, 144.

because in their present form, national groups tend to take over the world and overrun the harmony represented by individuals with their collective competitiveness.[660]

Ahad Ha'am suggested that the nation itself had a collective soul, or spirit, which could regenerate with a new *halachah* in the Zionist era.[661] Hayim Nachman Bialik seemed to take a similar approach.[662] Bialik and Ahad Ha'am could, in many ways, be deemed secular Jews, who viewed Jewish success and progress primarily through a nationalistic lens. Some argue that they were thus disenchanting the holy while preserving cultural structures of the past. Such an approach could in some ways be compared to that of Rabbi Mordechai Kaplan (1881-1983), the founder of Reconstructionist Judaism. What Bialik celebrates in his work *Halakhah ve'Aggadah* is the Jewish discipline that leads to creativity, but not the actual content (the *halachah*) itself. Others contend that Bialik and Ahad Ha'am were indeed engaging a deeply religious project, not merely a cultural or nationalist one.

This all emerges from Israel. For Jews in America, progress has been measured quite differently. An old joke tells of an Israeli hearing an American Jew talking about *tikkun olam* and asking, "How do you say *tikkun olam* in Hebrew?" For many segments of American Jewry, the religious work is not performing *mitzvot* as an end in themselves, not about bringing about a messianic era, and not about nationalism. Rather, it is about *tikkun olam* (reducing suffering, combatting oppression, liberating the confined). Here, the focus is not merely on *halachah* or on state, but rather on legislation, philanthropy, and education.

Here we see one of the greatest divides between the Israeli mindset and the American Jewry mindset. For many in Israel, the state of Israel and all it represents and produces is the answer. For many American Jews, it is what we do for others in the secular, even non-Jewish spheres of the Diaspora, notwithstanding of the State of Israel, that is redemptive.

For post-modernists, progress is an illusion. How can we witness the horrific bloodshed of the *Shoah* (Holocaust) and claim that we are progressing? Canadian psychologist and author Professor Steven Pinker, on the other hand, believes he can empirically prove that the world is becoming less violent over the centuries. For some Jewish traditionalists, we are in a state of *yeridat hadorot* (generational

---

[660] Tamar Ross, *Between Metaphysical and Liberal Pluralism: A Reappraisal of Rabbi A. I. Kook's Espousal of Toleration*, (Cambridge University Press, 1996) 96-100.
[661] Ahad Ha'am is the penname of Asher Zvi Hirsch Ginsberg (1856-1927), a foremost Hebrew essayist and thinker. See https://benyehuda.org/read/3105 for examples of his work.
[662] Hayim Nachman Bialik (1873-1934) was a famed Jewish poet and, like Ahad Ha'am, was an important Jewish thinker. See https://benyehuda.org/read/8585 for examples of his work.

decline). For others (mystics, messianists, and religious Zionists), we are rapidly headed forward toward the ultimate *geulah* (redemption).

Jews are a people of hope. Whether we root our hope in purely halachic observance, in state building, in universal acts for justice, or any combination thereof, we can be optimistic that we are moving forward. We must continue to engage in our holy work to lift up others and create a sanctification of God's name in the public sphere.

DEBATE 38.

The Individual vs. the Collective: Which Should We Value?

Should we make choices that are best for individuals or best for the collective? It is hard to answer such a massive question in the abstract. To be sure, Jewish tradition values both the individual and the collective.

The case for the individual is easy to make. The Midrash teaches:

> "And he observed a mourning period of seven days for his father."[663] This corresponds to the seven days of creation, for a person departs from the world that contains the seven days of creation, therefore we mourn over him for seven days.[664]

We learn from this midrash that the reason we mourn the passing of a loved one for seven days is because of the seven days of creation. Just as the world was created in seven days, so too, a world that is lost is mourned for seven days. An individual human being is a world unto themselves.

Maimonides taught, based on the Talmud:

> For this reason, Adam was created as an individual unique in the world—to teach that anyone who causes a single soul to be lost from the world is regarded as if he has caused an entire world to be lost, and anyone who sustains a single soul in the world is regarded as if they have sustained an entire world. Indeed, all who come into the world are created in the form of the original Adam, and no one's face is identical with that of his fellow—for this reason each and every one can say "The world was created for my sake"[665]

We are told in Genesis 1:27 that "God created man in his image. In the image of God, God created him." What does this famous verse about human dignity mean? What is it teaching us?

---

[663] Genesis 50:10.
[664] Midrash Lekach Tov on Parshat Vayechi, commentary on Genesis 50:10. Translation by Rabbi Yakov Chaim Hilsenrath's "Torah Ethics of Interpersonal Relationships," (Jerusalem: Ktav Publishing, 2021), 284.
[665] Mishnah, Sanhedrin 4:5. The intent of this teaching, that "the world was created for my sake," is a dual one. On one hand, we are charged here with each of us contributing to the world in our own way. On the other hand, the world indeed has something to offer each and every one of us. See Maimonides, Mishneh Torah, Laws of the Sanhedrin 12:3.

> For most of biblical history, this verse was taken as a tautology—the first half of the verse and the second were understood to express the same thought, that the human being was created in the image of God. But the Kotzker Rebbe saw the verse as expressing two different ideas. The first half, he said, means that each individual is created *in that individual's* own image. Then we receive the infusion of the Divine spark. In other words, our own uniqueness comes first. We are stamped with the image that will be only ours, and then we receive an ember of God.[666]

Each of us, then, is unique, but each of us is also connected to the totality, the Oneness. This is seemingly a great paradox. To complicate matters, the Baal Shem Tov taught: "Every detail that exists in the individual person also exists in the human race as a whole."[667]

Even further, it has been taught that the maturation of the individual is similar to the maturation of the collective. Rabbi Moshe Chaim Luzatto teaches:

> This is the fact that humanity as a whole can exist in four basic states. In this respect, the history of man is very much like the life of an individual. Like a single person, the entire human race is born and reaches maturity.[668]

With our individuality come unique spiritual channels to discover. Rabbi Steinsaltz taught that each of us has our own unique pathway into Judaism. His assistant, Rabbi Arthur Kurzweil, explains:

> In that interview, among other things, Rabbi Steinsaltz said, "Whether a Jew is knowledgeable about his tradition or not, there comes a time when has to re-meet and re-understand his tradition in a way that will be applicable to him and will say something to him as he is. You see, every person has to, at some time, re-create Sinai for himself." And he said, "We believe that the Law has at least 600,000 different paths within it for

---

[666] Rabbi David Wolpe, *Making Loss Matter: Creating Meaning in Difficult Times* (Riverhead Books, 1999), 113.
[667] *Toledot Yaakov Yosef*, Kedoshim (100a) as quoted in the *Sefer Baal Shem Tov*.
[668] Rabbi Moshe Chaim Luzatto, *Derech Hashem*, 171. As quoted in *God and Evil: A Unified Theodicy/Theology/Philosophy*, David Birnbaum (Hoboken, NJ: Ktav Publishing, 1989), 124.

individuals to enter.⁶⁶⁹ There is what is called the 'private gate' for each of us. And we each have to find our own gate."⁶⁷⁰

There is no Jewish manual telling us exactly which rules or values or practices to choose. We must learn to paint our own individual canvas of Jewish values with different colors, different tastes, and different intensities, connections, and memories. Each of us, in our uniqueness, must assemble our own system of values. This is the foundation of moral and theological pluralism.

At the same time, in our struggle to balance our individuality with our being a part of the whole, one might need to put themselves in some danger to save the masses. Rabbi Yaakov Emden, in 18th-century Germany, wrote:

> A Jew with political responsibility (*adam chashuv*) has the obligation to rescue the oppressed from the hands of the oppressor by all means available to him, whether by direct action or through political effort, regardless of whether the oppressed is Jewish. So, Job praised himself by saying "I have broken the teeth of evil," and the Torah says of Moses that "He arose and championed them," referring to the daughters of Jethro, even though they were the daughters of an idolatrous priest...⁶⁷¹

On the one hand, every individual is created *b'tzelem Elokim* (in the image of God and with infinite dignity) and is a world in and of themselves. On the other hand, we must not stand idly by (i.e., we must put ourselves at some risk to save others): "Do not stand idly by your peer's blood; I am God."⁶⁷²

> From where in Scripture do we learn that if one sees his friend drowning in a river, or being dragged by a wild animal, or attacked by bandits, that he is obligated to rescue them? This is the meaning of "Do not stand idly by your peer's blood."⁶⁷³

---

⁶⁶⁹ This number 600,000 corresponds to the number of men who departed from Egypt in the Exodus story. The idea being expressed here is that as we, the Jewish people, were leaving Egypt for our Journey to Sinai and then on to Eretz Yisrael, we were given the charge of each of us contributing to the world. We were now becoming one nation, but at the same time were informed that we can never lose sight of our own individuality.
⁶⁷⁰ Rabbi Arthur Kurzweil, *On the Road with Rabbi Steinsaltz* (San Francisco: Jossey-Bass, 2006), ix.
⁶⁷¹ Responsa *Sh'eilat Yaavetz* 2:51.
⁶⁷² Leviticus 19:16.
⁶⁷³ BT Sanhedrin 73a.

We are to emulate the Divine and engage in *yishuv ha'olam*,[674] promoting peace in the world:

> We Jews have been commanded to rescue the pursued from the hands of any who pursue them with intent to kill, [and] if necessary, [even] at the cost of the pursuer's life . . .
>
> Among the roots of this commandment is that God, Who is Blessed, created the world and willed that it be settled, and the settlement of the world is upheld by the championing of the weak against those stronger. Furthermore, the pursued will always have eyes and heart turned toward God to champion him against his pursuer, as Scripture says, "The Lord will seek out the pursued," meaning that the pursued seeks the Lord and prays. Therefore, God, Who is Blessed, has commanded us to assist the pursued.[675]

Consider how none other than Moshe himself put himself at great risk intervening in three injustices in a row.[676] He intervened regardless of who was involved in each case (Jews or gentiles).

From an ethical perspective, consider the dilemma of the trolley case. As the train conductor, I find myself in a major moral dilemma when I discover five people tied to the train tracks ahead. I can either passively keep going straight or switch to another track. In theory I'm not culpable because I'm not taking any action, but five people will die. Or I can switch tracks, killing only one person tied to the tracks. Here I may be culpable since I've made an active choice, but fewer people will be killed. What is one to do? Save more people but kill one actively? Or save fewer people but not actively kill anyone? This is a difficult matter.

The Lubavitcher Rebbe wrote about the value of both the individual and the collective.

> When an individual comes and joins a crowd, one might think: "Since there are so many Jews here, if so, what am I worth as an individual?" To this we respond, "Blessed is the one who

---

[674] The term *Yishuv ha'olam* literally means "settling the world," but is always and only used in the context of creating a peaceful world.
[675] *Sefer HaChinnukh* (13th-century Barcelona), Commandment #600.
[676] Exodus 2:11-17. The first injustice involved Moshe observing an Egyptian smiting a Jew. The second, on the very next day, involved Moshe observing two Jews quarreling. The third transpired when Moshe fled to Midian upon realizing that his killing the Egyptian (in the first injustice) was discovered and that Pharaoh wanted to kill him. In Midian, at the site of a well, Moshe witnesses shepherds chasing away Yitro's daughters and saves them.

comes." (Psalms, 118:26.) Though you are but one individual, even when you come to a place in which a crowd is found, your existence as an individual remains intact. Indeed, a special blessing is extended to you: "Blessed is the *one* who comes."

This is underscored by the saying of the Sages, "for this reason man was created alone," in order that all future generations should know that anyone who descends from Adam—which refers not only to Jews.... but to all the descendants of Adam, including non-Jews—is, "a complete world"....

When an individual comes and joins a crowd.... then he accrues the additional station, merit, and blessing of the community. In addition to fulfilling his mission as an individual he also fulfills his mission as a part of the collective entity... formed by several individuals who join together "like one man with one heart"[677] for a single purpose and telos, thereby creating an entirely new entity.[678]

We need both the individual and the collective, and each strengthens and reinforces one another.

To some degree, the notion of an individual, completely separate from the collective, is more fully developed in modernity. Rabbi Jonathan Sacks reflects:[679]

> People began writing autobiographies. Artists started painting self-portraits. Rembrandt (1606-69) did so repeatedly: over forty paintings, thirty-oe etchings, and seven drawings of himself. People lived, increasingly, in private rooms. The French psychologist Jacques Lacan argued that the sense of an "I" closely corresponded to the mass manufacture of glass mirrors.[680] All roads in the late seventeenth century, writes historian Christopher Hill, led to individualism: "More rooms in better-off houses, use of glass in windows.... replacement of benches by chairs—all this made possible greater comfort and privacy for at least part of the population." Privacy, he argues, "contributed

---

[677] Rashi on Exodus 19:2.
[678] Menachem Mendel Schneerson, *Torat menachem hitvaduyot 5744*, Vol. 4 (Brooklyn, NY: Kehot Publication Society, 1990), 2160-2161. Quote found in Philip Wexler's *Social Vision-The Lubavitcher Rebbe's Transformative Paradigm for the World*, (The Crossroad Publishing Company, 2019), Chapter 4, Section 5, 135-136.
[679] Rabbi Jonathan Sacks, *Morality: Restoring The Common Good In Divided Times* (New York: Basic Books, 2020), 75.
[680] Lionel Trilling, *Sincerity and Authenticity* (Cambridge: Harvard University Press, 1971), 24-5.

to the introspection and soul-searching of radical Puritanism, to the keeping of diaries and spiritual journals.[681]

No matter how much we account for the collective, we must never forget the individual. Rabbi Jonathan Sacks writes:

> Against that, God tells Moses to lift people's heads by showing that they each count; they matter as individuals. Indeed, in Jewish law, a *davar shebeminyan*, something that is counted, sold individually rather than by weight, is never nullified even in a mixture of a thousand or a million others.[682] In Judaism, taking a census must always be done in such a way as to signal that we are valued as individuals. We each have unique gifts. There is a contribution only I can bring. To lift someone's head[683] means to show them favor, to recognize them. It is a gesture of love.[684]

Looking at the political level, we see the dangers of extremes. We must reject the extreme version of both capitalism (which has left billions out to dry in destitute poverty while expanding the gap between the rich and poor) and communism (which suppresses the individual human spirit in the name of the collective). We need a new concept that involves responsibility to both the individual and the collective. *Acharayut* (responsibility) includes both *ach* (sibling) and *acher* (the other). To have the ability to respond ethically (response-ability) we must care for both our sibling and the stranger (the other), for the individual and the collective.

This work is crucial to rebuilding a healthy democracy that values both human dignity and collective responsibility. Quaker thinker Parker Palmer writes:

> These habits have a downside as well, as does everything human: individualism can slip into selfishness, and communalism can collapse into having no mind of one's own. Learning how to hold individualism and communalism in creative tension with each other—allowing each to check the other's dark potentials—is a key democratic habit of the heart.[685]

---

[681] Christopher Hill, *The Century of Revolution: 1603-1741* (Nelson, 1961), 253.
[682] BT Beitzah 3b. This concept has *halachic* ramifications in the area of kashrut. Generally, a food item which inadvertently falls into another food item (a drop of milk into a pot of chicken soup, for example) is nullified. A *davar shebeminyan* is an exception to this rule.
[683] Lifting one's head is the expression used (Exodus 30:11) regarding the *mitzvah* of the census. God tells Moshe, "When you lift the heads of the people of Israel..."
[684] Rabbi Lord Jonathan Sacks, *Lessons in Leadership* (New Milford, Connecticut: Maggid Books, 2015), 186.
[685] Parker J. Palmer, *Healing the Heart of Democracy* (San Francisco: Wiley, 2014), 43.

The Jewish author and thinker Dr. Erica Brown writes:

> This trend is not all surprising if you compare it to sociological trends in virtually every other area of American life. In *Habits of the Heart*, a bestseller about individualism and commitment in the United States, the authors argue that Americans have come to make sharp distinctions between private and public life, to the detriment of the latter. Fierce individualism has weakened the bonds of community responsibility and the notion of the collective, which results in, among other things, the Disney-themed funeral.[686]

Reform theologian Rabbi Dr. Eugene Borowitz writes:

> God's kingdom-to-be is not a private matter between one individual and God. It must be accomplished with all men and be manifest in our lives, or it is unworthy of the Lord of the universe. The individual man cannot understand himself, cannot properly know his own life's purpose unless he sees it within the context of all mankind and all of history. Isolated from his fellows, he isolates himself from God's social goals.[687]

Finally, Rav Kook offers us a poem on the relationship between our individuality and collectivity and how we might "find ourselves."

> Each individual finds himself within himself.
> Then he finds himself within his surroundings:
> His friends, community and people.
>
> The community finds itself within itself.
> Then it finds itself within all humanity.
>
> Humanity finds itself within itself—at least, at first.
> Then it finds itself within the world.
>
> The world finds itself within itself.
> Then it finds itself within all the worlds surrounding it.

---

[686] Dr. Erica Brown, *Happier Endings* (New York: Simon & Schuster, 2014), 38-39.
[687] Rabbi Dr. Eugene Borowitz, "The Individual and the Community in Jewish Prayer," *Rediscovering Judaism*, 1965.

> The entirety of universal encompassing finds itself within itself.
> Then it finds itself within the all-inclusive, supernal classification of all concepts of universe.
>
> The concept of universe finds itself within itself.
> Then it finds itself within the full treasury, the supernal light, the multitude of life as well as the source of its days, and in the divine illumination.
>
> All of these recognitions fuse together.
> They become one unit, whose inclusiveness is infinitely glorious, whose particular nature is strong, flawless, whole and outstanding—
> Endless and perpetual.
>
> The flow of life flows ever more strongly
> And the light of holiness grows ever more strongly.
> "The singers and flute-players [proclaim] together:
> All of my wellsprings are within you, [Zion]!" [688]

Each of us is called upon to actualize our unique gifts and talents. Each of us contains greatness that we should boldly and courageously pursue. On the other hand, each of us is called upon to be humble and serve the greater good and see ourselves as a tiny part of a massive collective. We should strive for the right balance each and every day.

---

[688] *Orot Hakodesh* II, 447.

DEBATE 39.

Hierarchy vs. Populism: Moshe vs. Korach

Moshe is working hard to lead the people, but is then met with a populous uprising from Korach (also spelled Korah) and his friends. Pirkei Avot reminds us of the value of debate, but at the same time cautions us to be sure that our arguments are made with good intentions, like those of Hillel and Shammai, and are not self-serving. The example given of the latter is Korach. "And which is the controversy that is not for the sake of Heaven? Such was the controversy of Korah and all his congregation."[689]

One of Korach's debate points was that holiness was not God-given, as Moshe and Aaron had claimed, but achieved through merit. Professor Yeshayahu Leibowitz, a 20th-century Jewish philosopher, prolific writer, and professor of science at Hebrew University, teaches about the debate of "who is holy" between Moshe and Korach. (This debate stems from the verse in Numbers 16:3, "All of the people are holy.")

> The [first concept] of holiness is not a fact, but a goal.
> In the [second concept] holiness is something granted to us; we are holy.
> The difference between the two is most profound. On the one hand holiness is expressed as the loftiest state that can be attained through man's decisions on religious faith; he is required to demand this goal of himself. On the other hand, we have holiness [in which] a person absolves himself of responsibility, of the mission imposed upon him and of the obligation to exert himself; he is smugly sure that he is already holy.[690]

It seems that Korach's argument is fair. "Hey, why do you call all the shots? Aren't all people holy?" But we must remember that holiness is something to work for and strive for, not purely innate. Yes, all humans are created in the Image of God, but holiness is so much more than that.

Rabbi Shlomo Riskin, the Chief Rabbi of Efrat, takes a similar approach.

> The conflict between Moses and Korah reflects a tug of war within the human spirit ... Korah denies the importance of the laws. He says, "Who needs this system of dos and don'ts,

---
[689] Pirkei Avot 5:17, trans. Dr. Joshua Kulp.
[690] Yeshayahu Leibowitz on Parshat Korah in *Weekly Parsha* (New York: Chemed, 1990), 143.

you shalls and you shall nots. We're holy already." Certainly this perspective was attractive to every Israelite who wanted to be left alone. Who wants to be told what to do and what not to do?[691]

But wait—doesn't Judaism encourage dissent and pushback? Why squash debate? In fact, the debates of Hillel and Shammai explored in the first debate of this book are referred to as being *"l'sheim shamayim"* (for the sake of heaven), and the entire corpus of the Talmud is written in a give-and-take debate style, with Talmudic rabbis often, sometimes heatedly so, disagreeing with one another. This pattern continued through the period of the *Rishonim* (medieval commentaries)[692] and beyond, and continues to this day.

Rabbi Bradley Artson, a Los Angeles-based Conservative rabbi, raises this question based on the Korach episode.

> Korah's challenge strikes to the heart of democratic values. . . . If all people are created equal, then, why should any one person have any authority over another? Why should one person ever have access to power, wealth, or prestige in a way that another person does not? . . . . each person has intrinsic worth . . . all people have equal value.[693]

Rabbi Harold Schulweis, a Holocaust survivor and a Los Angeles-based Conservative rabbi of the late 20th century, wrote:

> The lesson of Korah, then, is not that dissent must be squashed but that the character of the dissent and its motivations be sincere. Korah's dissent was manipulative and his intent self-serving. Where the dissent is moral, honest, and without ulterior motive, it is the will of God.[694]

As Jews, we must embrace debate, even among those with whom we most stridently disagree. However, when we see that someone is manipulative and narcissistic, we must caution ourselves. We also must caution ourselves toward humility to

---

[691] Rabbi Dr. Shlomo Riskin, as cited in Torah column, *Jerusalem Post*, July 1, 1989.

[692] Rabbeinu Tam (Rabbi Yaakov ben Meir, Rashi's grandson and French Tosafist), for example, often disagreed with his father Rashi on both the reading of a *Talmudic* passage and on *halachic* ruling. Perhaps their most famous debate is the order of the *parashiyot* (passages) in the *tefillin*. While all wear Rashi's *tefillin*, there are some who wear both Rashi's and Rabbeinu Tam's versions. And even the latter view is observed differently, with some wearing Rashi's *tefillin* first and then toward the end of the prayer service switching to Rabbeinu Tam's *tefillin*, and others wearing both at the same time.

[693] Rabbi Bradley Artson, as cited in Torah column, Bat Kol Institute, June 27, 2008.

[694] Rabbi Harold Schulweis, as cited in Torah column, *Jerusalem Report*, July 10, 1997.

know our place and role. Just because we have a voice doesn't mean we should challenge, unnecessarily, those who are experts and know far more than us. One midrash teaches:

> Four types of people are called wicked: One who stretches out his hand against his fellow to strike him... one who borrows and does not repay... one who is arrogant and is not ashamed in the presence of someone greater than himself... and one who is argumentative.[695]

We should be humbled before those greater than ourselves, the Midrash teaches. We cannot flippantly shout down people of great virtue and great wisdom.

Today, populism is on the rise in various forms. Rabbi Jonathan Sacks roots this phenomenon back in the Korach story:

> Korach was a populist, one of the first in recorded history, and populism has reemerged in the West, as it did in the 1930s, posing great danger to the future of freedom. What links populism on the one hand, and the phenomenon of "wokeness" discussed by Barack Obama on the other, is that they are both binary, both extreme. Both divide the world into good and evil, black and white, with no shades of gray. Both see themselves as the oppressed and their opponents as the oppressors. They see no saving grace on the other side.[696]

He continues:

> These are classic populist claims. First, implies Korach, the establishment, represented by Moses and Aaron, is corrupt. Moses has been guilty of nepotism in appointing his own brother as High Priest. He has kept the leadership roles within his immediate family instead of sharing them out more widely. Second, Korach presents himself as the people's champion. The whole community, he says, is holy. There is nothing special about you, Moses and Aaron. We have all seen God's miracles and heard his voice. We all helped build his Sanctuary. Korach is posing as the democrat - so that he can become the autocrat....

---

[695] Bamidbar Rabbah, Parshat Korach 18.
[696] Rabbi Jonathan Sacks, *Morality: Restoring The Common Good In Divided Times* (New York: Basic Books, 2020), 188.

> Nachmanides was undoubtedly correct when he says that such a challenge to Moses's leadership would have been impossible at any earlier point. Only in the aftermath of the episode of the spies, when the people realized that they would not see the Promised Land in their lifetime, could disconnect be stirred by Korach and his assorted fellow travelers. They felt they had nothing to lose. Populism is the politics of disappointment, resentment, and fear.[697]

Korach was a populist (something dangerously on the rise around the globe today), wherein outsiders (on whatever end of a political spectrum) just hate the establishment simply because it's the establishment, and want to take over, doing anything and stopping at nothing to achieve that end. It sounds righteous but the truth is it's only righteous if they're fighting something actually evil (and not just something established).

Rabbi Sacks dedicated so much of this, his last book before he passed, toward critiquing populism:

> Populist politics involves magical thinking. The belief that a strong leader, with contempt for the democratic process, divisive rhetoric, relaxed about the truth or otherwise of his or her utterances, ignoring the conventions of normal politics, appealing directly to the people, blaming the state of the nation on some subgroup of the nation, or perhaps on neighboring nations and peoples, and speaking not to the better angels of our nature but to the worst, can restore a nation's former greatness—that is magical thinking.[698]

Today, as western liberals, we, by and large, embrace egalitarianism and democracy in society. All people are equal and should have equal access. But embracing equality doesn't mean that we have to reject hierarchy or respect for greatness, or become populists working to derail hierarchy and authority. There are times for revolution in history and there are times for evolution. There are times for critique and debate and there are times for silence.

Korach had some valid points. He is so close to getting it right, but ultimately gets it all wrong. We should learn from that mistake in our times of polarization and divisiveness.

---

[697] Ibid., 189-190.
[698] Ibid., 127-128.

DEBATE 40.

Spinoza vs. the Rabbis of Amsterdam: Allowing Heresy or Preserving Communal Boundaries

Baruch (Benedict) Spinoza was a fascinating 17th-century philosopher who accomplished so much before passing at the young age of 44. A Dutch rationalist of Portuguese Sephardic origin, he was one of the early thinkers of the Haskalah (enlightenment) movement. His ideas were met with enormous controversy, as he was one of the early founders of biblical criticism, offered radical theologies (such as pantheism, equating God with nature), denied the immortality of the soul as well as Divine omnipotence and Divine providence, rejected the notion that the Torah is from God and that Jewish law is binding for Jews, and rethought the concept of self within the universe. On a behavioral level, he stopped contributing to the synagogue and attending synagogue services. He also renounced his father's heritage in adjudication, choosing a civil court over a *beit din* (rabbinic court).

It was not only the Jewish community who banned him; the Catholic Church added his writings to the Index of Forbidden Books. Many claimed that Spinoza was an atheist, although nowhere in his work does he argue that God does not exist.

In his magnum opus, *Ethics* (published posthumously), he argued against Descartes' view of mind-body dualism. He became so prominent after his life that the great philosopher Hegel even said of him: "The fact is that Spinoza is made a testing-point in modern philosophy, so that it may really be said: You are either a Spinozist or not a philosopher at all."[699]

Now, given how many existential threats the Jews historically faced, one can understand why the rabbinic establishment would want to combat a perceived threat from within. Further, it is very difficult for us living in the 21st century to fathom how big of a threat the advent of modernity and the Enlightenment was to Jewish survival. We are so removed from communal expulsions that they may only strike us as absurd. They can, however, be understood, at least on some level, within their own historical context. In fact, another form of sympathy for the rabbis here emerges from the community's fear of their own collective expulsion.

On July 27, 1656, the Talmud Torah congregation of Amsterdam issued a *cheirem* (ban) against Spinoza, who was a mere 23 years old at the time. The censure said:

---

[699] Georg Wilhelm Friedrich Hegel, in *Lectures on the History of Philosophy* (1896), Vol. 3, Ch. I : "The Metaphysics of the Understanding," § 2 : Spinoza, p. 283

> The Lords of the *ma'amad* [court], having long known of the evil opinions and acts of Baruch de Espinoza, have endeavored by various means and promises, to turn him from his evil ways. But having failed to make him mend his wicked ways, and, on the contrary, daily receiving more and more serious information about the abominable heresies which he practiced and taught and about his monstrous deeds... they became convinced of the truth of the matter; and after all of this has been investigated in the presence of the honorable *chachamim* [sages], they have decided, with their consent, that the said Espinoza should be excommunicated and expelled from the people of Israel. By the decree of the angels, and by the command of the holy men, we excommunicate, expel, curse and damn Baruch de Espinoza, with the consent of God, blessed be He, and with the consent of all the Holy Congregation, in front of these Holy Scrolls with the 613 precepts which are written therein, with the excommunication with which Joshua banned Jericho,[700] with the curse with which Elisha cursed the boys[701] and with all the curses which are written in the Book of the Law.[702]

Such a censure was not unusual, as the Talmud Torah congregation actually did this often, although the language used here is unusually harsh. Scholars actually say that such harsh language wasn't issued for anyone else.[703] It's also strange that while referring to "abominable heresies" and "monstrous deeds," the rabbis never actually state the specific heresies involved, leaving questions for us.

Interestingly enough, once Spinoza was banned by the Jewish community, he never sought conversion to Christianity, although he lived, worked and was even buried among Christians. Further, he never so much as advocated for secularism.

I believe we owe Spinoza a measured apology. Those of us who have remained religiously committed centuries after his life have all too often failed to investigate our own creed with adequate rigor. We have replaced inquiry with exclusivity. Rather than engaging in the courageous interrogation and bold inquiry of the

---

[700] Joshua 6:26: "And Joshua adjured them at that time, saying, cursed be the man before the Lord, that rises up and builds this city Jericho; he shall lay the foundation thereof in his firstborn, and in his youngest son shall he set up the gates of it."
[701] Kings 2, 23–24: "And as he [Elisha] was going up by the way, there came forth little children out of the city, and mocked him, and said unto him, 'Go up, thou bald head; go up, thou bald head.' And he turned back, and looked on them, and cursed them in the name of the Lord. And there came forth two she bears out of the wood, and tore forty and two children of them."
[702] Steven M. Nadler, *Spinoza: A Life*. (Cambridge University Press, 1999), 120.
[703] Nadler, 2.

most perplexing questions of the universe, we have alienated—all too often—those who have come to conclusions outside our conformed norms.

While I would disagree on many matters with Spinoza, I'd like to think we'd enjoy each other's company. He was a bold pioneer ushering in Enlightenment, and suffered for his intellectual authenticity. Excommunication from his Portuguese-Sephardic community when he was only a 23-year-old man must have been traumatic. In our time, being excommunicated is irrelevant for the majority of us, but in the 17th century, he had no real precedent. One had nowhere to go, no one to whom one could turn.

Dr. Rebecca Goldstein wrote:

> By what right is Benedictus Spinoza included in this series, devoted as it is to Jewish themes and thinkers? Can the seventeenth-century rationalist, who produced one of the most ambitious philosophical systems in the history of Western Philosophy, be considered, by any stretch of interpretation, a Jewish thinker? Can he even be considered a Jew? Benedictus Spinoza is the greatest philosopher the Jews ever produced, which adds a certain irony to his questionable Jewishness.[704]

But a Jew is a Jew regardless of their beliefs or behaviors. The Talmud teaches: "[E]ven when the Jewish people have sinned, they are still called "Israel."[705] Would we dare today to ban a scholar as great as Einstein who himself affirmed a major segment of the theology of Spinoza?

I believe in Spinoza's God who reveals himself in the orderly harmony of what exists, not in a God who concerns himself with fates and actions of human beings.[706]

Six decades ago, Israeli Prime Minister David Ben-Gurion asked the chief rabbi of the Portuguese-Spanish community to lift Spinoza's *cheirem*. He was unwilling. Ben-Gurion even called Spinoza "the first Zionist of the last 300 years." In 2012, the Portuguese-Israelite commune of Amsterdam asked the chief rabbi of the community (Pinchas Toledano) to remove the ban, but he declined. Rabbi Nathan Lopes Cardozo also asked the current Chief Rabbi to lift the ban. He was unwilling. One day, perhaps, his ideas will be understood and his legacy vindicated. Indeed, rather than shunning him, we should be thanking him. Referring to his scholarship, Rabbi Cardozo wrote:

---

[704] Rebecca Goldstein, *Betraying Spinoza* (New York: Schocken, 2006), 36.
[705] BT Sanhedrin 44a.
[706] Rabbi Barry L. Schwartz, *Judaism's Great Debates* (Philadelphia: Jewish Publication Society, 2012), 75.

> I love heresy because it forces us to rethink our religious beliefs. We owe nearly all of our knowledge not to those who have agreed but to those who have differed… I consider him [Spinoza] a secular *tzaddik*. He lived by his noble ideas, was dedicated to simplicity, and showed the most remarkable virtuous characteristics… He surely helped us to think more maturely about God, human nature, happiness, and the society in which we live.[707]

This specific debate is still alive today. In November 2021, the synagogue that banned Spinoza banned a Spinoza scholar as well:

> Yitzhak Melamed, a professor of philosophy at Johns Hopkins University, was informed he could not visit the synagogue after a film director asked for permission to film Melamed conducting research in the library's archives.[708]

The ban explains:

> The chachamim and parnassim of Kahal Kados Torah excommunicated Spinoza and his writings with the severest possible ban, a ban that remains in force and cannot be rescinded. You have devoted your life to the study of Spinoza's banned works and the development of his ideas.[709]

Rabbi Dr. Nathan Lopes Cardozo responded:

> It would seem that you may be ignorant of the fact that the famous former Chief Rabbi of Israel Rabbi Yitzhak HaLevi Herzog z.l. (1888-1959) has already stated that the ban was only in force halachically as long as Spinoza was alive. Furthermore, it would seem you are unaware of the story concerning the ban

---

[707] Nathan Lopes Cardozo, "It is time to lift the ban" (*The Jerusalem Post*, 2015). Rabbi Nathan Lopes Cardozo is a prolific writer and thinker. Born in Amsterdam (1946), he was ordained at Gateshead Talmudical College, and lives in Jerusalem.
[708] Shira Hanau, "A Jewish expert on Spinoza was named 'persona non grata' in Amsterdam's synagogue and library," *Jewish Telegraphic Agency*, November 29, 2021. https://www.jta.org/2021/11/29/global/a-jewish-expert-on-spinoza-was-named-persona-non-grata-in-amsterdams-synagogue-and-library?utm_source=JTA_Maropost&utm_campaign=JTA_DB&utm_medium=email&mpweb=1161-37307-13478
[709] Ibid.

and the many deliberations concerning the real cause of this ban and the very teachings of Spinoza himself.

As for Prof. Melamed, it may be necessary to inform you that he is a deeply religious Jew who was raised in the ultra-Orthodox Bnei Brak in Israel and studied in Yeshivot.

Your view that the ban on Spinoza's works is still in force clearly indicates that you are not familiar with his writings, and are thus completely incapable of expressing an opinion about his philosophy.[710]

In the end, the organization overrode the rabbi and apologized to Professor Melamed and they welcomed him in.[711]

If I believe his ideas did harm to Judaism, I believe the proclamation for his banishment did more. Those who don't understand the subtle complexities of his ideas appear to ban them simply for being foreign and threatening. But are such individuals spiritually xenophobic? His philosophy must, at the least, be understood. For doesn't Judaism thrive most amidst an open marketplace of ideas where critiques, protests, and counterpoints are not only to be welcomed but encouraged? Is not this the source of our intellectual sustenance? The ban on Spinoza has, for centuries, represented fear. And Judaism must embrace a bold and fearless journey forward.

Judaism, at its best, urges us to avoid clinging blindly to dogmas and the notions of religious exclusivity. Our normative practices reflect the intellectual ideals we hold dear. We must make clear, then, that the precepts of Torah embrace autonomy, open thinking, hermeneutical diversity, and engaging with ideas that may be outside the comfortable framework that is all too prevalent in contemporary Jewish thought. Thus, defending Spinoza, one might argue, is defending the essence of Judaism itself.

Today, does our moral and political tolerance match our theological tolerance? If a rabbi declared themselves an atheist, do we think they should leave their position? If a Jewish leader comes out as anti-Israel, or on the flip side, as a right-wing extremist on Israel, should their public position be altered? What if an academic who joins the community comes out as a Holocaust denier? Should they be given an *aliyah* (be called up to recite a blessing on the Torah) in the congregation? For those who believe we cannot shun those for their beliefs, what if they use

---

[710] Nathan Lopes Cardozo: "An open letter to Rabbi Serfaty of Amsterdam," *The Times of Israel*, 2021.
[711] Cnaan Liphshiz, "The Spinoza scholar who was banned from Amsterdam synagogue is now invited to visit it," *Jewish Telegraphic Agency*, December 3, 2021, https://www.jta.org/2021/12/03/global/the-spinoza-scholar-who-was-banned-from-amsterdam-synagogue-is-now-invited-to-visit-it?utm_source=JTA_Maropost&utm_campaign=JTA_DB&utm_medium=email&mpweb=1161-37511-13478.

our communal spaces to proselytize for their ideas that we find beyond the pale? Sometimes we might choose to be legislative (to ban) and other times we might be more persuasive (avoiding a ban but countering the ideas head-on).

Today, our community knows all too well the importance of setting moral boundaries at work and in the community. But what are the intellectual and theological boundaries? Many liberal Jewish communities would suggest there should be none. Many traditional Jewish communities would indeed embrace *halakhic* and *hashkafic* (legal and ideological) boundaries to maintain a respect for communal norms. Should an atheist be allowed to have an *aliyah*? Should one who rejects the Divinity of the Torah be trusted on *kashrut*? Should one who rejects Divine Providence be hired as a day school Torah teacher? There is a huge range of approaches taken on such matters today. There must be room for these debates to take place. And when they do, indeed, they are following in the tradition of the debate of the rabbis versus Spinoza. Everyone is complicated and no one is pure. We must learn to hold the light and the dark simultaneously rather than hiding only within one.

Conclusion

We reflected on forty debates just as we lived for forty years in the desert. Just as we need a desert to transition from the powerlessness of slavery in Egypt to the responsibility of sovereignty in Israel, we need forty debates, immersing in Jewish wisdom, to prepare ourselves to see our own moral and spiritual lives with fresh eyes.

The goal here is to ensure not only that we're debating and not remaining in our own silos, but also that we're debating for the sake of heaven. The Talmudic rabbis teach us:

> Every dispute that is for the sake of Heaven, will in the end endure; But one that is not for the sake of Heaven, will not endure.[712]

Further, engaging in debate helps to remind us of the complexity, and often times the plurality, of truth.

> For three years Beit Shammai and Beit Hillel disagreed. These said: The *halakha* is in accordance with our opinion, and these said: The *halakha* is in accordance with our opinion. Ultimately, a Divine Voice emerged and proclaimed: Both these and those are the words of the living God. However, the *halakha* is in accordance with the opinion of Beit Hillel.[713]

Rabbi Samson Raphael Hirsch, 18th-century German rabbi and community leader, explains the value of debates that have integrity:

> When in a controversy both parties are guided by pure motives and seek noble ends... and when both parties seek to find the truth, then, of course... only one of the two opposing views can and will prevail in practice.
> But actually, both views will have permanent value because, through the arguments each side has presented, both parties will have served to shed new light on the issue under debate, and will have contributed to the attainment of the proper

---
[712] Pirkei Avot 5:17 trans. Dr. Joshua Kulp.
[713] BT Eruvin 13b.

understanding of the question discussed. They shall be remembered as . . . advancing the cause of the genuine knowledge of truth.[714]

Judaism is not a monolithic tradition that teaches absolutes (absolute laws or absolute values). Rather, Judaism offers the world an alternative: dialectical tensions. Jews, immersed in Jewish learning, can be trained to think about the tensions between laws, and the tensions between values. This can make us more open-minded, more intellectually honest, and more compassionate as we strive to hold empathy for all people. This is a crucial task given recent growing political and social polarization. These forty debates offer only a small sample of the countless debates throughout our tradition, but reflecting on them can help us to see and embrace others, from the past and in our contemporary moments.

May the debates among the Jewish people only grow. May we ensure that they not create unnecessary conflict but rather enable us to return to Torah, return to God, and return to ourselves. May they expand us spiritually and intellectually, and may they bring us all closer together as a people.

---

[714] Samson Raphael Hirsch, "Commentary on Pirkei Avot (5:20)," as quoted in Jewish Theological Seminary Torah Commentary, June 10, 2010.

Recent books from *Ben Yehuda Press*

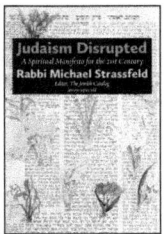

Judaism Disrupted: A Spiritual Manifesto for the 21st Century by Rabbi Michael Strassfeld. "I can't remember the last time I felt pulled to underline a book constantly as I was reading it, but *Judaism Disrupted* is exactly that intellectual, spiritual and personal adventure. You will find yourself nodding, wrestling, and hoping to hold on to so many of its ideas and challenges. Rabbi Strassfeld reframes a Torah that demands breakage, reimagination, and ownership." —Abigail Pogrebin, author, *My Jewish Year: 18 Holidays, One Wondering Jew*

The Way of Torah and the Path of Dharma: Intersections between Judaism and the Religions of India by Rabbi Daniel Polish. "A whirlwind religious tourist visit to the diversity of Indian religions: Sikh, Jain, Buddhist, and Hindu, led by an experienced congregational rabbi with much experience in interfaith and in teaching world religions." —Rabbi Alan Brill, author of *Rabbi on the Ganges: A Jewish Hindu-Encounter*

Liberating Your Passover Seder: An Anthology Beyond The Freedom Seder. Edited by Rabbi Arthur O. Waskow and Rabbi Phyllis O. Berman. This volume tells the history of the Freedom Seder and retells the origin of subsequent new haggadahs, including those focusing on Jewish-Palestinian reconciliation, environmental concerns, feminist and LGBT struggles, and the Covid-19 pandemic of 2020.

Duets on Psalms: Drawing New Meaning from Ancient Words by Rabbis Elie Spitz & Jack Riemer. "Two of Judaism's most inspirational teachers, offer a lifetime of insights on the Bible's most inspired book." — Rabbi Joseph Telushkin, author of *Jewish Literacy*. "This illuminating work is a literary journey filled with faith, wisdom, hope, healing, meaning and inspiration." —Rabbi Naomi Levy, author of *Einstein and the Rabbi*

Weaving Prayer: An Analytical and Spiritual Commentary on the Jewish Prayer Book by Rabbi Jeffrey Hoffman. "This engaging and erudite volume transforms the prayer experience. Not only is it of considerable intellectual interest to learn the history of prayers—how, when, and why they were composed—but this new knowledge will significantly help a person pray with intention (*kavvanah*). I plan to keep this volume right next to my siddur." —Rabbi Judith Hauptman, author of *Rereading the Rabbis: A Woman's Voice*

Renew Our Hearts: A Siddur for Shabbat Day edited by Rabbi Rachel Barenblat. From the creator of *The Velveteen Rabbi's Haggadah*, a new siddur for the day of Shabbat. *Renew Our Hearts* balances tradition with innovation, featuring liturgy for morning (*Shacharit* and a renewing approach to *Musaf*), the afternoon (*Mincha*), and evening (*Ma'ariv* and *Havdalah*), along with curated works of poetry, art and new liturgies from across the breadth of Jewish spiritual life. Every word of Hebrew is paired with transliteration and with clear, pray-able English translation.

Forty Arguments for the Sake of Heaven: Why the Most Vital Controversies in Jewish Intellectual History Still Matter by Rabbi Shmuly Yanklowitz. Hillel vs. Shammai, Ayn Rand vs. Karl Marx, Tamar Ross vs. Judith Plaskow... but also Abraham vs. God, and God vs. the angels! Movements debate each other: Reform versus Orthodoxy, one- two- and zero-state solutions to the Israeli-Palestinian conflict, gun rights versus gun control in the United States. Rabbi Yanklowitz presents difficult and often heated disagreements with fairness and empathy, helping us consider our own truths in a pluralistic Jewish landscape.

Recent books from *Ben Yehuda Press*

Reaching for Comfort: What I Saw, What I Learned, and How I Blew it Training as a Pastoral Counselor by Sherri Mandell. In 2004, Sherri Mandell won the National Jewish Book award for *The Blessing of the Broken Heart*, which told of her grief and initial mourning after her 13-year-old son Koby was brutally murdered. Years later, with her pain still undiminished, Sherri trains to help others as a pioneering pastoral counselor in Israeli hospitals. "What a blessing to witness Mandell's and her patients' resilience!" —Rabbi Dayle Friedman, editor, *Jewish Pastoral Care: A Practical Guide from Traditional and Contemporary Sources*

Heroes with Chutzpah: 101 True Tales of Jewish Trailblazers, Changemakers & Rebels by Rabbi Deborah Bodin Cohen and Rabbi Kerry Olitzky. Readers ages 8 to 14 will meet Jewish changemakers from the recent past and present, who challenged the status quo in the arts, sciences, social justice, sports and politics, from David Ben-Gurion and Jonas Salk to Sarah Silverman and Douglas Emhoff. "Simply stunning. You would want this book on your coffee table, though the stories will take the express lane to your soul." —Rabbi Jeff Salkin

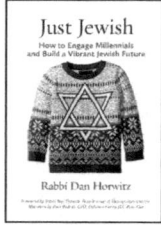

Just Jewish: How to Engage Millennials and Build a Vibrant Jewish Future by Rabbi Dan Horwitz. Drawing on his experience launching The Well, an inclusive Jewish community for young adults in Metro Detroit, Rabbi Horwitz shares proven techniques ready to be adopted by the Jewish world's myriad organizations, touching on everything from branding to fundraising to programmatic approaches to relationship development, and more. "This book will shape the conversation as to how we think about the Jewish future." —Rabbi Elliot Cosgrove, editor, *Jewish Theology in Our Time*.

Put Your Money Where Your Soul Is: Jewish Wisdom to Transform Your Investments for Good by Rabbi Jacob Siegel. "An intellectual delight. It offers a cornucopia of good ideas, institutions, and advisers. These can ease the transition for institutions and individuals from pure profit nature investing to deploying one's capital to repair the world, lift up the poor, and aid the needy and vulnerable. The sources alone—ranging from the Bible, Talmud, and codes to contemporary economics and sophisticated financial reporting—are worth the price of admission." —Rabbi Irving "Yitz" Greenberg

Why Israel (and its Future) Matters: Letters of a Liberal Rabbi to the Next Generation by Rabbi John Rosove. Presented in the form of a series of letters to his children, Rabbi Rosove makes the case for Israel — and for liberal American Jewish engagement with the Jewish state. "A must-read!" —Isaac Herzog, President of Israel. "This thoughtful and passionate book reminds us that commitment to Israel and to social justice are essential components of a healthy Jewish identity." —Yossi Klein Halevi, author, *Letters to My Palestinian Neighbor*

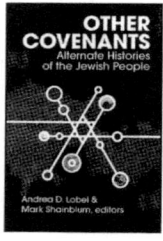

Other Covenants: Alternate Histories of the Jewish People by Rabbi Andrea D. Lobel & Mark Shainblum. In *Other Covenants*, you'll meet Israeli astronauts trying to save a doomed space shuttle, a Jewish community's faith challenged by the unstoppable return of their own undead, a Jewish science fiction writer in a world of Zeppelins and magic, an adult Anne Frank, an entire genre of Jewish martial arts movies, a Nazi dystopia where Judaism refuses to die, and many more. Nominated for two Sidewise Awards for Alternate History.

Reflections on the weekly Torah portion from *Ben Yehuda Press*

An Angel Called Truth and Other Tales from the Torah by Rabbi Jeremy Gordon and Emma Parlons. Funny, engaging micro-tales for each of the portions of the Torah and one for each of the Jewish festivals as well. These tales are told from the perspective of young people who feature in the Biblical narrative, young people who feature in classic Rabbinic commentary on our Biblical narratives and young people just made up for this book.

Torah & Company: The weekly portion of Torah, accompanied by generous helpings of Mishnah and Gemara, served with discussion questions to spice up your Sabbath Table by Rabbi Judith Z. Abrams. Serve up a rich feast of spiritual discussion from an age-old recipe: One part Torah. Two parts classic Jewish texts. Add conversation. Stir... and enjoy! "A valuable guide for the Shabbat table of every Jew." —Rabbi Burton L. Visotzky, author *Reading the Book*

Torah Journeys: The Inner Path to the Promised Land by Rabbi Shefa Gold. Rabbi Gold shows us how to find blessing, challenge and the opportunity for spiritual transformation in each portion of Torah. An inspiring guide to exploring the landscape of Scripture... and recognizing that landscape as the story of your life. "Deep study and contemplation went into the writing of this work. Reading her Torah teachings one becomes attuned to the voice of the Shekhinah, the feminine aspect of God which brings needed healing to our wounded world." —Rabbi Zalman Schachter-Shalomi

American Torah Toons 2: Fifty-Four Illustrated Commentaries by Lawrence Bush. Deeply personal and provocative artworks responding to each weekly Torah portion. Each two-page spread includes a Torah passage, a paragraph of commentary from both traditional and modern Jewish sources, and a photo-collage that responds to the text with humor, ethical conscience, and both social and self awareness. "What a vexing, funny, offensive, insightful, infuriating, thought-provoking book." —Rabbi David Saperstein

The Comic Torah: Reimagining the Very Good Book. Stand-up comic Aaron Freeman and artist Sharon Rosenzweig reimagine the Torah with provocative humor and irreverent reverence in this hilarious, gorgeous, off-beat graphic version of the Bible's first five books! Each weekly portion gets a two-page spread. Like the original, the Comic Torah is not always suitable for children.

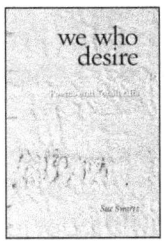

we who desire: Poems and Torah riffs by Sue Swartz. From Genesis to Deuteronomy, from Bereshit to Zot Haberacha, from Eden to Gaza, from Eve to Emma Goldman, *we who desire* interweaves the mythic and the mundane as it follows the arc of the Torah with carefully chosen words, astute observations, and deep emotion. "Sue Swartz has used a brilliant, fortified, playful, serious, humanely furious moral imagination, and a poet's love of the music of language, to re-tell the saga of the Bible you thought you knew." —Alicia Ostriker, author, *For the Love of God: The Bible as an Open Book*

Eternal Questions by Rabbi Josh Feigelson. These essays on the weekly Torah portion guide readers on a journey that weaves together Torah, Talmud, Hasidic masters, and a diverse array of writers, poets, musicians, and thinkers. Each essay includes questions for reflection and suggestions for practices to help turn study into more mindful, intentional living. "This is the wisdom that we always need—but maybe particularly now, more than ever, during these turbulent times." —Rabbi Danya Ruttenberg, author, *On Repentance and Repair*

Jewish spirituality and thought from *Ben Yehuda Press*

The Essential Writings of Abraham Isaac Kook. Translated and edited by Rabbi Ben Zion Bokser. This volume of letters, aphorisms and excerpts from essays and other writings provide a wide-ranging perspective on the thought and writing of Rav Kook. With most selections running two or three pages, readers gain a gentle introduction to one of the great Jewish thinkers of the modern era.

Ahron's Heart: Essential Prayers, Teachings and Letters of Ahrele Roth, a Hasidic Reformer. Translated and edited by Rabbi Zalman Schachter-Shalomi and Rabbi Yair Hillel Goelman. For the first time, the writings of one of the 20th century's most important Hasidic thinkers are made available to a non-Hasidic English audience. Rabbi Ahron "Ahrele" Roth (1894-1944) has a great deal to say to sincere spiritual seekers far beyond his own community.

A Passionate Pacifist: Essential Writings of Aaron Samuel Tamares. Translated and edited by Rabbi Everett Gendler. Rabbi Aaron Samuel Tamares (1869-1931) addresses the timeless issues of ethics, morality, communal morale, and Judaism in relation to the world at large in these essays and sermons, written in Hebrew between 1904 and 1931. "For those who seek a Torah of compassion and pacifism, a Judaism not tied to 19th century political nationalism, and a vision of Jewish spirituality outside of political thinking this book will be essential." —Rabbi Dr. Alan Brill, author, *Thinking God: The Mysticism of Rabbi Zadok of Lublin*

Return to the Place: The Magic, Meditation, and Mystery of Sefer Yetzirah by Rabbi Jill Hammer. A translation of and commentary to an ancient Jewish mystical text that transforms it into a contemporary guide for meditative practice. "A tour de force—at once scholarly, whimsical, deeply poetic, and eminently accessible." —Rabbi Tirzah Firestone, author of *The Receiving: Reclaiming Jewish Women's Wisdom*

Enlightenment by Trial and Error: Ten Years on the Slippery Slopes of Jewish Mysticism, Postmodern Buddhist Meditation, and Heretical Flexidox Spirituality by Rabbi Jay Michaelson. A unique record of the 21st-century spiritual search, from the perspective of someone who made plenty of mistakes along the way.

The Tao of Solomon: Finding Joy and Contentment in the Wisdom of Ecclesiastes by Rabbi Rami Shapiro. Rabbi Rami Shapiro unravels the golden philosophical threads of wisdom in the book of Ecclesiastes, reweaving the vibrant book of the Bible into a 21st century tapestry. Shapiro honors the roots of the ancient writing, explores the timeless truth that we are merely a drop in the endless river of time, and reveals a path to finding personal and spiritual fulfillment even as we embrace our impermanent place in the universe.

Embracing Auschwitz: Forging a Vibrant, Life-Affirming Judaism that Takes the Holocaust Seriously by Rabbi Joshua Hammerman. The Judaism of Sinai and the Judaism of Auschwitz are merging, resulting in new visions of Judaism that are only beginning to take shape. "Should be read by every Jew who cares about Judaism." —Rabbi Dr. Irving "Yitz" Greenberg

www.ingramcontent.com/pod-product-compliance
Lightning Source LLC
Chambersburg PA
CBHW050548160426
43199CB00015B/2582